Visual Reconstruction

The MIT Press Series in Artificial Intelligence
Edited by Patrick Henry Winston and Michael Brady

Artificial Intelligence: An MIT Perspective, Volume I: Expert Problem Solving, Natural Language Understanding, Intelligent Computer Coaches, Representation and Learning edited by Patrick Henry Winston and Richard Henry Brown, 1979

Artificial Intelligence: An MIT Perspective, Volume II: Understanding Vision, Manipulation, Computer Design, Symbol Manipulation edited by Patrick Henry Winston and Richard Henry Brown, 1979

NETL: A System for Representing and Using Real-World Knowledge by Scott Fahlman, 1979

The Interpretation of Visual Motion by Shimon Ullman, 1979

A Theory of Syntactic Recognition for Natural Language by Mitchell P. Marcus, 1980

Turtle Geometry: The Computer as a Medium for Exploring Mathematics by Harold Abelson and Andrea diSessa, 1981

From Images to Surfaces: A Computational Study of the Human Early Visual System by William Eric Leifur Grimson, 1981

Robot Manipulators: Mathematics, Programming and Control by Richard P. Paul, 1981

Computational Models of Discourse edited by Michael Brady and Robert C. Berwick, 1982

Robot Motion: Planning and Control edited by Michael Brady, John M. Hollerbach, Timothy Johnson, Tomás Lozano-Pérez, and Matthew T. Mason, 1982

In-Depth Understanding: A Computer Model of Integrated Processing for Narrative Comprehension by Michael G. Dyer, 1983

Robotics Research: The First International Symposium edited by Michael Brady and Richard Paul, 1984

Robotics Research: The Second International Symposium edited by Hideo Hanafusa and Hirochika Inoue, 1985

Robot Hands and the Mechanics of Manipulation by Matthew T. Mason and J. Kenneth Salisbury, Jr., 1985

The Acquisition of Syntactic Knowledge by Robert C. Berwick, 1985

The Connection Machine by W. Daniel Hillis, 1985

Legged Robots that Balance by Marc H. Raibert, 1986

Robotics Research: The Third International Symposium edited by O. D. Faugeras and Georges Giralt, 1986

Machine Interpretation of Line Drawings by Kokichi Sugihara, 1986

ACTORS: A Model of Concurrent Computation in Distributed Systems by Gul A. Agha, 1986

Knowledge-Based Tutoring: The GUIDON Program by William Clancey, 1987

AI in the 1980s and Beyond: An MIT Survey edited by W. Eric L. Grimson and Ramesh S. Patil, 1987

Visual Reconstruction by Andrew Blake and Andrew Zisserman, 1987

Visual Reconstruction

Andrew Blake and Andrew Zisserman

The MIT Press
Cambridge, Massachusetts
London, England

© 1987 Massachusetts Institute of Technology

Library of Congress Cataloging-in-Publication Data

Blake, Andrew.
  Visual reconstruction.

  (The MIT Press series in artificial intelligence)
  Bibliography: p.
  Includes index.
  1. Pattern perception.   I. Zisserman, Andrew.
II. Title.   III. Series.
Q327.B53   1987   001.53′4   87-4079
ISBN 0-262-02271-0

Contents

1 Modelling Piecewise Continuity   **1**

  1.1 What is Visual Reconstruction?   3

  1.2 Continuity and cooperativity   6

      1.2.1 Cooperativity in physical models   6

      1.2.2 Regression   8

      1.2.3 Cooperative networks that make decisions   10

      1.2.4 Local interaction in models of continuity   11

  1.3 Organisation of the book   15

2 Applications of Piecewise Continuous Reconstruction   **17**

  2.1 Detecting discontinuities in intensity   18

  2.2 Surface reconstruction   21

      2.2.1 Grimson's method   25

      2.2.2 Terzopoulos' method   25

      2.2.3 Why reconstruct a surface anyway?   26

      2.2.4 Surface descriptions   28

      2.2.5 Localising discontinuities   28

  2.3 Surface reconstruction from dense range data   29

  2.4 Curve description   33

3 Introduction to Weak Continuity Constraints   **39**

  3.1 Detecting step discontinuities in 1D   39

  3.2 The computational problem   40

  3.3 Eliminating the line process   43

  3.4 Convexity   43

  3.5 Graduated non-convexity   46

4 Properties of the Weak String and Membrane   **51**

  4.1 The weak string   55

      4.1.1 Energy of a continuous piece   55

	4.1.2	Applying continuity constraints	56
	4.1.3	Sensitivity to an isolated step	58
	4.1.4	Interaction of adjacent steps	58
	4.1.5	The gradient limit	62
4.2	Localisation and spurious response in noise	63
	4.2.1	Localisation in scale space: uniformity property . . .	63
	4.2.2	Localisation in noise	70
	4.2.3	Spurious responses in noise	72
4.3	The weak membrane	72
	4.3.1	Penalties for discontinuity	73
	4.3.2	Energy of a continuous piece	74
	4.3.3	Sensitivity of the membrane in detecting steps . . .	75
	4.3.4	Localisation and preservation of topology	76
4.4	Choice of parameters for edge detection	78
	4.4.1	Adaptive thresholding	80
4.5	Sparse data	81
	4.5.1	Hyperacuity	84
4.6	Hysteresis maintains unbroken edges	87
4.7	Viewpoint invariance in surface reconstruction	90

5 Properties of the Weak Rod and Plate   **97**
5.1	Energy of the weak rod/plate	98
5.2	Scale and sensitivity in discontinuity detection	100
	5.2.1	Sensitivity to an isolated step	100
	5.2.2	Interaction of adjacent steps	100
	5.2.3	Sensitivity to an isolated crease	101
	5.2.4	Interaction of adjacent creases	101
5.3	Mixed 1st and 2nd order energy performs poorly	103
5.4	Hysteresis	105
5.5	1st order plate	106
5.6	Viewpoint invariance	107

6 The Discrete Problem   **111**
6.1	Discretisation and elimination of line variables	112
	6.1.1	Extending 1D methods to 2D	114
	6.1.2	Higher order energies: weak rod and plate	117
	6.1.3	First order plate	120
	6.1.4	Sparse data	120
6.2	Minimising convex energies	121
	6.2.1	Algorithms based on gradient descent	121
	6.2.2	Multi-grid algorithms	122
6.3	Overcoming non-convexity	125

	6.3.1	The GNC algorithm	125
	6.3.2	Simulated annealing	126
	6.3.3	Hopfield's neural model	127
	6.3.4	Dynamic programming	128

7 The Graduated Non-Convexity Algorithm   **131**

7.1	Convex approximation	132
	7.1.1 Weak string	132
	7.1.2 General method	134
	7.1.3 Convex approximation for sparse data	136
7.2	Performance of the convex approximation	137
7.3	Graduated non-convexity	141
7.4	Why GNC works	142
	7.4.1 Isolated discontinuity	143
	7.4.2 Interacting discontinuities	146
	7.4.3 Noise	149
	7.4.4 Summary	150
7.5	Descent algorithms	152
7.6	Convergence properties	158
	7.6.1 Continuous problems	158
	7.6.2 Adding weak constraints	161
	7.6.3 Granularity of the $F^{(p)}$ sequence	163
	7.6.4 Activity flags	163

8 Conclusion   **167**

8.1	Further applications in vision	167
8.2	Hardware Implementation	168
8.3	Mechanical or probabilistic models?	168
8.4	Improving the model of continuity	170
	8.4.1 Psychophysical models	170
	8.4.2 The role of visual reconstruction	171

References   **173**

APPENDIX

A Energy Calculations for the String and Membrane   **183**

A.1	Energy calculations for the string	183
A.2	Energy calculations for the membrane	189
A.3	Infinite domain calculations for the membrane	190

CONTENTS

B Noise Performance of the Weak Elastic String **195**
B.1 Localisation 195
B.2 Spurious response 198
B.3 Comparison with a linear operator 200

C Energy Calculations for the Rod and Plate **203**
C.1 Energy calculations for the rod 203
C.2 Energy calculations for the plate 204

D Establishing Convexity **207**
D.1 Justification of "worst-case" analysis of the Hessian 207
D.2 Positive definite Hessian is sufficient for convexity 207
D.3 Computing circulant eigenvalues 209
D.4 Treating boundary conditions 211

E Analysis of the GNC Algorithm **213**
E.1 Setting up the discrete analysis 213
E.2 Constraining the discrete string 215
E.3 Isolated discontinuity 215
E.4 Cost function sequence 216
E.5 Discreteness of the function sequence 216
E.6 Checking for continuity of the discrete solution 218

Glossary of notation **221**

Index **223**

Series Foreword

Artificial intelligence is the study of intelligence using the ideas and methods of computation. Unfortunately, a definition of intelligence seems impossible at the moment because intelligence appears to be an amalgam of so many information-processing and information-representation abilities.

Of course psychology, philosophy, linguistics, and related disciplines offer various perspectives and methodologies for studying intelligence. For the most part, however, the theories proposed in these fields are too incomplete and too vaguely stated to be realized in computational terms. Something more is needed, even though valuable ideas, relationships, and constraints can be gleaned from traditional studies of what are, after all, impressive existence proofs that intelligence is in fact possible.

Artificial intelligence offers a new perspective and a new methodology. Its central goal is to make computers intelligent, both to make them more useful and to understand the principles that make intelligence possible. That intelligent computers will be extremely useful is obvious. The more profound point is that artificial intelligence aims to understand intelligence using the ideas and methods of computation, thus offering a radically new and different basis for theory formation. Most of the people doing artificial intelligence believe that these theories will apply to any intelligent information processor, whether biological or solid state.

There are side effects that deserve attention, too. Any program that will successfully model even a small part of intelligence will be inherently massive and complex. Consequently, artificial intelligence continually confronts the limits of computer science technology. The problems encountered have been hard enough and interesting enough to seduce artificial intelligence people into working on them with enthusiasm. It is natural, then, that there has been a steady flow of ideas from artificial intelligence to computer science, and the flow shows no sign of abating.

The purpose of this MIT Press Series in Artificial Intelligence is to provide people in many areas, both professionals and students, with timely, detailed information about what is happening on the frontiers in research centers all over the world.

Patrick Henry Winston
Michael Brady

Preface

For now we see through a glass darkly; but then face to face.
1st letter of Paul to the Corinthians, ch. 13, v. 12.

We count it a great privilege to be working in a field as exciting as Vision. On the one hand there is all the satisfaction of making things that work - of specifying, in mathematical terms, processes that handle visual information and then using computers to bring that mathematics to life. On the other hand there is a sense of awe (when time permits) at the sheer intricacy of creation. Of course it is the Biological scientists who are right in there; but computational studies, in seeking to define Visual processes in mathematical language, have made it clear just how intrinsically complex must be the chain of events that constitutes "seeing something".

Our appreciation of Vision owes much to encouragement received from other research workers. Very special mention must be made of John Mayhew and John Frisby who have been a continual source of enthusiasm and insight. Bernard Buxton and Michael Brady have made many valuable comments on our work. We are grateful for helpful discussions with Alan Yuille, John Porril, Christopher Longuet-Higgins, John Canny and Chris Taylor. We derived much benefit from the software expertise of Gavin Brelstaff. Stephen Pollard and Chris Brown supplied many digitised images and Olivier Faugeras supplied laser rangefinder data. For diligent proof-reading we thank Fiona Blake, Michael Brady, Gavin Brelstaff, Robert Fisher, John Hallam, Constantinos Marinos and David Willshaw. Finally, we gratefully acknowledge the support of the Science and Engineering Research Council, the Royal Society of London (for their IBM Research Fellowship for AB) and the University of Edinburgh.

Chapter 1

Modelling Piecewise Continuity

This is a book about the problem of vision. How is it that a torrent of data from a television camera, or from biological visual receptors, can be reduced to perceptions - the recognition of familiar objects and the concise description of unfamiliar ones? There is of course an immense literature in psychophysics[1], neurophysiology and neuroanatomy that provides some answers in the case of biological systems (see Uttal (1981) for a taxonomy). For instance, the functioning of light-sensitive cells in mammalian vision is understood in some detail (Marks et al. 1964); and the elegant, orderly, spatial correspondence of feature detectors in the brain with the array of cells in the retina, is well known (Hubel and Wiesel 1968). There has also been much dialogue between psychophysics and neurophysiology/neuroanatomy. Examples are the discovery of spatial bandpass channels (Campbell and Robson 1968, Braddick et al. 1978), and understanding the perception of coloured light (Livingstone and Hubel 1984, Jameson and Hurvich 1961) and surface colour (Land 1983, Zeki 1983). These instances are but parts of a very large body of knowledge of biological vision.

Over the last two decades, computers have introduced a new strand into the study of vision. The earliest work (Roberts, 1965) produced systems able to recognise simple objects and manipulate them in a controlled way (Ambler et al. 1975). These systems were, of course, vastly inferior to the biological systems studied by the psychophysicists, neuroanatomists

---

[1]Psychophysics is the application of physical methods to the study of psychological properties. Visual psychophysics typically probes the mechanisms of human vision by noting a subject's perception of specially designed patterns, under controlled experimental conditions.

and neurophysiologists. They were rather slow, and very brittle. Nonetheless, the availability of computers affects the study of vision in three, very important ways:

1. It provides a rich and precise language in which to express visual problems and processes.   Marr distinguishes three levels at which this is done (Marr 1982). At the top "computational theory" level, subtasks are described in terms of their function in processing information. At the next level a subtask, once specified, can be carried out by an appropriately designed "algorithm" - a mathematical recipe. Finally, at the implementation level, any given algorithm might be "realised physically" on any of a great variety of machines, which may be quite dissimilar in their internal architecture, and of vastly differing computing power.

2. Discussion of vision problems can be isolated from design of computing hardware.   The beauty of the enriched language for specifying subtasks is that a subtask can be discussed in isolation from the structure of the machine that is to perform it, whether biological or electronic. It can be specified with mathematical precision, and the consequences of the specification can be made inescapably plain by logical predictions. Ullman (1979b), expanding Marr's philosophy (Marr 1976a), puts it like this:

> Underlying the computational theory of visual perception is the notion that the human visual system can be viewed as a symbol-manipulating system. The computation it supports is, at least in part, *the construction of useful descriptions of the visible environment*. An immediate consequence of this view is the distinction that can be drawn between the physical embodiment of the symbols manipulated by the system on the one hand, and the meaning of these symbols on the other. One can study, in other words, the *computation* performed by the system almost independently of the physical *mechanisms* supporting the computation.

Furthermore, task specifications can be tested in practice by executing an algorithm that implements them, on a computer. All this has led to considerable enrichment of studies of human vision (e.g. Marr and Poggio 1979, Mayhew 1982, Hildreth 1984, Ullman 1979b, Koenderinck and van Doorn 1976).

3. Complete, though simple, vision systems can be built and tested.   The restriction to study the visual systems that nature has kindly provided is removed. It is possible to construct a system to test a particular issue and to reach a theoretical understanding of the system's behaviour. One of the issues studied in this book is how different ways of modelling the *continuity* of surfaces might affect the stability of their perception as the viewer moves. This is as important to vision by machines as to human vision - it is a generic problem in vision. Furthermore, computer vision systems are now gaining maturity. They appear at last to be approaching widespread practicability in industrial automation and robotics.

This book deals with vision as a computational problem. Little further mention will be made of psychophysics or neurophysiology. But we hope and believe that the new ways of modelling continuity presented here could eventually have a bearing, not only on computer vision, but on biological vision too.

1.1   What is Visual Reconstruction?

Visual Reconstruction will be defined as the process of

> *reducing visual data to stable descriptions.*

"Visual data" comes in various forms, including:

- Raw intensity data direct from photoreceptors, in the form of an array of numbers

- "Optic flow" - measures of velocities of points in an image, obtained perhaps from a suitable spatio-temporal filter (e.g. Buxton and Buxton 1983).

- A depth map, consisting of points embedded, usually sparsely, in the viewer's coordinate-frame. At each point, depth (distance from the viewer) is known. Depth maps may be produced by stereopsis, in which images obtained from two slightly different viewpoints (e.g. two eyes) are compared and matched (Marr and Poggio 1979, Mayhew and Frisby 1981, Baker 1981, Grimson 1981); triangulation is then used to compute the depths. Alternatively depths may be obtained by appropriate processing of optic flow (Bruss 1983) or, artificially, from an optical rangefinder.

- Sets of discrete points making up curves in a 2D image, or in 3D ("space-curves").

In each case, data must be reduced in quantity, with minimal loss of meaningful content, if a concise, symbolic representation is to be attained. It is not enough merely to achieve compression - for example by "run-length encoding", in which an array

$$\{0, 0, 0, 0, 0, 4, 4, 4, 4, 4, 7, 7, 7, 7, 0, 0, 0\}$$

is represented more briefly as

$$\{0 \times 5, 4 \times 5, 7 \times 4, 0 \times 3\}.$$

Rather, in any vision system that is to perform in a consistent manner, it is necessary that the compressed form should be *stable*. This means that it should be *invariant* to (undisturbed by) certain distortions or variations that are likely to be encountered in the image-formation process. These include:

- sampling grain, varying in density due to perspective effects or to inhomogeneity of receptor spacing, as in the eye.

- optical blurring

- optical distortion and sensor noise

- rotation and translation in the image plane

- rotation in 3D (not including, at this point, occlusion effects in which one surface obscures another)

- perspective distortions

- variation in photometric conditions (principally in illumination of the visible scene)

Raw intensity data is affected by all these factors. Ultimately, invariance to all of them must be achieved to produce descriptions of visible surfaces that are, as far as possible, independent of imaging effects. For example, the description of a particular surface patch should not change dramatically if the image is gradually blurred by defocussing; rather it should "degrade gracefully" (Marr 1982). Those blurred snapshots of the baby still look more like a baby than, say, a table. As for 3D rotation invariance, it is required for any system that works in real-time, so that viewed surfaces appear stable as the viewer moves. Less obviously, for analysis of static images, it is still necessary to achieve descriptions that are relatively independent of viewpoint. All the factors mentioned above are relevant to the particular reconstruction processes dealt with in this book.

A prominent theme in following chapters will be *continuity*. In order to reconstruct descriptions that are not only invariant, but also relatively unambiguous, it is necessary to make simplifying assumptions about the world. Assumptions of continuity underlie visual processes of different kinds. Stereopsis is facilitated by constraints on the continuity of surfaces (Marr 1982) and, in particular, by figural continuity - continuity along curves and surface features (Mayhew and Frisby 1981). Analysis of optical flow also appears to require assumptions of continuity, either in regions (Horn and Schunk 1981, Longuet-Higgins 1984) or along curves (Hildreth 1984). Computation of lightness, the perceptual correlate of surface reflectivity (i.e. surface colour), needs constraints on continuity both of the reflectivity itself, and of the incident illumination (Land 1983).

It is clearly unreasonable, in each of these cases, to assume unremitting, global continuity. Depth, optical flow and surface colour all undergo some sudden changes across a scene. It is natural to think of them as continuous in patches. Marr (1982) used the term "continuous almost everywhere". This is not the same as "piecewise continuous" in the mathematical sense, for there is the additional expectation that "the fewer pieces the better". To put it another way, simple descriptions are best, and fewer pieces make simpler descriptions. The challenge, then, is to reach a satisfactory formalisation of "continuity almost everywhere". We do that here by borrowing the idea of a "weak constraint" - a constraint that can be broken occasionally - from Hinton (Hinton 1978). With an appropriate class of continuous surface patches, this leads to "weak continuity constraints" (Blake 1983b) - preferring continuity, but grudgingly allowing occasional discontinuities if that makes for a simpler overall description.

Another important theme emerges later in the book - *cooperativity*. Whereas the "weak continuity constraint" belongs at Marr's "computational theory" level, cooperativity is an algorithmic property. A cooperative process is a computation performed in parallel by a network of independent processing cells. Each cell is connected to just a few of its neighbours, and continually computes some function of its own state, its own input signal, and signals received from its neighbours. The attraction is that rapid computation is achievable, not only by using fast cells, but by using many cells in a large network, all sharing the computational load. The remarkable property of cooperative processes, well known in mathematics and in physical modelling, is this: despite the purely local connectivity of the cells, the network can perform global computations. It is clear that messages could pass between successive neighbours and so propagate across the network. What is more surprising is that propagation can be coordinated, unhindered by collisions between messages, to achieve a useful effect.

Networks of this kind have received much attention in theories of Psychophysics (e.g. Julesz 1971, Marr 1976b) Cognitive Science (e.g. Hinton and Sejnowski 1983, Hopfield 1984), Pattern Recognition (e.g. Rosenfeld et al. 1976) and Computer Science (e.g. Brookes et al. 1984, Milner 1980). In vision, there have been cooperative algorithms for optical flow computation (Horn and Schunk 1981), analysis of shading (Woodham 1977, Ikeuchi and Horn 1981), analysis of motion (Ullman 1979a), computation of lightness (Horn 1974, Blake 1985c) and reconstruction of stereoscopically viewed surfaces (Grimson 1981, Terzopoulos 1983). The implementation of weak continuity constraints can be achieved very naturally too, we shall see, by cooperative networks.

1.2   Continuity and cooperativity

1.2.1   Cooperativity in physical models

Two physical examples will help to provide a more concrete insight into basic properties of cooperative computations.

The first (figure 1.1) is an elastic sheet - a soap film for instance -

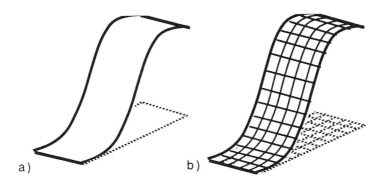

a)   b)

Figure 1.1: A physical example of cooperative computation. A wire frame (a) is covered by an elastic sheet (b). The shape that the sheet assumes can be calculated by an array of locally connected cells.

stretched over a wire frame. The sheet takes up a minimum energy configuration, which happens to be a solution of Laplace's equation[2]. This configuration can be computed in a local-parallel fashion, in what is called

---

[2]Strictly, the solution of Laplace's equation approximates to the minimum energy configuration.

a "relaxation algorithm". The shape taken up by the sheet is represented by its height at each point on a rectangular grid. Initially some rough estimate of those heights is made. The following local computation is then done, repeatedly, at each grid point: its height value is replaced by the average of the values at the four neighbouring positions. While this is going on, the heights of points on the wire frame itself remain fixed (a "boundary condition" for the cooperative process). Imagine simple computational cells, whose sole function is to accept signals from four neighbours and output their average. They repeat this perpetually. The result is that the influence of the wire frame propagates inwards on the sheet, until finally the sheet comes to rest at its true equilibrium position.

Several general properties of cooperativity are illustrated here:

Propagation - in this case from the boundary to the interior. Propagation can also occur, in certain systems, over shorter ranges, more like pressing on a mattress to produce a dent in the region of the hand. The extent of the dent depends on how elastic the mattress is. Truly global propagation (as on the soap film) occurs in visual processes - the computation of lightness is an example. Propagation over a restricted range (as on the mattress) is what occurs when weak continuity constraints are in force.

Local interaction: cells communicate only with their immediate neighbours.

Parallelism: the cells compute continuously, and independently except for the exchange of signals with neighbours.

Energy minimisation: the relaxation algorithm progressively reduces the elastic energy of the sheet, until equilibrium is reached.

The second physical example is one proposed by Julesz (Julesz 1971) as a model for stereoscopic vision, and is known in physics as an Ising model. Magnetic dipoles arranged on pivots (figure 1.2) interact with one another in such a way that they prefer to align with their neighbours. Springs on the magnets tend to return them to their natural orientations. The angles of the magnets take the place, here, of the heights in the example of figure 1.1. In just the same way, the stable states of the system of magnets can be computed cooperatively. But there is an important difference. There are not one, but many stable states. Whereas the elastic sheet always returns, after a deflection, to the same equilibrium position, the system of magnets can flip from one stable state to another. A stable state will usually consist

Figure 1.2: A more complex example of cooperativity. Bar magnets, arranged on a grid, tend to align with one another, but are also subject to restoring forces from the springs around their pivots.

of a patchwork of regions ("domains") each containing magnets of similar orientation. Orientation changes abruptly across domain boundaries. The size of the domains is determined by the strength of the magnetic interaction, compared with the strength of the springs: the stronger the magnetic force, the larger the domains tend to be. And all this is very much how a system behaves under weak continuity constraints - regions of continuous variation, with abrupt changes at boundaries.

1.2.2   Regression

Visual reconstruction processes of the sort discussed in this book are founded on least-squares regression. In its simplest form, regression can be used to choose the "best" straight line through a set of points on a graph. More complex curves may be fitted - quadratic, cubic or higher order polynomials. More versatile still are splines (de Boor 1978) - sequences of polynomials joined smoothly together. There is an interesting connection between cubic splines and elastic systems like the sheet in figure 1.1 (Poggio et al. 1984, Terzopoulos 1986). A flexible rod, such as draughtsmen commonly use to draw smooth curves is an elastic system. If it is loaded or clamped at several points, it takes up a shape - its minimum energy configuration - which is in fact a cubic spline[3] (figure 1.3a). Each load-point forms a "knot" in

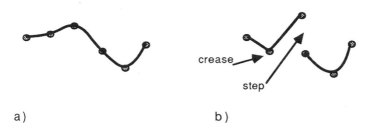

crease

step

a)   b)

Figure 1.3: A flexible rod, under load, forms a spline. (a) A continuous spline. (b) A spline with crease and step discontinuities, controlled by multiple knots.

the spline, where one cubic polynomial is smoothly joined to the next. So spline fitting can be thought of in terms of minimising an elastic energy - the energy of a flexible rod.

Yet a further generalisation of regression, and the most important one for visual reconstruction, is to include discontinuities in the fitted curve. In spline jargon, these are "multiple knots", generating kinks ("crease" discontinuities) or cutting the curve altogether ("step" discontinuities) as in figure 1.3b. Incorporation of multiple knots, *if* it is known exactly *where* along the curve the discontinuities are, is standard spline technology. A more interesting problem is one in which the positions of discontinuities are not known in advance. In that case, positioning of multiple knots must be done automatically. An algorithm to do that might consist of constructing an initial spline fit, and then adding knots until the regression error measure reached an acceptably small value (Plass and Stone 1983). This would ensure a spline that closely fitted the data points.

For visual reconstruction that is not enough. The requirement for *stability* has already been discussed, which means that the multiple knots must occur in "canonical" (natural) positions, robust to small perturbations of the data and to the distortions and transformation listed earlier. Only then are they truly and reliably descriptive of the data.

The stability requirement is met by imposing weak continuity constraints on an elastic system like the rod. Leaving the details to later chapters, it is sufficient for now to draw on the magnetic dipole system as an analogy. Typically, it has many locally stable states with groups of dipoles of various sizes, aligned in various directions. Among these states,

---

[3] Again, this is an approximation.

there is a ground state, the state of lowest energy. As energy is reduced, the system is liable to stick in a locally stable state, before the ground state is reached. Similarly, an elastic material under weak continuity constraints has a ground state - its favourite configuration - which is usually very stable. A spline, for example, may have its knots arranged so as to reach its ground state, forming (by definition!) the best, stable description of the data.

Finding the ground state is a problem. Procedures for direct improvement of knot positions (Pavlidis 1977) are prone to be caught in a state other than the ground-state. But provided the system can be jostled or drawn into the ground state, the positions of discontinuities will be stable in the required manner. And this is precisely what is achieved by certain statistical algorithms (Kirkpatrick et al. 1982, Geman and Geman 1984), and the deterministic "Graduated Non-convexity" (GNC) algorithm, proposed in this book. Some examples of the operation of the GNC algorithm, reconstructing various kinds of visual data, are shown in the next chapter. A definition of the algorithm itself, however, must be delayed until chapter 3.

1.2.3   Cooperative networks that make decisions

Visual reconstruction must be more than linear filtering if it is to generate usable features for subsequent visual processes. At some point there must be an element of commitment; decisions must be made - either a feature is present or it is not. In particular, in visual reconstruction, it is necessary repeatedly to decide whether or not a discontinuity is present in a particular location. An example should clarify the distinction between mere linear filtering and feature detection. Consider the task of locating a thin, bright bar in an image. A suitable linear filter could be found which transforms an image into a new image, in which such bars, or their edges, stand out even more brightly. This is not enough. A vision system must make a decision at some point - either there is a bar (in a certain location) or there isn't. Rather than being simply "enhanced", bars must be "labelled". An elegant example due to Poggio and Reichardt (1976) illustrated a similar point. They showed that even so simple a function as detecting the direction of local motion cannot be achieved by any linear system[4].

So purely linear systems are inadequate for visual reconstruction. There must be some non-linearity, even if it is just a thresholding operation. This is what occurs in the Perceptron (Rosenblatt 1962, Minsky and Papert 1969), a simple, neuron-like switching element that computes a weighted

---

[4]A linear system is one that simply outputs a weighted sum of its inputs.

sum of its inputs, and produces the output 1 or 0, according to whether the sum exceeds some threshold. Similarly, in the computation of lightness (Land 1983), thresholding (used to detect edges in the conventional manner) is an adequate form of non-linearity.

Generally, *any* network that makes decisions cannot be entirely linear. Suppose the network acts to minimise an energy $F(\mathbf{x}, \mathbf{y})$, where $\mathbf{x}$ is a vector of inputs to the network, and $\mathbf{y}$ is the vector of outputs. Then the output is defined (not necessarily uniquely) as that vector $\mathbf{y}$ which minimises $F(\mathbf{x}, \mathbf{y})$ - for a given, fixed $\mathbf{x}$. If F were a quadratic polynomial in the variables $\mathbf{x}$, $\mathbf{y}$ then $\mathbf{y}$ would be a linear function of $\mathbf{x}$ - the solution of the linear system

$$\partial F/\partial \mathbf{y} = 0.$$

It has already been said that a linear system cannot make decisions[5]. In fact it cannot make decisions as long as F is both "strictly convex" and smooth (differentiable in the variables $\mathbf{x}$, $\mathbf{y}$). In that case, the minimum always exists, and every input/output pair $\mathbf{x}$, $\mathbf{y}$ is a "Morse point" of the function F (Poston and Stewart 1978) which means that $\mathbf{y}$ varies continuously with $\mathbf{x}$. There is no discontinuous or sudden or catastrophic switching behaviour.

We know now that the energy function F for any system under weak continuity constraints must be either undifferentiable or non-convex or both. This is illustrated in figure 1.4.

1.2.4   Local interaction in models of continuity

Geman and Geman (1984) have forged an elegant link, via statistical mechanics, between mechanical systems like the soap film or splines, and probability theory. They have shown, in effect, that signal estimation by least squares fitting of splines is exactly the right way to behave if you have certain *a priori* probabilistic beliefs about the world in which the signal originated. Specifically, the beliefs are: that the signal - the one that is being estimated - is sampled from a "Markov Random Field" (MRF) and that Gaussian noise was added, in the process of generating the data.

What exactly is an MRF? It is a probabilistic process in which all interaction is local; the probability that a cell is in a given state is entirely determined by probabilities for states of neighbouring cells. An example based on one given by Besag (1974) illustrates this. Imagine a field full of cabbages, planted by a very methodical farmer on a precise, square grid. (A hexagonal grid would, of course, have given better packing density, but his ageing tractor runs best in straight lines.) Unfortunately, an outbreak

---

[5]This assumes that the system is unconstrained.

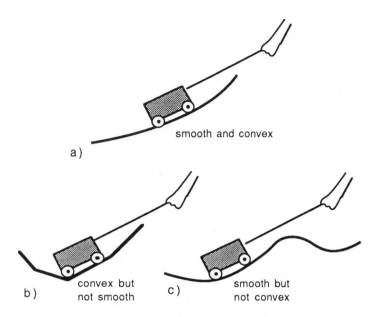

a)
smooth and convex

b)
convex but
not smooth

c)
smooth but
not convex

Figure 1.4: A smooth, convex energy function cannot cause discontinuous behaviour. The cart's position is a continuous function of the hand's position in (a), but jerky motion occurs in (b) and (c).

of CMV (Cabbage Mosaic Virus), which is particularly virulent when cabbages are arranged in a regular tesselation, has afflicted his crop. At a certain stage in the progress of the disease, its spread can be characterised as follows. The probability that any given cabbage has the disease depends entirely on the probability of disease of its four immediate neighbours. This is because the disease passes, with a certain probability, from neighbour to neighbour.

Qualitatively, the spread of the disease has much in common with the soap film example given earlier. In both cases, *direct* interaction occurs only between immediate neighbours. But global effects can still occur as a result of propagation. Just as the position of the wire frame influences the position of the interior of the soap film, so the introduction of disease at the edge of the field can spread, from neighbour to neighbour, towards the middle.

Formally, what Geman and Geman show is that elastic systems can also be considered from a probabilistic point of view. The link between spline energy E and probability Π is that

$$\Pi \propto e^{-E/T} \qquad (1.1)$$

(T is a constant). The lower the energy of a particular signal (that was generated by a particular MRF), the more likely it is to occur. Highly deformed elastic sheets have high energy and are intrinsically "unlikely" to occur. What is more, weak continuity constraints can also be understood in probabilistic terms: they are consistent with the belief that there is a "line-process", also an MRF but not directly observable in the data, determining the positions of discontinuities.

It comes as something of a shock, when happily using splines as a very natural, mechanical model for smooth, physical surfaces, to find that this is inescapably equivalent to making certain probabilistic assumptions! The most disturbing thing is that one is *forced* to accept that the surface model is a probabilistic one, and therefore includes an element of randomness. This may be appropriate for modelling texture (Derin and Cole 1986), but in a model of smooth surfaces it has rather counter-intuitive consequences, illustrated in figure 1.5. A "1st order" MRF[6], for instance, ranks a noisy but horizontal plane more probable than a smooth inclined one. This is because the 1st order MRF is sensitive only to gradients. Later in the book, this "gradient limit" problem is discussed in some detail. It can be cured by moving to 2nd order, but then it just recurs in a different form, as

---

[6] 1st order, here, means that direct interaction occurs only between immediate neighbours; 2nd order means that there is direct interaction between neighbours separated by 2 steps.

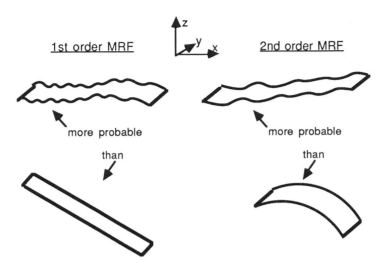

Figure 1.5: MRF models of surfaces can be somewhat counter-intuitive. A smooth but inclined or curved surface may have a *lower* MRF probability than a rough, noisy one.

in the figure. It is not clear what order of MRF would be sufficiently high to avoid the problem, if any. In any case, the higher the order, the greater the range of interaction between cells, and the more intractable the problem of signal estimation becomes. In practice, anything above 1st order is more or less computationally infeasible, as later chapters will show. What the probabilistic viewpoint makes quite clear, therefore, is that a spline under weak continuity constraints (or the equivalent MRF) is not quite the right model. But it is the best that is available at the moment.

As for choosing between mechanical and probabilistic points of analogies, we are of the opinion that the mechanical one is the more natural for representation of *a priori* knowledge about visible surfaces, or about distributions of visual quantities such as intensity, reflectance, optic flow and curve orientation. The justification of this claim must be left, however, until the concluding chapter. In the meantime, this book pursues Visual Reconstruction from the mechanical viewpoint.

1.3   Organisation of the book

Throughout the book, even in later chapters which are more technical, our aim has been to avoid obstructing the text with undue mathematical detail. Longer mathematical arguments are delayed until the appendix.

Chapter 2.   Examples are given, with copious illustrations, of the applications of weak continuity constraints in Visual Reconstruction. Problems discussed include edge detection (analysis of variations in image intensity), stereoscopic vision, passive rangefinding and describing curves. This chapter is free of mathematical discussion; it should be easily accessible to most readers.

Chapter 3.   The simplest possible discontinuity detection scheme is described - detecting step discontinuities in 1D data, using a "weak string". The idea of a weak continuity constraint is expanded. A simple algorithm, using Graduated Non-convexity (GNC), is described. There is some mathematics in this chapter, but nothing too difficult.

Chapter 4.   The theoretical properties of the weak string and its 2D analogue, the "weak membrane", are discussed in some detail. Application of variational calculus enables exact solutions to be obtained for certain data - for example step edges and ramps. These solutions, in turn, enable the two parameters in the weak string/membrane energy to be interpreted. Far from being arbitrary, in need of unprincipled tweaking, they have clear roles in determining scale, sensitivity and resistance to noise. Moreover, it is shown that, under weak continuity constraints, the positions of discontinuities are localised with impressive accuracy. In 2D, the geometry and topology (connectivity) of discontinuities is faithfully preserved - something that, it seems, cannot be achieved by more conventional means.

Chapter 5.   The "weak rod" and the "weak plate" are even more powerful means of detecting discontinuities. ("Creases" can be detected, as well as "steps".) Analytical results can again be obtained for certain cases and, as before, lead to an interpretation of parameters in the energy.

Chapter 6.   So far, energy minimisation has been treated as a variational problem. For computational purposes it must be made discrete. This is done using "finite elements", together with "line-variables" to handle discontinuities. Existing minimisation algorithms are reviewed.

Chapter 7.   The effectiveness of the GNC algorithm is explained. For a substantial class of signals (step discontinuities in noise), it is shown that GNC produces precisely the correct optimal solution.

Some details of designing GNC algorithms for weak membrane and plate are given. In particular, it is necessary to approximate a non-convex energy by a convex function. We explain how this is done. Both serial and parallel algorithms are dealt with, together with a full discussion of convergence properties.

Chapter 8.   Some conclusions and open questions.

Appendix.   The appendix contains a substantial body of work supporting, in particular, variational analysis (appendix A,B,C) and analysis of the GNC algorithm (appendix D,E).

Chapter 2

Applications of Piecewise Continuous Reconstruction

In practical terms, the application of weak continuity constraints, by means of the GNC algorithm, constitutes a powerful class of filters. Their power lies in their ability to detect discontinuities and *localise* them *accurately* and *stably*. This is an important property for visual reconstruction tasks, as this chapter seeks to illustrate.

A conventional means of finding discontinuities would be to blur the signal, and then look for features such as points of steepest gradient (figure 2.1). Unfortunately, the blurring, whilst having the beneficial effect of removing noise, also distorts the data. This can result in substantial error in the positions of marked discontinuities. The weak string, however, preserves discontinuities without any prior information about their existence or location. They are localised accurately, even in the presence of substantial noise, and when the effective spatial scale of the filter is large. This is illustrated in figure 2.2.

The weak rod has the capabilities of the weak string, and some more besides. A string resists stretching, whereas a rod also resists bending. This means that it tends to be continuous, and also to have a continuous gradient. Weak constraints can therefore be applied to continuity both of the signal, and of its derivative. Broken constraints mark "steps" and "creases" respectively (figure 2.3). Fitting a weak rod in a single computational process is possible in principle, and has been achieved in practice. But it is far more efficient to split the computation into two stages. The first stage

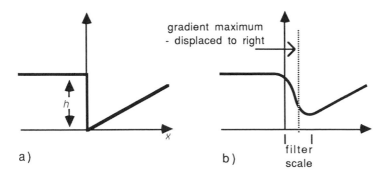

Figure 2.1: Conventional edge detection for locating discontinuities. Signal (a) is blurred (b) to remove noise, and then points of greatest slope are labelled as positions of discontinuities. But blurring distortion causes errors in those positions.

is just to apply the weak string as before, detecting steps, and producing a smooth reconstruction. The second stage detects creases, as in figure 2.3.

The string and rod also have analogues, the membrane and plate, which filter 2D data. The family of 1D and 2D filters has important application in vision. Four "canonical" visual reconstruction processes have been implemented using one or more of the filters. They are

- detection of discontinuities in intensity

- segmentation of 'sparse' range data (stereoscopic reconstruction)

- segmentation of 'dense' range data (reconstruction from optical rangefinder data)

- description of curves in images

2.1   Detecting discontinuities in intensity

Many methods have been proposed for detecting discontinuities (edges) in (2D) intensity data. Step discontinuities in intensity are important because they mark sudden changes in the visible surfaces. For instance, where one surface ends and another begins (e.g. the roof of the van and the wall behind, in figure 2.4) there is a sudden change in intensity. This is an "occluding" boundary, where one surface obscures another. Similarly a crease

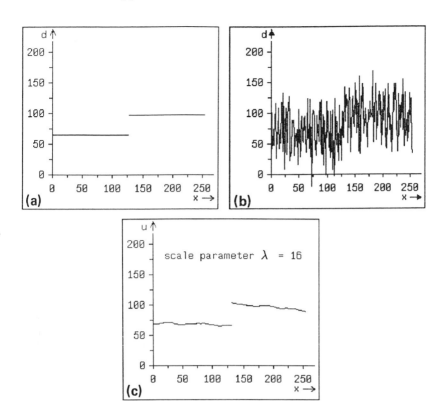

Figure 2.2: The weak string is a discontinuity preserving filter for one-dimensional data. Original data (a). Data immersed in noise (b). The signal-to-noise ratio is approximately 1. The weak string works by producing a reconstruction (c) in which discontinuities are preserved, without blurring, and accurately localized.

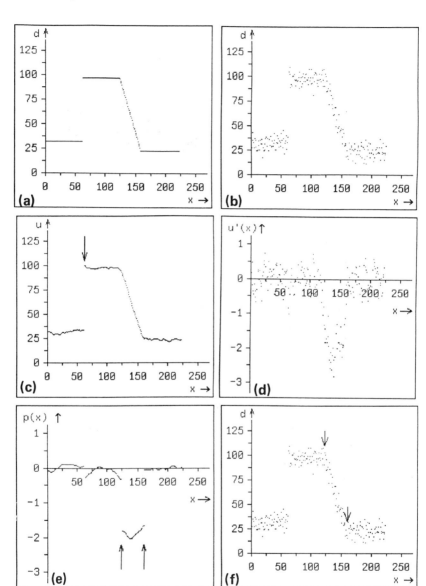

Figure 2.3: The weak rod detects "steps" and "creases". Signal (a) in noise (b). Signal-to-noise ratio is 10:1. First the weak string reconstruction labels step discontinuities (c), as before. This is differentiated (d) (within continuous pieces) and a second reconstruction stage recovers discontinuities (e), correctly marking creases in the original data (f).

in a smooth surface (e.g. an edge of a cube) generates a discontinuity in intensity. Such a crease is called a "connect" edge. Finally, where a surface suddenly changes colour, there is again a discontinuity in intensity. Having located discontinuities, it may also be useful to organise them further - for example by noting "bar" features (e.g. a thin white stripe on a dark background), consisting of two parallel discontinuities, back-to-back.

There are basically three kinds of filter for labelling discontinuities. Those of the first kind use blurring (linear filtering), naturally extending to 2D the use of blurring that we have already seen in 1D (Haralick 1980, Canny 1983, Marr and Hildreth 1980). The second kind use regression to fit step-shaped templates, locally, to intensity data (Hueckel 1971, O'Gorman 1978, Leclerc 1985, Gennert 1986). Where the template fits well, there must be a step discontinuity in the data. The third kind, also uses regression, but acts globally across the data, without the need for arbitrarily choice of neighbourhoods in which template fitting can take place. Elastic surfaces under weak continuity constraints are of the third kind. They act globally, by propagation, as we saw earlier. Global schemes of this sort have recently attracted much interest both in Vision and in Image Processing (Blake 1983a,b, Geman and Geman 1984, Mumford and Shah 1985, Blake and Zisserman 1985a, Smith et al. 1983, Burch et al. 1983).

The results of edge detection by fitting a weak membrane (that is, an elastic membrane under weak continuity constraints) are shown in figures 2.4 and 2.5.

As in 1D (the weak string), discontinuities are localised accurately. This is especially significant in large amplitude noise which, if noise is to be effectively suppressed, calls for the use of large filters, which necessarily blur on a large scale. Linear filters, under these conditions, make significant systematic errors in localisation of discontinuities: corners are rounded, T-junctions are disconnected, and displacements occur near intensity gradients. The magnitude of these errors is of the order of the spatial scale of the filter. Such problems are avoided when weak continuity constraints are used, as shown in figure 2.6. The weak membrane also has an intrinsic tendency to produce the shortest possible discontinuity contours consistent with the data. This has the effect of producing edges that are smooth curves.

2.2   Surface reconstruction

Stereo image pairs can be matched to generate sparsely distributed points of known depth, rather like the spot heights on a topographical map. It may be useful to produce a dense depth map from that data, filling in

Figure 2.4: The weak membrane as an edge detector. The image in (a) and its discontinuities (b). Reconstructed intensity (c) is the filtered version of (a), preserving the discontinuities marked in (b). Both (b) and (c) are produced simultaneously by the weak membrane.

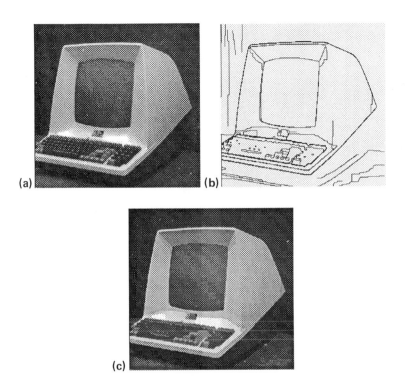

Figure 2.5: Edge detection again: (a), (b) and (c) as in figure 2.4.

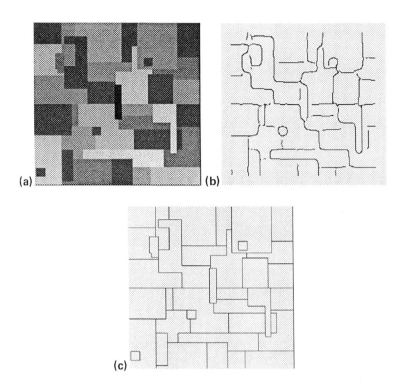

Figure 2.6: Localisation accuracy. A "Mondrian" test image (a) including noise and intensity gradients. Discontinuities found by marking points of maximum gradient, after linear (directional gaussian) filtering show considerable distortion (b). This is not present in the fitted weak membrane (c). (Comparable operator scales were used in (b) and (c).)

between the sparse points. Algorithms to do this were first proposed by Grimson (1981), and developed further by Terzopoulos (1983). But the main purpose of producing a depth map, this book argues, is to mark discontinuities in the visible surface. They may either be steps or creases, corresponding either to occlusions in the visible surface, or to connect edges (discontinuities of surface orientation). Both types can be recovered by applying weak continuity constraints to a suitable elastic sheet, which is then attached by springs to the sparse depth points.

2.2.1   Grimson's method

Grimson's algorithm produces an *explicit* representation of the visible surface, as a depth map. This is an encoding of depth z (distance from the viewer) as a function of image coordinates x, y, at each point on a fine grid (as in figure 1.1). Imagine that the wire frame in figure 1.1a is the boundary of some surface patch. The boundary appears in left and right views, and can be stereoscopically matched to obtain depth. So the position and shape of the boundary curve, in 3D space, is known. Assume, furthermore, that *within* the boundary curve, over the surface patch itself, no features are visible. There are no discontinuities in intensity. Grimson's "no news is good news" constraint can be invoked: the surface patch must be smooth. The question is, therefore, what smooth surface would fit inside the boundary curve? Of course there are many possibilities. A plausible one is that formed by a membrane, tacked onto the wire frame. Still better than a membrane, which is prone to creasing, would be a thin plate which bends but cannot crease. This is what Grimson proposes. It remains to describe the algorithm which actually computes the shape of a plate, welded onto a given piece of wire (see chapter 6). Suffice it to say, for the present, that it is an elaboration of the simple "relaxation" algorithm, described earlier, that computes the shape of a soap film by repeated averaging.

2.2.2   Terzopoulos' method

Terzopulos extended Grimson's method in various ways. The most significant was the impressive improvement in efficiency gained by "multi-grid" techniques (see chapter 6). He also began to consider the effects of surface discontinuities on reconstruction. Suppose it were known (somehow), before reconstruction began, that the surface to be reconstructed was not entirely continuous as Grimson supposed, but discontinuous along a certain, known line. The thin plate could be arranged to break along that line. Similarly if the surface were known to be creased along a certain line, a thin strip of membrane could be sewn into the plate (figure 2.7). (We have found that the more direct strategy of building a "hinge" into the plate also works well.)

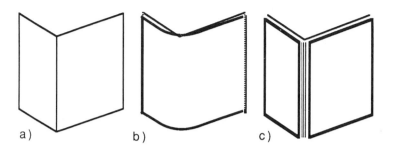

Figure 2.7: Creases in reconstruction. Data (a) contains two planes joined at a crease. A thin plate cannot crease (b) without a special modification. For instance a thin strip of membrane can be "sewn in" (c).

The real problem, the major concern of this book, is to find surface discontinuities when they are *not* already known to exist. Terzopoulos proposed looking for points of high stress in a plate, indicating that stereoscopic data is "trying" to break it. This can be shown, formally, to be equivalent to applying a linear filter and picking out points of steepest gradient - just as with discontinuities of intensity. In fact computation can be saved by using a membrane (cheaper than a plate) to fill in the sparse depth data, followed by conventional linear filtering (McLauchlan et al. 1987). But as with any method based on linear filtering, accuracy is spoilt by blurring distortion. This drawback can be avoided by using weak continuity constraints.

2.2.3   Why reconstruct a surface anyway?

We argue that the usefulness of *explicit* reconstruction (generating a depth-map) is somewhat restricted:

> Explicit reconstruction is applicable to textured surface patches only, with the primary purpose of detecting step and crease discontinuities.

Effective application of reconstruction therefore presupposes prior detection of texture, and control of focus of attention, to restrict computation to appropriate image areas. There are several reasons for advancing this view.

Ambiguity   Reconstruction of untextured, smooth surfaces presents a severe ambiguity problem. A given circle in space, for instance, could be the boundary of any one of infinitely many smooth patches (figure 2.8). Grimson/Terzopoulos thin plate reconstruction would plump for a disc.

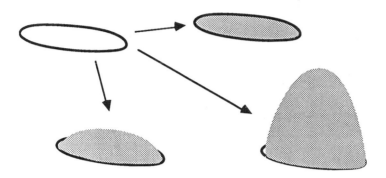

Figure 2.8: Ambiguity in surface reconstruction.

This dangerously eliminates all the other possibilities - a violation of Marr's principle of "least commitment" (Marr 1982).

In fact the shape of the boundary curve, plus the smoothness constraint, constitute the best available description of the surface patch. There is little further to be deduced about the shape of the patch. This is nothing to be ashamed of - descriptions of this sort are already a powerful handle for matching visible surfaces to one another (Pollard et al. 1987) and to stored models (Brooks 1981). New sources of information, such as analysis of surface shading, might add usefully to such descriptions - but that possibility must be left for discussion elsewhere (Ikeuchi and Horn 1981, Ikeuchi 1983, Blake et al. 1985d). And, of course, if the surface is visibly textured the shape ambiguity is resolved by stereoscopic vision, because the texture elements constitute features that can be stereoscopically matched.

Texture masking of monocular features   Texture aids stereoscopic vision - but impedes monocular vision. It masks the intensity discontinuities generated by surface features (occluding edges etc.). Imagine walking down carpeted stairs. The front of each step is an occluding edge, giving rise to a discontinuity in intensity, but mixed up with intensity changes due to the texture of the carpet. Monocularly, the occluding edge is difficult to pick out. (A picture illustrates this shortly). Stereoscopically, however, the sudden change in depth at the occluding edge, falling off one step onto the next, is quite unambiguous. (Motion parallax similarly facilitates perception of occluding edges (Longuet-Higgins and Prazdny 1980)).

2.2.4   Surface descriptions

There are two distinct types of usage of information about visible surfaces: reasoning about visible objects, and path planning or collision avoidance. In the first, the goal is to match visible surfaces to one another, or to stored object-descriptions. The second concerns the "mapping out" of a world in which many objects are unknown; it imposes weaker requirements on visual processing than the first: it is not necessary to identify the vase on the table as a precious Chinese porcelain merely to avoid knocking it off. It is enough to know that it occupies a certain portion of space.

Different descriptions are appropriate in each case. For reasoning about objects, an adequate description might consist of the shapes and positions of occluding and connect edges and *compact* descriptions of the shapes of smooth patches, together with other features such as colour and texture quality. The cumbersome depth-map has no place here. In this context it is merely a means to an end, the end of recovering monocularly masked features.

It is less clear what is the best form of description for path-planning and collision avoidance. A depth-map may be useful for computing the point of collision of a given path in space, with the visible surface. Greater efficiency is achieved, though, if the visible surface can be "protected" by a bounding polygon, computed directly from sparse depths (Boissonat 1984), without the use of an intermediate depth map.

The point is that direct applications for depth maps, as descriptions of visible surfaces, are at best limited and at worst, perhaps, non-existent.

2.2.5   Localising discontinuities

Incorporation of discontinuities into the reconstructed surface by means of weak continuity constraints was originally suggested in (Blake 1983a). Such ideas have recently been developed from (Geman and Geman 1984) by Marroquin (1984). Alternative approaches have been suggested by Grimson and Pavlidis (1985) and Terzopoulos (1985). The special problems presented by the fact that stereoscopic data is sparse are discussed fully in chapters 4 and 7.

Fitting a weak membrane to sparse depth data is illustrated in figure 2.9, and for a real image in figures 2.10 and 2.11.

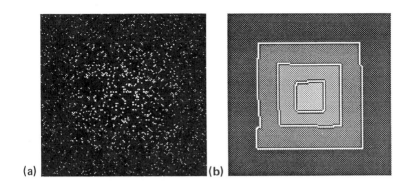

Figure 2.9: Fitting a membrane to sparse depth data. Artificially generated, sparse depth data (a) in which displayed grey-level encodes depth, contains
a sequence of layers, like a wedding cake viewed from above. After fitting with a
weak membrane, the piecewise continuous surface is recovered (b), together with
discontinuities between layers.

A weak membrane is sufficient for labelling occluding edges only; they
appear as tears in the membrane. To detect connect edges as well, a thin
plate must be used, capable both of tearing and of buckling. An example
of the application of a weak plate to stereoscopic images is given in figure
2.12.

2.3   Surface reconstruction from dense range data

Optical range-finders produce raw arrays of depth values. These require
organisation before they are usable for path-planning and collision avoidance, or for matching to object models. It is desirable to make explicit the
discontinuities in depth and its derivative; they correspond to occlusions
and creases between surfaces in the scene. This is quite like the problem of
detecting discontinuities of intensity. But, in addition, invariance to change
of viewpoint (Blake 1984) must be ensured, in order to maintain stability
under viewer motion. This would be of crucial importance in a real time
system, but is important even for analysis of single frames, if surface descriptions are to be robust.

Figure 2.13 shows the results of fitting a plate to laser rangefinder data,
under weak continuity constraints. A weak plate is used (rather than a weak

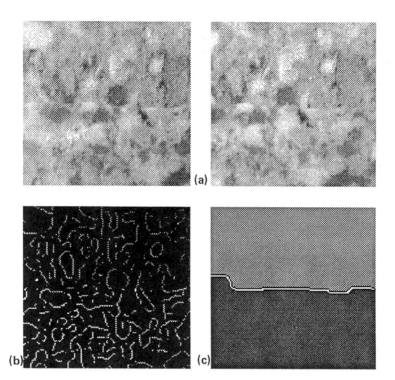

Figure 2.10: Weak membrane reconstruction of real stereo data. A stereo pair (a) of a foam block, with a step discontinuity across the middle, that is all but invisible monocularly. Stereo correspondence using a state-of-the-art matching algorithm (Pollard et al. 1985) produces depths along sparse contours (b). The reconstructed surface is shown with its contour of discontinuity (c).

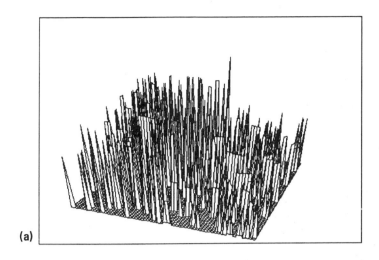

(a)

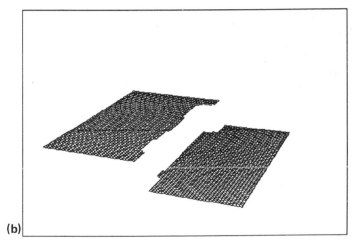

(b)

Figure 2.11: Isometric plots of the stereoscopic data from figure 2.10b and the reconstructed surface in figure 2.10c.

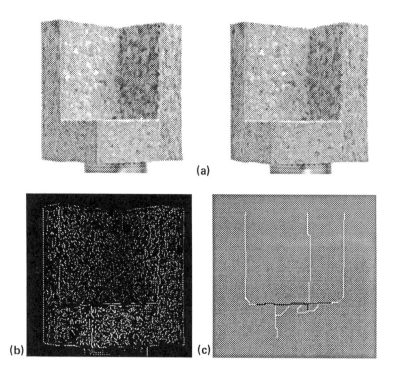

(a)

(b)   (c)

Figure 2.12: Applying a weak plate to sparse, stereoscopic depths.
(a) Stereo image-pair. (b) Stereoscopically matched features. Both steps and
creases are recovered by the plate (c), shown superimposed on the reconstructed,
dense depth-map. Creases are marked as thin white lines, whilst steps are marked
as thick, black lines. A few spurious creases have been generated as a result of
"ghost" matches in the stereoscopically viewed texture.

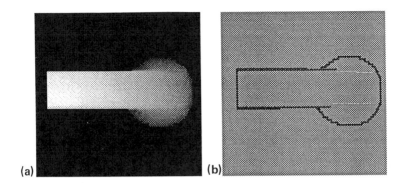

Figure 2.13: Fitting a weak plate to a laser rangefinder depth-map.
The depth map (a) is of a telephone handset. Both steps and creases are recovered
by the plate (b), giving a piecewise smooth approximation to the data. (Creases
are marked as white lines, whilst steps are marked as black lines.)

membrane) so that both step and crease discontinuities can be recovered.

2.4   Curve description

At an early stage of visual processing, descriptions of the shape and connectivity of curves are needed. For example, connect and occluding edges, obtained by surface reconstruction, are unorganised. They are simply chains
of points arranged on a grid. The chains must be aggregated to form compact, stable descriptions, consisting of the positions of corners, junctions
and curve endings, together with the approximate shape of smooth curve
segments.

Discontinuities again have a primary role. Commonly, a curve is con-
verted to tangent angle/arc-length (θ, s) form, and filtered to detect corners (step discontinuities in θ) and possibly also curvature discontinuities
(Perkins 1978, Asada and Brady 1986, Ramer 1975, Zucker et al. 1977,
Zucker 1982, Blake et al. 1986a). This may be done at a variety of spatial
scales in order to obtain both coarse and fine views of the curve's shape.
Corners, for instance, appear as step discontinuities in tangent angle θ.
Sharp corners look discontinuous at all scales, but rounded ones only at
coarse scale. Just as with discontinuities in intensity and in visible surfaces,
discontinuities in tangent angle can be detected by linear filtering, followed
by labelling of gradient maxima. But again, blurring distortion causes localisation errors which are avoided when weak continuity constraints are

used instead.

In figure 2.14 a simple hand drawn curve is shown. Corners have been detected by fitting a weak elastic string to the (θ, s) data. Results at a variety of scales are plotted in "scale-space" (figure 2.14d). Note the remarkably uniform structure of the scale-space - this agrees with theoretical predictions. Uniformity has the advantage that tracking features in scale-space becomes trivial. Tracking is essential to maintain correct correspondence between features at coarse and fine scales. But under linear filters such as the gaussian and its derivatives, complex structure arises, which is difficult to track and harder still to interpret (Asada and Brady 1986, Witkin 1983). A weak string scale-space for a silhouette taken from a real image, is shown

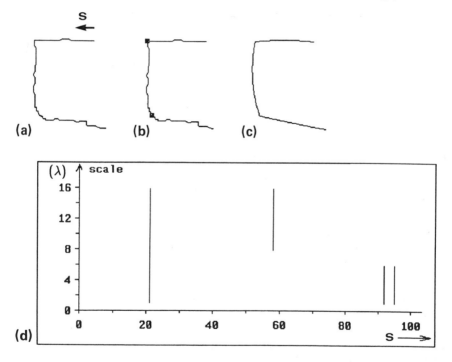

(a)   (b)   (c)

(d)

Figure 2.14: Scale-space filtering. The hand drawn curve (a) segmented at coarse scale (b) and reconstructed by fitting arcs between discontinuities (c). When weak elastic strings are fitted at a variety of spatial scales, the discontinuities trace out a uniform "fingerprint" (straight vertical lines) in "scale-space" (d). Notice that, as expected, the fingerprint of the small notch on the curve appears only at small scales; the rounded corner's fingerprint appears only at large scales.

in figure 2.15.

The weak string curve filter, in addition to running on clean, isolated curves as in figures 2.14, 2.15, can also operate on edges embedded in an image. This is shown in figures 2.16 and 2.17. A simple linear filter runs along the edges, estimating local tangent angles. The weak string is then applied to the "graph" of edges, just as they are, embedded in the image. Corners show up as discontinuities of tangent angle as before. In addition, T-junctions generate 3-way discontinuities (continuous tangent angle along the crossbar, but discontinuous at the top of the downstroke). At a Y-junction, tangent angles on all 3 arms are discontinuous.

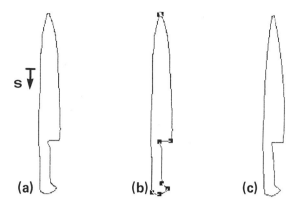

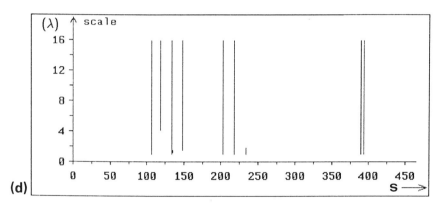

Figure 2.15: Weak string scale-space applied to a real image. Sillhouette (a) segmented at coarse scale (b) and reconstructed by fitting arcs between discontinuities (c). It is apparent that discontinuities and arcs together constitute a compact but accurate representation of the silhouette. (d) Scale-space. Most features, in this case, are visible at both coarse and fine scale, except for the curved base of the handle, visible at coarse scale only. (Data after Asada and Brady (1986).)

 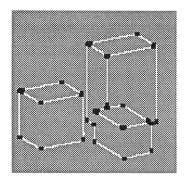

Figure 2.16: Corner and junction detection: synthesised image. Dark blobs mark discontinuities in tangent angle, obtained from fitting weak strings to the entire "graph" of edges.

 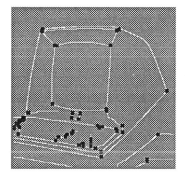

Figure 2.17: Corner and junction detection: real image.

Chapter 3

Introduction to Weak Continuity Constraints

For illustrative purposes, consider the simplest weak continuity problem: detection of step discontinuities (edges) in 1D data. The aim is to construct a piecewise smooth 1D function $u(x)$ which is a good fit to some data $d(x)$. This is achieved by modelling $u(x)$ as a "weak elastic string" - an elastic string under weak continuity constraints. Discontinuities are places where the continuity constraint on $u(x)$ is violated. They can be visualised as breaks in the string. The weak elastic string is specified by its associated energy; the problem of finding $u(x)$ is then the problem of minimising that energy.

3.1 Detecting step discontinuities in 1D

The behaviour of the elastic string over an interval $x \in [0, N]$ is defined by an energy, which is a sum of three components:

P: the sum of penalties α levied for each break (discontinuity) in the string.

D: a measure of faithfulness to data.

$$D = \int_0^N (u - d)^2 dx$$

S: a measure of how severely the function $u(x)$ is deformed.

$$S = \lambda^2 \int_0^N u'^2 dx.$$

This is the elastic energy of the string itself, that is stored when the string is stretched. The constant λ^2 is a measure of elasticity or "stretchability" or willingness to deform[1].

The problem is to minimise the total energy:

$$E = D + S + P \tag{3.1}$$

- that is, for a given $d(x)$, to find that function $u(x)$ for which the total energy E is smallest. Without the term P (if the energy were simply $E = D + S$) this problem could be simply solved using the calculus of variations. For example fig 3.1c shows the function u that minimises $D + S$, given the data $d(x)$ in fig 3.1a. It is clearly a compromise between minimising D and minimising S - a trade-off between sticking close to the data and avoiding very steep gradients. The precise balance of these 2 elements is controlled by λ. If λ is small, D (faithfulness to data) dominates. The resulting $u(x)$ is a close fit to the data $d(x)$. In fact, λ has the dimensions of length, and it will be shown that it is a characteristic length or scale for the fitting process.

When the P term is included in E, the minimisation problem becomes more interesting. No longer is the minimisation of E straightforward mathematically. E may have many local minima. For example, for the problem of fig 3.1, b) and c) are both local minima. Only one is a global minimum; which one that is depends on the values of α, λ and the height h of the step in a). If the global minimum is b) then the reconstruction $u(x)$ contains a discontinuity; otherwise, if it is c), $u(x)$ is continuous.

3.2   The computational problem

The "finite element method" (Strang and Fix 1973) is a good means of converting continuous problems, like the one just described, into discrete problems. In the case of the string it is relatively easy. The continuous interval $[0, N]$ is divided into N unit sub-intervals ("elements") $[0, 1], ..., [N-1, N]$, and nodal values are defined: $u_i = u(i), i = 0...N$. Then $u(x)$ is represented by a linear piece in each sub-interval (fig 3.2). The energies defined earlier

---

[1] Really, interpreting S as a stretching energy is only valid when the string is approximately aligned with the x axis. Another way to think of S is that it tries to keep the function $u(x)$ as flat as possible.

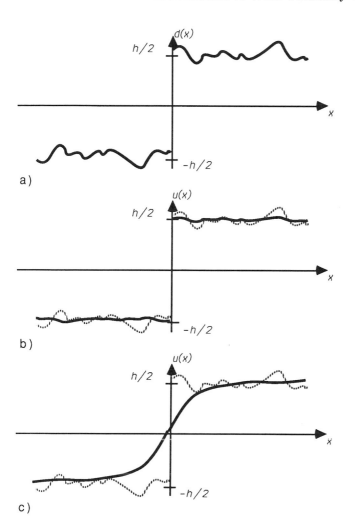

Figure 3.1: Calculating energy for data consisting of a single step. (a) Data. (b) A reconstruction with one discontinuity. (c) A continuous reconstruction.

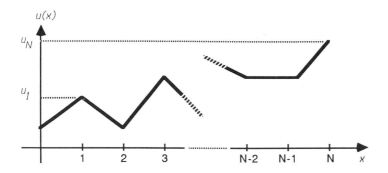

Figure 3.2: Dividing a line into sub-intervals or "elements".

now become:

$$D = \sum_{0}^{N}(u_i - d_i)^2 \qquad (3.2)$$

$$S = \lambda^2 \sum_{1}^{N}(u_i - u_{i-1})^2(1 - l_i) \qquad (3.3)$$

$$P = \alpha \sum_{1}^{N} l_i \qquad (3.4)$$

where l_i is a so-called "line-process". It is defined such that each l_i is a boolean-valued variable.

Either: $l_i = 1$ indicating that there is a discontinuity in the sub-interval $x \in [i - 1, i]$.

or: $l_i = 0$ indicating continuity in that subinterval - u_i, u_{i-1} are joined by a spring.

Note that when $l_i = 1$ the elastic string is "broken" between nodes $i - 1$ and i and the relevant energy term in (3.3) is disabled. (Geman and Geman (1984) coined the term "line-process" as a set of discrete variables describing edges in 2D; here we have a simple case, appropriate in 1D.)

3.3   Eliminating the line process

The problem, now in discrete form, is simply:

$$\min_{\{u_i, l_i\}} E.$$

It transpires that the minimisation over the $\{l_i\}$ can be done "in advance". The problem reduces simply to a minimisation over the $\{u_i\}$. Exactly how this is achieved will be explained in chapter 6. The reduced problem is more convenient for two reasons:

- The computation is simpler as it involves just one set of real variables $\{u_i\}$, without the boolean variables $\{l_i\}$.

- The absence of boolean variables enables the "graduated non-convexity algorithm", described later, to be applied.

It will be shown that once the line-process $\{l_i\}$ has been eliminated, the problem becomes

$$\min_{\{u_i\}} F, \text{ where } F = D + \sum_{1}^{N} g(u_i - u_{i-1}). \tag{3.5}$$

The neighbour interaction function g will be defined precisely in chapter 6 but to give some idea of how it acts, it is plotted in figure 3.3. The term $S + P$ in (3.1) has been replaced by the $\sum g(..)$ term in (3.5). Note that nothing of value has been thrown away by eliminating line variables. They can very simply be explicitly recovered from the optimal $\{u_i\}$ (this is also explained in chapter 6).

3.4   Convexity

The discrete problem has been set up. The task now is to minimise the function F; but that proves difficult, for quite fundamental reasons. Function F lacks the mathematical property of "convexity". What this means is that the system u_i may have numerous stable states, each corresponding to a local minimum of energy F. Such a state is stable to small perturbations - give it a small push and it springs back - but a large perturbation may cause it to flip suddenly into a state with lower energy.

There may be very many local minima in a given F. In fact there is (in general) one local minimum of F corresponding to each state of the line process l_i - 2^N local minima in all! The goal of the weak string computation is to find the *global* minimum of F; this is the local minimum with the lowest

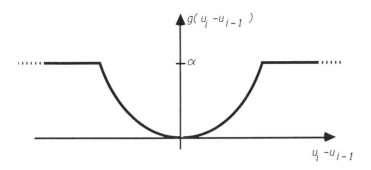

Figure 3.3: Energy of interaction between neighbours in the weak string. The central dip encourages continuity by pulling the difference $u_i - u_{i-1}$ between neighbouring values towards zero. The plateaus allow discontinuity: the pull towards zero difference is released, and the weak continuity constraint has been broken.

energy. Clearly it is infeasible to look at all the local minima and compare their energies.

How do these local minima arise? The function F can be regarded as the energy of a system of springs, as illustrated in figure 3.4a. We will see that, like the magnetic dipole system in chapter 1, it has many stable states. Vertical springs are attached at one end to anchor points, representing data d_i which are fixed, and to nodes u_i at the other end. These springs represent the D term in the energy F (3.5). There are also lateral springs between nodes. Now if these springs were just ordinary springs there would be no convexity problem. There would be just one stable state: no matter how much the system were perturbed, it would always spring back to the configuration in figure 3.4a. But in fact the springs are special; they are the ones that enforce weak continuity constraints. Each is initially elastic but, when stretched too far, gives way and breaks, as specified by the energy g in figure 3.3. As a consequence, a second stable state is possible (figure 3.4b) in which the central spring is broken. In an intermediate state (figure 3.4c) the energy will be higher than in either of the stable states, so that traversing from one stable state to the other, the energy must change as in figure 3.4d. For simplicity, only 2 stable states have been illustrated, but in general each lateral spring may either be broken or not, generating the plethora of stable states mentioned above.

No local descent algorithm will suffice to find the minimum of F. Local descent tends to stick, like the fly shown in figure 3.4, in a local minimum,

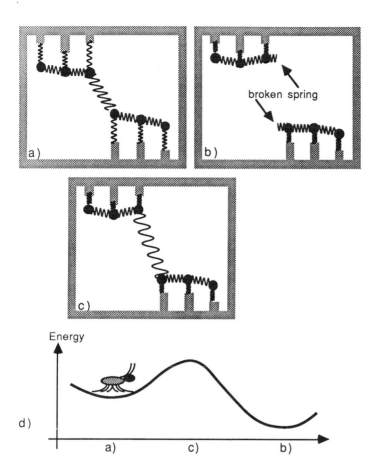

Figure 3.4: Non-convexity: the weak string is like a system of conventional vertical springs with "breakable" lateral springs as shown. The states (a) and (b) are both stable, but the intermediate state (c) has higher energy than either (a) or (b). Suppose the lowest energy state is (b). A myopic fly with vertigo, crawling along the energy transition diagram (d) thinks state (a) is best - he has no way of seeing that, over the hump, he could get to a lower state (b).

and there could be as many as 2^N local minima to get stuck in. Somehow some global "lookahead" must be incorporated. The next section explains how the Graduated Non-Convexity (GNC) algorithm does this.

3.5   Graduated non-convexity

A method of minimising F is needed which avoids the pitfall of sticking in local minima. Stochastic methods such as "Simulated Annealing" (Kirkpatrick et al. 1982) avoid local minima by random fluctuations, spasmodic injections of energy, to shake free of them (figure 3.5a). Although this guarantees to find the global minimum eventually, the amount of computation required may be very large (Geman and Geman 1984). It would

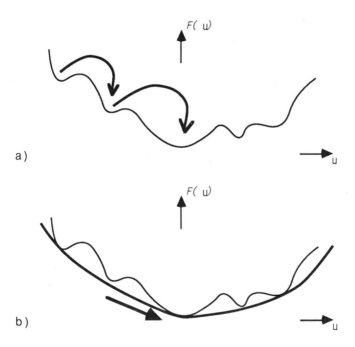

Figure 3.5: a) Stochastic methods avoid local minima by using random motions to jump out of them. b) The GNC method constructs an approximating convex function, free of spurious local minima.

appear, however, to be in the interests of computational efficiency to use a non-random method. GNC, rather than injecting energy randomly, uses a modified cost function (fig 3.5b).

In the GNC method, the cost function F is first approximated by a new function F^* which is *convex* and hence can only have one local minimum, which must also be a global minimum[2]. Descent on F^* (descending, that is, in the $(N+1)$-dimensional space of variables $\{u_i\}$) must land up at that minimum. Now, for certain data d_i this minimum may also be a *global* minimum of F - which is what we were after. There is a simple test to detect whether or not this has succeeded (fig 3.6a,b). In fact (see chapter 7) success is most likely when the scale parameter λ is small.

A more general strategy, that works for small or large λ, is to use a whole *sequence* of cost functions $F^{(p)}$, for $1 \geq p \geq 0$. These are chosen so that $F^{(0)} = F$, the true cost function, and $F^{(1)} = F^*$, the convex approximation to F. In between, $F^{(p)}$ changes, in a continuous fashion, between $F^{(1)}$ and $F^{(0)}$. The GNC algorithm is then to optimise a whole sequence of $F^{(p)}$, for example $\{F^{(1)}, F^{(1/2)}, F^{(1/4)}, F^{(1/8)}, F^{(1/16)}, F^{(1/32)}\}$, one after the other, using the result of one optimisation as the starting point for the next. As an example, optimisation of a non-convex F, using a sequence of just 3 functions, is illustrated in fig 3.6c. Initially, optimisation of $F^{(1)} \equiv F^*$ produces u^* but (let us suppose) this happened not to be the global optimum of F. (Note that *any* starting point will do for optimising $F^{(1)}$. That is because $F^{(1)}$, being convex, has only one minimum, which will be attained by descent, regardless of where descent starts.) But successive optimisation of $F^{(p)}$ as p decreases "pulls" towards the true global optimum of F. Exactly how the functions $F^{(p)}$ are constructed must be left until later. It all depends on making F^* a good convex approximation to F. Suffice it to say that, like F in (3.5), F^* and all the $F^{(p)}$ are sums of local functions:

$$F^{(p)} = D + \sum_1^N g^{(p)}(u_i - u_{i-1}), \qquad (3.6)$$

and this is important when it comes to considering optimisation algorithms. Of course, the trick is to choose the right neighbour interaction function $g^{(p)}$. This is all explained at some length in chapter 7.

There are numerous ways to minimise each $F^{(p)}$, including direct descent and gradient methods. Direct descent is particularly straightforward to implement and runs like this: propose a change in one of the nodal values u_i, see if that leads to a reduction in $F^{(p)}$ (this only involves a local computation); if it does then make the change. A simple program which

---

[2] Actually there are some details to take care of here, distinguishing between convexity and strict convexity.

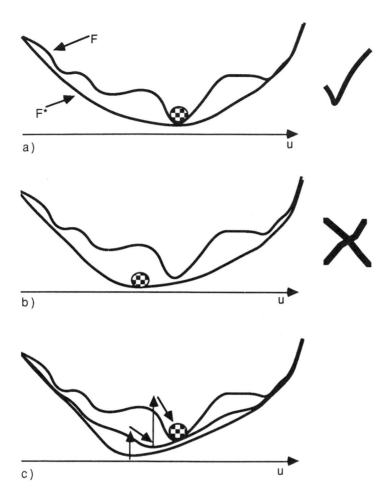

Figure 3.6: The minimum of a non-convex function F may be found by minimising a convex approximation F^* (a). If that does not work (b), the minimum may still be found by the GNC algorithm, which runs downhill on each of a sequence of functions (c), to reach the true global optimum.

implements GNC by direct descent is outlined in fig 3.7. It can be made to

```
for p ∈ {1, 1/2, 1/4, 1/8, 1/16, 1/32} do
  for δ := 1; δ ≥ δ_min; δ := δ/2 do
    changed := true
    while changed do
    changed := false
    for i = 0...N do
      if F^(p)(u_1, .., u_i + δ, .., u_N) < F^(p)(u_1, .., u_i, .., u_N) then
      u_i := u_i + δ
      changed := true
      else if F^(p)(u_1, .., u_i − δ, .., u_N) < F^(p)(u_1, .., u_i, .., u_N) then
      u_i := u_i − δ
      changed := true
```

Figure 3.7: A direct descent algorithm for GNC - see text for details

run quite satisfactorily with fixed point arithmetic. As $F^{(p)}$ is expressed as a sum over $i = 0, ..., N$ of local terms (3.6), the effect of altering a particular u_i (tested in the **if** and **else if** statements) can be computed from just a few of those terms. For example u_i appears only in $g^{(p)}(u_i - u_{i-1})$, $g^{(p)}(u_{i+1} - u_i)$ and, in D, in the term $(u_i - d_i)^2$. Not only does this simplify the computation of the effect on $F^{(p)}$ of changing u_i, but it is also possible to perform such computations on many u_i in parallel. More efficient algorithms, based on gradient descent methods, are described in chapter 7.

Figure 3.8 shows the GNC method in operation, solving the 1D weak elastic string problem. The successive gradient descent scheme (SOR) of chapter 7 is used. For small values of the scale parameter λ the total time for execution[3] is about $0.001N$ seconds, where N is the length of the data vector. This works out at about 50 arithmetic operations per data element.

---

[3]On a SUN2 computer, with SKY floating point board

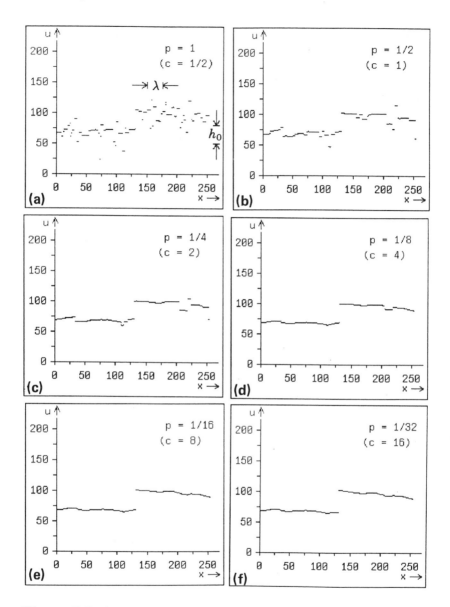

Figure 3.8: Snapshots of GNC: Initial data as in figure 2.2 on page 19. As GNC progresses, parameter p is decreased. (The significance of parameters h_0 and c is explained in subsequent chapters.)

Chapter 4

Properties of the Weak String and Membrane

The previous chapter introduced the weak string as a 1D discontinuity detecting filter. This chapter examines both it and its 2D equivalent, the weak membrane, as variational problems. Recall that the energy of the weak string is described by the function

$$E \;=\; D + S + P \qquad (4.1)$$

$$=\; \int (u(x) - d(x))^2 \; dx + \lambda^2 \int u'^2(x) \; dx + \alpha Z \qquad (4.2)$$

where α and λ are constants - parameters of the system - and integration is between suitable limits. The first two terms D, S specify the behaviour of each continuous section of the piecewise elastic string $u(x)$, attached by "springs" to the data $d(x)$. The last term is a measure of the set of discontinuities in $u(x)$; Z is taken to be simply the total number of points x at which $u(x)$ is discontinuous. In 1D, this definition of Z is more or less the only sensible one. It will be seen that, in 2D, with the membrane, there is more than one reasonable way of defining Z.

So far it has appeared that constants α, λ are arbitrary parameters; it is not clear how they should be fixed. But variational analysis of the weak string's behaviour with certain specially chosen data $d(x)$ allows extremal energy E to be predicted, as a function of α, λ. This can be done both for continuous u and when u includes one or more discontinuities. The weak string/membrane will adopt the lowest energy configuration. So comparison of energies, with and without discontinuities, determines exactly what effect λ and α have on the detection of discontinuities. Most of our results (but not their derivations) were reported in (Blake and Zisserman 1985a, 1986b).

The principal conclusions of this chapter are that

- The parameter λ is a characteristic length or *scale* (figure 4.1).

- The ratio $h_0 = \sqrt{2\alpha/\lambda}$ is a "contrast" sensitivity threshold, determining the minimum contrast for detection of an isolated step edge. A step edge in the data counts as isolated if there are no features within λ of it - and this property itself reinforces the interpretation of λ as a characteristic length. In addition to being a characteristic length for *smoothing* continuous portions of the data, λ is also a characteristic distance for *interaction* between discontinuities.

- When two similar steps in the data are only a apart ($a \ll \lambda$) they interact as follows: the threshold for detection (labelling the steps as discontinuities) is increased by a factor $\sqrt{\lambda/a}$, compared with the contrast threshold for an isolated step. This constitutes a proof that the weak string is *not* equivalent to any linear operator followed by thresholding, for which the corresponding factor would be proportional to $1/a$, not $1/\sqrt{a}$. It is complementary to the finding of Mumford and Shah (1985) that the weak string does behave like a linear operator with thresholding, but *only* for isolated, non-interacting discontinuities. Such distinctive, non-linear behaviour is a property also of the membrane, with interacting discontinuities in 2D.

- The ratio $g_l = h_0/2\lambda$ is a limit on gradient, above which spurious discontinuities may be generated. This property is inferred from behaviour when fitting data in the form of a ramp: if the gradient exceeds g_l one or more discontinuities may appear in the fitted function.

- It can be shown that, in a precise sense, localisation accuracy (for given signal-to-noise) is high. In fact it is qualitatively as good as the "difference of boxes" operator - but without any false zero-crossings problem (see (Canny 1983)). Non-random localisation error is also minimised. Given asymmetrical data, gaussians and other smooth linear operators make consistent errors in localisation. The weak string, based as it is on least squares fitting, does not.

- The parameter α is a measure of immunity to noise. If the mean noise has standard deviation σ, then no spurious discontinuities are generated provided $\alpha > 2\sigma^2$, approximately. This theoretical prediction is borne out in the computer implementation (e.g. figure 4.2).

- The membrane has a hysteresis property - a tendency to form unbroken edges. This is an intrinsic property of membrane elasticity, and

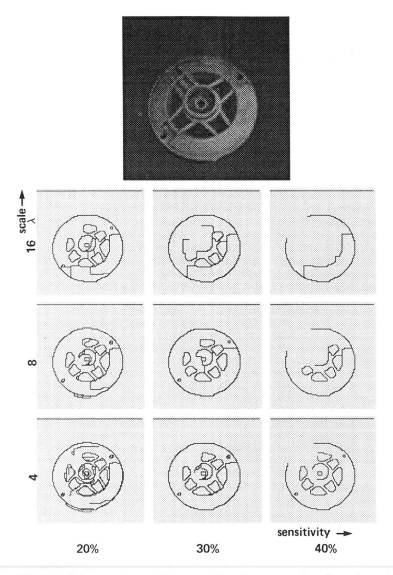

Figure 4.1: Weak membrane edge detector: the effect of varying scale (λ) and contrast sensitivity is shown. (Data $d(x,y)$ was approximately the *logarithm* of image intensity. The image is 128 pixels square.)

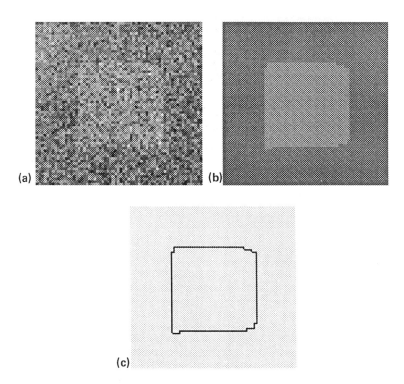

Figure 4.2: A light square on a dark background, with added noise (a). Signal-to-noise ratio is 1. A weak membrane is well able to reconstruct the signal (b). (c) Labelled discontinuities. ($\alpha/\sigma^2 \approx 4$.)

happens *without* any need to impose additional cost on edge terminations.

- The weak string or membrane can be used with sparse data. The
  density of stereo depth data (depths obtained from matching a stereoscopic image pair) is limited by the density of strongly localised features in images. Also hyperacuity - sub-pixel localisation of discontinuities - can be implemented by forming a fine grid on which the
  data (intensity or depth) is distributed sparsely.

- Finally the weak string/membrane is quite unable to label crease
  discontinuities. This is because a membrane conforms quite happily
  to a crease without any associated energy increase. The weak plate,
  however, can be used to detect creases. This is because it has a
  2nd order energy (a function of 2nd derivatives) unlike the membrane
  energy which is 1st order; but that must be left until the next chapter.

4.1   The weak string

4.1.1   Energy of a continuous piece

Suppose the positions of all discontinuities were given in advance. Then
the energy of each continuous piece of u could be computed separately.
One way of doing this[1] is to construct the solution $u(x)$, in each piece, by
convolving d with a Green's function G:

$$u(x) = \int G(x, x')d(x')\, dx' \tag{4.3}$$

where, in the case of a bi-infinite interval,

$$G(x, x') = \frac{1}{2\lambda}e^{-|x-x'|/\lambda} \tag{4.4}$$

which is plotted in figure 4.3. The characteristic length or scale of the filter
is simply the parameter λ. In the case of a finite interval, the filter shape
is similar, but modified near interval boundaries (see appendix A). Having
obtained $u(x)$ the energy is (appendix A)

$$E = \int_{-\infty}^{\infty} d(x)(d(x) - u(x))\, dx. \tag{4.5}$$

This can be used to compute energies for various forms of data $d(x)$.

---

[1] An alternative Fourier method is given in appendix A.

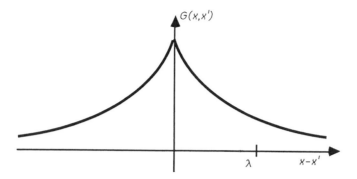

Figure 4.3: Green's function for the string. The elastic string has the effect of smoothing data d with the filter shown.

4.1.2   Applying continuity constraints

The behaviour of the weak string depends on the size of the energy increase when a discontinuity is removed so that $u(x)$ is forced to be continuous across an interval boundary. A closely related question is: how much does the energy of the string, in some interval, increase when the position of one end is fixed? The answers to both questions, remarkably, turn out to be virtually independent of the precise form of the data d. They will therefore be satisfyingly general.

Suppose the string $u(x)$, $x \in [0, L]$ is fixed at one end, so that $u(0) = z$ (figure 4.4a). Its energy is (appendix A):

$$E = \mathcal{E}(z - \overline{z})^2 + E_0 \tag{4.6}$$

where $E_0, \overline{z}$ are values of E, z when the string is unconstrained and $\mathcal{E}$ is a constant depending *only* on L, λ - quite independent of the data:

$$\mathcal{E} = \lambda \tanh\left(\frac{L}{\lambda}\right) \tag{4.7}$$

$$\approx \lambda \text{ when } L \gg \lambda. \tag{4.8}$$

As expected, energy E is smallest in the "resting" position $z = \overline{z}, u = \overline{u}$, and increases quadratically as z is displaced.

When u is forced to be continuous at the join of two intervals, u is effectively fixed, at the ends of both intervals, to the common value z that minimizes the total increase in energy (figure 4.4b). It is easily shown

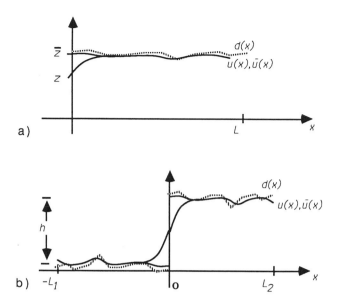

Figure 4.4: Fixing one end of a string increases its energy (a). Enforcing continuity fixes ends of two strings to some common value (b).

(appendix A) that this total increase in energy is

$$\Delta E = h^2 \left(\frac{1}{\mathcal{E}_1} + \frac{1}{\mathcal{E}_2} \right)^{-1}, \qquad (4.9)$$

where $h = |\bar{z}_2 - \bar{z}_1|$ - the "effective" step height.

If both intervals have lengths $L_1, L_2 \gg \lambda$, then, from (4.8), $\mathcal{E}_1 = \mathcal{E}_2 = \lambda$ and the energy increase is just

$$\Delta E = \frac{1}{2} h^2 \lambda. \qquad (4.10)$$

4.1.3   Sensitivity to an isolated step

The simplest possible data comprises a single isolated step discontinuity as in figure 4.4b. The lowest energy solution contains a discontinuity at the step if and only if the energy increase $\Delta E - \alpha$ on removing the discontinuity satisfies $\Delta E - \alpha > 0$. (Remember, from chapter 3, that the α term represents the energy penalty for one discontinuity.) From (4.10) the condition is met when

$$h > h_0 = \sqrt{\frac{2\alpha}{\lambda}}. \qquad (4.11)$$

So the existence of an isolated discontinuity in weak string reconstruction u of data d, at a particular point, depends entirely on whether the effective step height h exceeds the threshold h_0. It can also be shown that

$$\Delta E = 2\lambda^3 \left(\bar{u}'(0) \right)^2, \qquad (4.12)$$

(where $\bar{u}(x)$ is now the continuous reconstruction of $d(x)$) so an equivalent condition is that

$$\bar{u}'(0) > \frac{h_0}{2\lambda}. \qquad (4.13)$$

Of course it has been assumed so far that only one possible site for the discontinuity is under consideration. The question of exactly where discontinuities choose to form has not been answered - it will be dealt with later in the chapter. Detection of a discontinuity appears, so far, to depend on a remarkably simple threshold rule. In fact that is true only for isolated sites. When two sites for discontinuities come within interaction range (λ) behaviour is somewhat modified.

4.1.4   Interaction of adjacent steps

A top hat (figure 4.5a) consists of two steps back to back. The energy of a

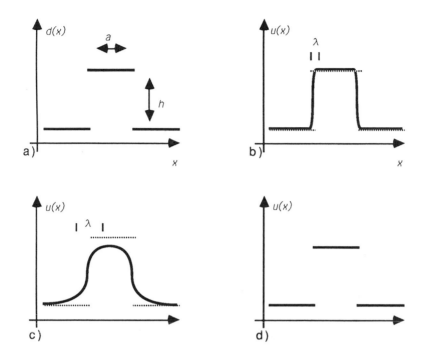

Figure 4.5: 1D top hat data. (a) shows a 1D top hat and (b) and (c) are continuous elastic strings fitted to the data, with small and large λ respectively. (d) shows the fitted string with two discontinuities.

continuous string fitted to such data is given by

$$E = h^2\lambda(1 - e^{-a/\lambda}) \tag{4.14}$$

where h is the height of the steps and a their separation. Typical continuous solutions for $u(x)$ are shown in figure 4.5b,c. The energy (4.14) is due both to the deviation from the data and to the cost of not being flat.

The weak membrane can break at both steps (figure 4.5d) and then the only contribution to the energy (for this special data) is from the penalty 2α. In this case, therefore,

$$E = 2\alpha. \tag{4.15}$$

Comparison of the two energies (4.14) and (4.15) determines whether or not a solution with discontinuities has the lowest energy.

If $\lambda \ll a$ then (4.14) reduces to

$$E = h^2\lambda \tag{4.16}$$

which is independent of a and is simply the energy of two steps. Comparison of equations (4.15) and (4.16) shows that the lowest energy solution will have discontinuities at the steps - and so the steps will be detected - if

$$h > h_0 = \sqrt{\frac{2\alpha}{\lambda}}$$

This is the same as the threshold for a single step (4.11). Consequently, if the step separation is large compared to λ then the steps do not interfere with each other - they are treated independently by the weak string.

If the steps are close to each other $(a \ll \lambda)$ the energy (4.14) is reduced and the steps interfere. The energy in that case is

$$E = h^2 a, \tag{4.17}$$

independent of λ. Comparing this with the penalty 2α, the discontinuous solution (with 2 steps) has lower energy if $h > h_0\sqrt{\lambda/a}$. The contrast threshold is increased by a factor $\sqrt{\lambda/a}$, compared with that for isolated steps.

The interference effect extends the interpretation of λ, already established by the form of the Green's function, as a scale parameter. If discontinuities are separated by distances which are large compared to λ then they do not interfere with each other and are considered independently by the system.

Although this result has been obtained for an ideal top hat it can be generalised just as threshold behaviour for an isolated discontinuity applied, not only for an ideal step, but also for general data (figure 4.4b). The generalisation of the top hat would include any pair of discontinuities with the same effective step height. It is possible to generalise still further (appendix A, equation (A.23)) to cover any pair of interacting discontinuities. In that case it is possible that both, one or neither discontinuities may be detected. For example, in the case that the spacing between discontinuities satisfies $a \ll \lambda$, so that the interaction is strongest, the number of discontinuities detected depends on which of the following energies is least:

$$
\left\{
\begin{array}{llll}
\text{none}: & \text{if } \frac{1}{2}\lambda(h_1 - h_2)^2 + a h_1 h_2 & \text{is least} \\
\text{one}: & \text{if } a h_1^2 + \alpha & \text{is least} & (4.18) \\
\text{two}: & \text{if } 2\alpha & \text{is least}
\end{array}
\right.
$$

where h_2, h_1 are effective step heights with $h_2 > h_1$ (figure 4.6).

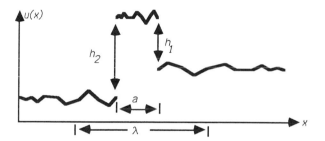

Figure 4.6: Interaction of a pair of step discontinuities (see text).

Double steps generated by digitisation: A particular case of interest are spurious steps (figure 4.7) which occur frequently in digitised data. (Discrete analysis should really be used here, but in fact it makes little difference to the outcome.) Comparing energies with one (central) discontinuity, which can be shown to be

$$
E = \alpha + \frac{1}{4}h^2 a
$$

and with two discontinuities

$$
E = 2\alpha,
$$

the undesirable effect is eliminated provided

$$
\frac{h}{h_0} < \sqrt{\frac{2\lambda}{a}}. \tag{4.19}
$$

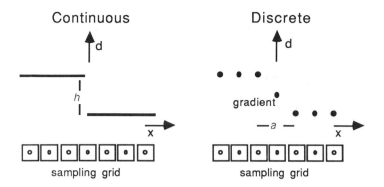

Figure 4.7: Double edges can occur on gradients caused by digitisation effects. They are suppressed by using a sufficiently large scale parameter λ.

The larger λ is, the larger the step height h can be, before a double edge occurs.

4.1.5   The gradient limit

Data in the form of a ramp of finite extent is shown in figure 4.8a. As before the energy of the continuous solution (figure 4.8b) is compared with that of a solution with a single discontinuity (figure 4.8c). The minimum energy solution with one step discontinuity has its step placed symmetrically at the centre of the ramp. The energies for the two cases are

$$E = g^2\lambda^2(a - \lambda(1 - e^{-a/\lambda})) \tag{4.20}$$

for the continuous membrane and, with a single step discontinuity,

$$E = \alpha + g^2\lambda^2(a - 2\lambda e^{-\frac{a}{2\lambda}}(2\cosh\frac{a}{2\lambda} - 2 + \sinh\frac{a}{2\lambda})) \tag{4.21}$$

where a is the extent of the ramp, h its height and g its gradient ($g = h/a$).

Again, consider the limits of large and small λ relative to a. If $\lambda \gg a$ then the ramp looks (at a scale of λ) like a step. As expected, the contrast threshold $h > h_0$ applies.

If $\lambda \ll a$ then a step is detected if

$$g > g_l = \sqrt{\frac{\alpha}{2\lambda^3}} = \frac{h_0}{2\lambda}. \tag{4.22}$$

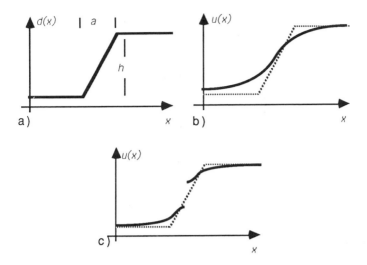

Figure 4.8: 1D finite ramp data (a) with continuous string fitted to it (b). (c) shows the lowest energy solution with a single discontinuity.

This is the "gradient limit" effect: if the gradient of a ramp exceeds the limit, a discontinuity appears in its reconstruction. And if g is *much* greater than g_l then a solution with multiple breaks might have smallest energy. This is a fundamental limitation of the weak string/membrane - a steep ramp with large extent (relative to λ) will be detected as a multiple step. The rod/plate (chapter 5) does not have this disadvantage.

Performance of the weak string and membrane, as characterised by variational analysis so far, is summarised in figure 4.9.

4.2 Localisation and spurious response in noise

4.2.1 Localisation in scale space: uniformity property

The introductory discussion of the applications of weak continuity included a brief reference to the task of curve description. A variation on Asada and Brady's use of gaussian scale-space filtering (Asada and Brady 1986)

Data: $\quad\mid\ \lambda\ \mid$	Continuous energy	Discontinuous energy	Criterion for step detection
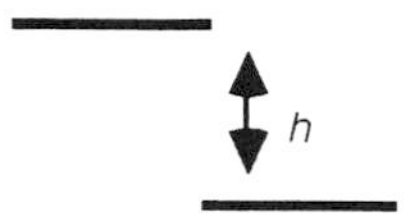 h	$h^2\lambda/2$	α	$h > \sqrt{2\alpha/\lambda}$
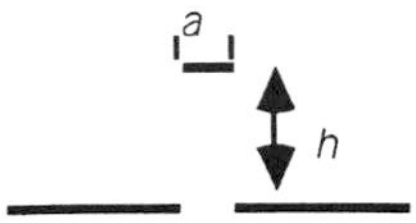 a h	h^2a	2α	$h > \sqrt{2\alpha/a}$
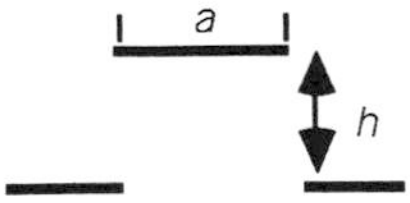 a h	$h^2\lambda$	2α	$h > \sqrt{2\alpha/\lambda}$
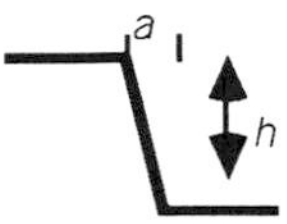 a h	as for step - but double step if $h/h_0 \gg 1$		
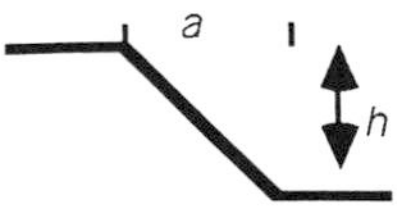 a h	E_s	$E_s + \alpha$ $-2h^2\lambda^3/a^2$	$g > \sqrt{\alpha/2\lambda^3}$ $(g = h/a)$
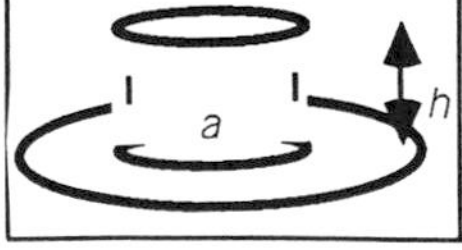 a h	$\pi a h^2 \lambda$	$2\pi a\alpha$	$h > \sqrt{2\alpha/\lambda}$

Figure 4.9: Summary of the performance of a weak string/membrane.

employs a weak string as the filter (Blake et al. 1986a). Typical results were displayed in figure 2.14 on page 34. Its most interesting property is that of *uniformity*; lines in the scale space diagram (figure 2.14d) are vertical. That is a graphical representation of the fact that the positions of discontinuities do not vary as the filter scale λ varies. Localisation across scale is very accurate. This is in distinct contrast to the behaviour of scale-space under a gaussian (or other smooth) linear filter. If an asymmetric signal $d(x)$ is filtered (figure 4.10a) there is a systematic error in localisation of the discontinuity (Asada and Brady 1986) which is proportional to the filter scale w.

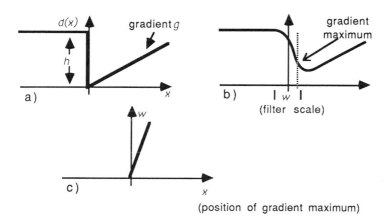

Figure 4.10: An asymmetric step (a) filtered by a gaussian filter of scale w generates a gradient maximum which can be used to mark the discontinuity (b). But the mark has an error of localisation which increases with w, as shown in the scale space diagram (c).

Such error can, in principle, be removed by tracking from coarse scale, where noise is well suppressed, to fine scale, where localisation is good. In practice it is possible only to sample scale-space at a few discrete scales, so that correct tracking becomes a difficult problem (figure 4.11). No such problem occurs under weak continuity constraints because of uniformity - tracking is trivial. Indeed, the weak string does not *demand* an entire scale space at all, in the sense that Gaussian filtering does. One or two scales λ may suffice for the purposes of interpretation - a fine and a coarse view perhaps. The examples given in chapter 2 (figures 2.14 and 2.15) needed only a single scale to achieve an accurate reconstruction.

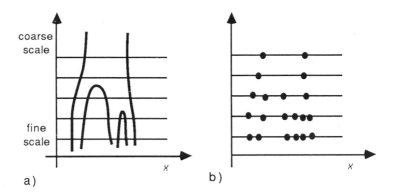

Figure 4.11: Tracking a sampled Gaussian scale-space. In principle, fingerprints can be tracked from coarse to fine scale (a). In practice, sampling makes this a much more difficult task (b).

When a similar asymmetric step is filtered by a weak string, the discontinuity in the string remains precisely on the step, regardless of the scale parameter λ in the string energy. That is the underlying reason for the uniformity property. Intuitively this is made clear in figure 4.12.

The intuitive argument can be made more precise. This is done in two different ways. First the now familiar variational approach is used to derive the energy $E(\epsilon)$ of the weak string, as a function of discontinuity location ϵ, for the data in figure 4.10. The global minimum is shown to exist stably at $\epsilon = 0$, having a V-shaped profile as in figure 4.12c, regardless of λ. Second, variational results show that the discontinuity in the string clings to $\epsilon = 0$ even in the presence of small variations in $d(x)$ near the step.

The effect of the weak string on the asymmetric step is analysed by means of (A.15) and (A.16) of appendix A, which gives the energy of a continuous string stretched over a step/ramp as in figure 4.10. The energy $E(\epsilon)$ for the asymmetric step of figure 4.12 can be shown to have the form

$$E(\epsilon) = \begin{cases} \text{const.} - \frac{1}{2}(h - g\lambda)^2 \lambda \exp\left(\frac{-2|\epsilon|}{\lambda}\right) & \text{for } \epsilon < 0 \\ \text{const.} - \frac{1}{2}(h + g\lambda)^2 \lambda \exp\left(\frac{-2|\epsilon|}{\lambda}\right) & \text{for } \epsilon > 0 \end{cases} . \tag{4.23}$$

(This assumes that λ is much less than the total extent of data $d(x)$ on either side of the step.) Energy $E(\epsilon)$ is clearly monotonic increasing with $|\epsilon|$ so that the global minimum is at $\epsilon = 0$. Curious degenerate cases occur when $h = \pm g\lambda$, and the stability of the global minimum is lost. To first

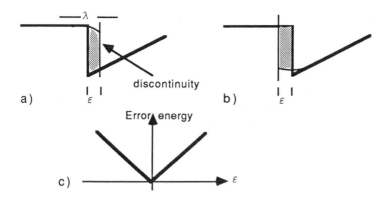

a) b) c)

discontinuity

Error energy

Figure 4.12: Localisation of the weak string: consider a weak string fitted to data $d(x)$ containing a step, but with its discontinuity displaced ϵ from the step (a) or (b). The hatched "error area" is roughly a rectangle $h \times \epsilon$, and so generates a square error contribution to the energy of approximately $h^2|\epsilon|$. The minimum energy is clearly at $\epsilon = 0$ (c).

order in $|\epsilon|$ the energy is

$$E(\epsilon) = E(0) + \begin{cases} (h - g\lambda)^2|\epsilon| & \text{for } \epsilon < 0 \\ (h + g\lambda)^2|\epsilon| & \text{for } \epsilon > 0. \end{cases} \tag{4.24}$$

This means that locally, around $\epsilon = 0$, the V-shape of the minimum (figure 4.12c) is preserved, albeit somewhat skewed. This holds for any λ (which is not too large and avoids the degeneracies just mentioned) so that precise localisation is maintained right across scale space (figure 4.12c).

Mumford and Shah (1985) derive an extremality condition which is necessary for the existence of a global minimum of energy $E(\epsilon)$. It assumes that the discontinuity at $x = \epsilon$ is isolated (on the scale of λ). The condition, in our notation, is that

$$u_c''(\epsilon) = 0 \tag{4.25}$$

where $u_c(x)$ is the configuration of a *continuous* string fitted to the data $d(x)$. This is directly related to the earlier result (4.12) which, applied here, shows that the energy gain on allowing a discontinuity at $x = \epsilon$ is

$$2\lambda^3 \left(u_c'(\epsilon) \right)^2 .$$

Equation (4.25) is therefore simply a necessary condition for maximising that energy gain. But since, from the Euler-Lagrange equation (A.2), $u_c'' =$

$\lambda^{-2}(u_c - d)$ the condition (4.25) can be re-expressed as

$$u_c(\epsilon) = d(\epsilon) \qquad (4.26)$$

- that the continuous string crosses the data at $x = \epsilon$. For data $d(x)$ with a step discontinuity (figure 4.13a) the condition is met *only* at the step. Hence there cannot be a global minimum anywhere other than at $\epsilon = 0$,

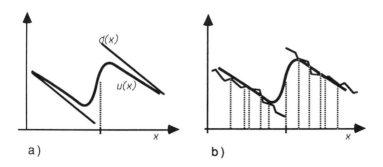

a)   b)

Figure 4.13: Necessary condition for an energy minimum: a minimum of $E(\epsilon)$ can occur only where the continuous string $u_c(x)$ crosses data $d(x)$, as at the step in (a). But in the presence of noise the condition will also be met in numerous spurious locations (b).

confirming what has already been concluded from (4.23). Moreover this property is clearly robust to small changes in the data $d(x)$, in the vicinity of the discontinuity.

   Next we consider localisation accuracy in the presence of noise. In this case Mumford and Shah's condition cannot be used, and for a rather interesting reason. We know that $u_c'' = \lambda^{-2}(u_c - d)$ - the second derivative depends linearly on the data d, raw and unfiltered, including any noise it may contain. Now the peak values of a noise signal $n(x)$ are theoretically unbounded, even for quite small amounts of noise, and in practice they are bounded only as a result of what little filtering has already been applied to the data, probably by sampling. This means that the noise will very frequently cross u_c (figure 4.13b) producing a high density of spurious zero-crossings of u_c''. Nonetheless, localisation accuracy is maintained in the presence of noise (figure 4.14). To explain this, it will be necessary to fall back on the first method - computing energy E as a function of localisation error ϵ - but now with added noise.

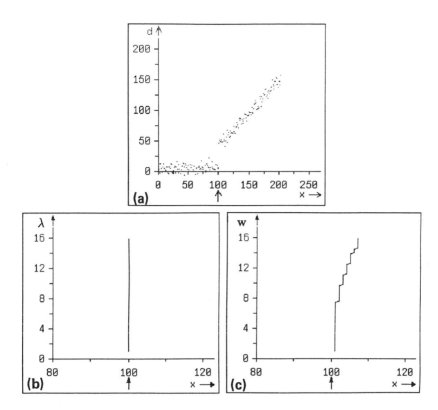

Figure 4.14: Uniformity in scale-space. An asymmetric step (a), (signal-to-noise ratio is 6:1), filtered by the weak string, is accurately localised (b) over a range of scales, as expected. Gaussian filtering produces error of the order of the filter size (c).

4.2.2   Localisation in noise

Consider an input signal $d(x), x \in [-L, L]$ consisting of a step of height h, which is then immersed in noise $n(x)$, as in figure 4.15a. The energy $E(u_\epsilon)$

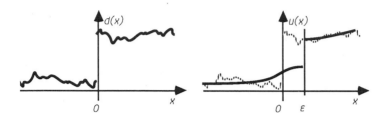

Figure 4.15: Localisation error in noise is estimated by applying variational analysis to a noisy ideal step.

varies with respect to the position $x = \epsilon$ of the discontinuity. In the noise free case the variation is denoted $E(u_{\epsilon,d})$ and is

$$E(u_{\epsilon,d}) \doteq E(u_{0,d}) + h^2 |\epsilon| \tag{4.27}$$

(equation (4.23) with $g = 0$). There is a sharp (V-shaped) minimum at $x = 0$. Any small variations in the data $d(x)$ around $x = 0$ simply add a small $O(\epsilon)$ term to energy $E(u_{\epsilon,d})$ above. This does not affect the position of the V-shaped minimum which remains at $\epsilon = 0$. It is the sharpness of the minimum at $\epsilon = 0$ that makes for such tenacious stability of the discontinuity at $x = 0$. In scale-space, this is what produced uniformity.

Having obtained $E(u_{\epsilon,d})$, for the noise-free case, it remains to calculate the equivalent energy $E(u_\epsilon)$ in the presence of additive noise. It is shown in appendix B that provided

$$\frac{h}{n_0} > 2$$

- that is that the signal-to-noise ratio exceeds 2 - then

$$\forall |\epsilon| > 0, \ E(u_\epsilon) > E(u_0).$$

(The quantity n_0 is the standard deviation of the noise[2].) There is negligible localisation error, when the signal-to-noise ratio is not too small. Results are shown in figure 4.16.

---

[2]This is not to be confused with the standard deviation of the *mean* noise, σ; $n_0 = \sqrt{\rho}\sigma$, where ρ is a coherence length. But typically $\rho = 1$ pixel, so σ, n_0 are numerically equal.

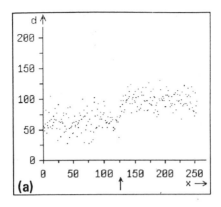

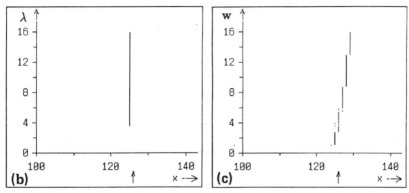

Figure 4.16: Localisation in noise. (a) Data: a noisy step, signal-to-noise ratio 2:1, with the position of the step marked for clarity. Uniform scale space (b) for the weak string - there is no localisation error. Gaussian scale space (c) - as theory predicts, localisation error increases with scale.

Now for smooth linear operators followed by labelling of gradient maxima, localisation error $\delta x \propto (h/n_0)^{-1}$. For an equivalent directional gaussian operator ($w = \lambda$ - see appendix B), at signal-to-noise ratio $h/n_0 = 2$, localisation error is already $\sqrt{w}/2$. (This assumes the coherence length of the noise is $\rho = 1$ pixel.)

Only for an operator like the difference of boxes, which is not smooth, is localisation as good as for the weak string. The difference of boxes operator was shown by Canny (1983) to be unusable because of the overwhelming incidence of spurious gradient maxima, when noise is present. But the spurious zero crossings problem simply doesn't arise with weak continuity constraints - zero crossings are not used.

4.2.3   Spurious responses in noise

Consider the data $d(x) = 0$, clearly free of discontinuities, in the presence of additive noise $n(x)$. If the penalty α is close to zero, then there is little to discourage the formation of discontinuities in $u(x)$. Discontinuities in $u(x)$ will be generated by the noise. But as α increases (for a given λ) it is to be expected that fewer and fewer discontinuities should form. For sufficiently large α the probability of spurious discontinuities becomes negligible. It is shown that the value of such an α depends on σ (the standard deviation of mean noise) only, independent of λ.

Two energies are computed: $E(u_\epsilon)$, the minimal energy of a u with a discontinuity at $x = \epsilon$, and $E(u_c)$ the minimal energy of a continuous u. Using the finite Green's function for the stretched string, it is shown in appendix B that

$$\alpha - E(u_\epsilon) + E(u_c) = R^2,$$

where R is a gaussian random variable whose standard deviation is $\sigma/\sqrt{2}$. Now the condition for a spurious discontinuity at $x = 0$, is $E(u_\epsilon) < E(u_c)$. The conclusion is that, for $\sqrt{2\alpha} > 2\sigma$ (2σ is approximately the two tail 95% confidence limit) that is, for

$$\alpha > 2\sigma^2,$$

there is less than 5 percent probability that the condition is satisfied.

4.3   The weak membrane

The energy $E = D + S + P$ of a string (4.2) can be generalised for a membrane in 2D. The appropriate generalisation of the elastic component $D + S$ of the energy is obvious:

$$D = \int (u - d)^2 \, dA \qquad (4.28)$$

$$S = \lambda^2 \int (\bigtriangledown u)^2 \, dA. \tag{4.29}$$

But there are a number of ways in which the penalty term $P = \alpha Z$ can be generalised.

4.3.1 Penalties for discontinuity

The quantity Z becomes a measure of the set of contours in the plane along which $u(x, y)$ is discontinuous. It might be defined in any of the following ways:

- **As a measure of total contour length:** this is the simplest reasonable measure, and is the one we use. Minimising the energy E then tends to minimize contour length. There is therefore an elastic energy associated with the contours of discontinuity in u.

- **Including a measure of contour curvature:** for example Z might have a $(d\theta/ds)^2$ component, where s is arc length and θ is tangent orientation along a contour. This ensures that contours are smooth as well as just short. But a reliable estimator for θ requires reasonably large neighbourhood convolutions, in order to avoid excessive quantisation error. (In statistical terms this would mean a higher order Markov random field). Experience with the weak plate (see later chapters on discrete computation) suggests that computation time increases very sharply indeed as neighbourhood sizes increase. Even the plate which is only 2nd order (interaction between a pixel, its neighbours and its neighbours' neighbours) is already more or less intractable in its "pure" form.

- **A weak constraint on contour smoothness:** essentially this would be an extension of the contour curvature energy above, but including a cost associated with tangent discontinuities (corners). Of course it is likely to be computationally infeasible for the same reasons.

- **Including costs for certain topological features:** costs can be levied for contour terminations for example, effectively imposing a weak connectedness constraint on the contour. Geman and Geman (1984) do this by means of their line process and its associated costs. Such a line process is too complex for use in the GNC algorithm. This is because the line-process elimination step, introduced for the weak string in chapter 3 and extended for the membrane in chapter 6, can no longer be performed. Fortunately there is no real need for such a complex line process. We will see that the membrane already imposes a weak connectedness constraint, as a natural consequence of its elastic behaviour. This "hysteresis" effect is the analogue of the propagation of a tear in an elastic material. It occurs without the need to associate any costs with terminations in the line process.

- **Global length measures:** a cost that increases non-linearly with contour length has possible uses - for example in introducing a graduated bias away from short edges (although the hysteresis effect already does this to some degree). But the global nature of the measure would increase computational cost enormously, by removing the restriction to local interaction.

The proposed weak membrane scheme achieves almost the best of all worlds, in the following manner. Computational simplicity is retained by having $Z \propto$ (contour length) - the first of the options above. This produces contours of minimal length, and with a tendency, due to hysteresis, to be unbroken. Then, contours produced with that Z are subjected to a subsequent process, in which the contours are regarded as fixed, and tangent orientation along contours is to be estimated. At this stage the $(d\theta/ds)^2$ energy can be applied, with weak continuity constraints on θ. This is in fact simply the application of weak strings along contours, to θ data. This generates descriptions of the contours as smoothly curved arcs, vertices and junctions. It can be made to operate in parallel over all contours in an image, labelling both corners and T junctions (figure 2.16 on page 37).

Some elegance has been sacrificed. The contour description process can no longer "feed back" to the discontinuity detecting membrane. But in return, the resulting two part scheme is computationally feasible.

4.3.2   Energy of a continuous piece

The energy of the weak membrane, with the simplest line process as above, is given by

$$E = \int \{(u - d)^2 + \lambda^2 (\nabla u)^2\} \, dA + \alpha \int dl \qquad (4.30)$$

where the first integral is evaluated over the area in which data d is defined, and the second along the length of all discontinuities. The penalty is now α per unit length of discontinuity.

There are still only two parameters and, just as with the weak string, the way they influence the weak membrane can be determined by comparing energies, with and without discontinuities. Broadly, the conclusion will be that behaviour in 2D is qualitatively like it was in 1D: λ still acts as a scale parameter and h_0, g_l are contrast threshold and gradient limit respectively, as before.

The energy of a continuous piece of membrane can be calculated, using the 2D Green's function. Given data d, the membrane configuration u is given by

$$u(\mathbf{x}) = \int G(\mathbf{x}, \mathbf{x}') d(\mathbf{x}') \, dA \qquad (4.31)$$

where the Green's function is

$$G(\mathbf{x}, \mathbf{x}') = \frac{1}{2\pi\lambda^2} K_0 \left(\frac{|\mathbf{x} - \mathbf{x}'|}{\lambda} \right) \qquad (4.32)$$

and K_0 is a modified Bessel function of the second kind (Watson 1952). The energy is

$$E = \int d(\mathbf{x}) (d(\mathbf{x}) - u(\mathbf{x})) \, dA \qquad (4.33)$$

This is a straightforward analogue of the 1D method. Further details are given in appendix A. The Green's function has the important asymptotic property that

$$K_0(x) \rightarrow \sqrt{\frac{\pi}{2x}} e^{-x} \qquad x \gg 1.$$

This means that for distances which are large compared to λ the Green's function falls off exponentially (in fact faster). So, as in 1D, λ acts as a scale parameter. Features separated by a distance that is large compared with λ, do not interact.

Note that for data with a constant cross section (i.e $d(x,y) \equiv d(x)$) the membrane fitting problem is essentially 1D. Contrast threshold and gradient limit behaviour must clearly apply in this case, as for the string. It will now be shown that genuinely 2D data can exhibit similar properties.

4.3.3   Sensitivity of the membrane in detecting steps

As a simple example we consider a cylindrical top hat. This consists of a flat circular patch of radius a at a height h above its surroundings (figure 4.5a rotated about a vertical axis). The energy of the continuous solution in this case is shown in appendix A to be

$$E_c = 2\pi a^2 h^2 K_1 \left(\frac{a}{\lambda} \right) I_1 \left(\frac{a}{\lambda} \right)$$

where I_1 is a modified Bessel function of the first kind (Watson 1952). Again it is most useful to consider limits. If a is large compared to λ

$$E_c = \pi a \lambda h^2.$$

Note that, unlike the 1D top hat (4.16), a appears in the energy expression for E. The cylindrical top hat is the swept volume of a 1D one of appropriate size, rotated through π radians. Hence E above is the energy in (4.16) multiplied by πa, a half-circumference.

The minimum energy solution, allowing discontinuities, has a step around the circumference of the patch. There is no deviation from the original data, no gradient, only the penalty term is left in (4.30). This energy is

$$E_s = 2\pi a \alpha,$$

which is α multiplied by the circumference. Comparing these two energies E_c, E_s, the contrast threshold

$$h_0 = \sqrt{\frac{2\alpha}{\lambda}}$$

determines step detection, as in 1D. Now, at the opposite limit, when a is very much less than λ, the continuous energy is

$$E_c = \pi a^2 h^2$$

which is independent of λ - as in 1D. The energy of the discontinuous solution is smallest (less than E_c above) only if

$$h > \sqrt{\frac{2\alpha}{a}}$$

So a top-hat whose radius a is small compared to λ will only be detected if

$$h > h_0 \sqrt{\lambda/a},$$

and this is again just the same as the behaviour of interacting steps in 1D. The general inference is that small scale features are detected only if they have high contrast. Such behaviour is consistent with the requirement to reject noise.

4.3.4   Localisation and preservation of topology

The good localisation properties of the weak string are, of course, inherited by the weak membrane. But there are also localisation defects, which are particular to linear edge detectors in 2D, and which do not occur with the weak membrane. They are: a tendency to distort curved edges, particularly at corners, and a tendency to disconnect one arm of a trihedral junction. The latter is particularly injurious, for instance when T junctions are used as evidence of occlusion. Since most edge detecting filters are designed to match isolated, straight edge-segments, it is not surprising that they filter curves and junctions badly. It has been argued that a family of appropriately structured filters could overcome this (Leclerc 1985, Gennert 1986) but a large number of them would be needed to cover all possible configurations of curves and junctions.

It is clear, for instance in figure 2.6 on page 24, that the weak membrane accurately preserves localisation and topology. This is so even in the presence of a considerable amount of noise, requiring large scale filters for adequate suppression, for which errors in linear filtering are substantial. The reason for the lack of distortion of corners, in the weak membrane, is illustrated in figure 4.17.

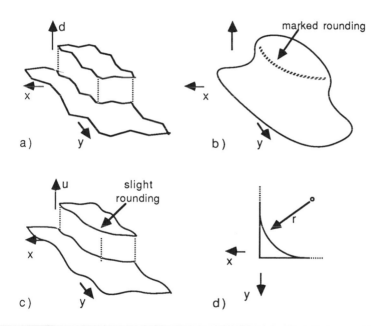

Figure 4.17: Localisation at corners: a corner in data d (a) is blurred by linear filtering (b), producing distortion. The weak membrane (c) tends to preserve discontinuities, although corners are slightly rounded (d).

One way to look at this is that the weak membrane does not blur across discontinuities. Alternatively think of it in terms of energy, the 2D analogue of the earlier 1D localisation argument (figure 4.12): any dislocation of the discontinuity in u relative to steps in the data d, generates a large error term $D = \int (u - d)^2$ in the energy E. However, it is somewhat compensated by a reduction in P, which favours the shortest possible discontinuity contour. This is related to Weierstrass's famous isoperimetric problem - what is the shortest arc bounding a given area? The answer is: a circular one. So corners are rounded as in figure 4.17d. What is the radius r of the corner, assuming ideal data, consisting of a raised block, with step height h? The change in energy due to rounding is approximately

$$\Delta E = h^2 (1 - \frac{\pi}{4})r^2 - \alpha(2 - \frac{\pi}{2})r$$

which is minimised when

$$r = \frac{\lambda}{2} \left(\frac{h}{h_0} \right)^{-2}$$

so that the displacement of the corner is

$$r(\sqrt{2} - 1) \approx 0.2\lambda \left(\frac{h}{h_0} \right)^{-2}. \tag{4.34}$$

Localisation error is therefore approximately 0.2λ at worst, falling off very rapidly as step height h increases above the contrast threshold h_0. This is very much better than localisation error for an equivalent directional gaussian of half-width $w = \lambda$: the error can be shown to be about 0.5λ - fixed, however large h is.

Distortion at T junctions due to linear filtering is similarly a matter of blurring across discontinuities, as in figure 4.18. Preservation of connectedness in the weak membrane is related to the hysteresis effect, described later. In both cases there is a tendency to inhibit gaps in edges.

4.4   Choice of parameters for edge detection

There are two degrees of freedom in the membrane energy, represented by the two parameters α, λ. Five different aspects of performance in discontinuity detection have been seen to depend on those two parameters. This is summarised in the following table:

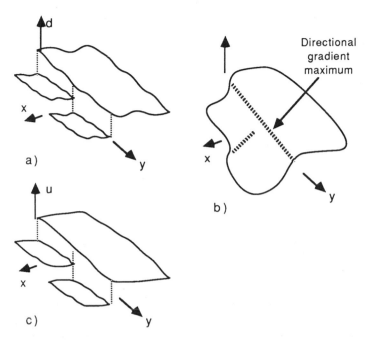

Figure 4.18: Preservation of topology: Data (a) at a T junction is blurred by linear filtering (b); but the weak membrane (c) does not blur across discontinuities.

Aspect of performance	Performance measure
Sensitivity	$h_0 = \sqrt{2\alpha/\lambda}$
Scale	λ
Gradient limit	$g_l = h_0/2\lambda$
Resistance to noise	α
Contrast above which double edges occur	$h_0\sqrt{2\lambda}$

In practice, sensor noise magnitude is unlikely to be a limiting factor in detection of discontinuities. Modern solid-state sensor arrays generate relatively little electrical noise. The major source of "noise" is the inaccuracy of the MRF model implied by the membrane energy. It is unreasonable to believe that intensity distributions really originate from an MRF model with fixed parameters. It is to accommodate such latitude in the *model* that tolerance to "noise" is required. Therefore, rather than considering noise resistance specifically, it is more natural to specify contrast sensitivity. For example, proportional sensitivity to reflectance change η of 5-20% may be adequately low to detect reflectance changes at most boundaries between materials.

Of the five performance parameters in the table above, those constrained most strongly by the requirements of edge detection are sensitivity h_0, the need to avoid double edges (which demands large λ), and the requirement to keep scale λ as small as possible in order to raise the gradient limit, procure maximum resolution, and avoid excessive computational expense (chapter 7).

4.4.1   Adaptive thresholding

Maintenance of a fixed sensitivity to *proportional* changes of reflectance, as is done in the computation of lightness (Land 1983), suggests applying the weak membrane to data

$$d(x,y) = \log(I(x,y)).$$

A small differential in the data

$$\Delta d = \Delta \log(I) = \frac{\Delta I}{I}$$

then corresponds to a proportional change in intensity. Threshold h_0 therefore applies to proportional changes in I - what is termed "Weber's law" in psychophysics.

However, the logarithm transformation greatly amplifies noise at low intensities. The following strategy achieves a similar effect without noise problems.

- Data is $d(x, y) = I(x, y)$ - simply the intensity.

- A *continuous* membrane, at relatively large scale, is used to compute a local average of intensity $I_{av}(x, y)$. The contrast threshold h_0 is then set adaptively across the image to

$$h_0(x, y) = \eta I_{av}(x, y)$$

where η is an approximate proportional measure of sensitivity to changes in intensity. The smoothing effect of the membrane removes problems with noise at low intensity.

- The weak membrane is applied. This is done by means of the GNC algorithm (see later chapters), suitably modified to cope with spatially varying h_0.

- Intensity difference h of detected edges must now lie approximately in the range $h \in [h_0, 2h_0/\eta]$ so that, from the table above, double edges should not occur if

$$\frac{2h_0}{\eta} \le h_0 \sqrt{2\lambda},$$

that is, if

$$\eta \ge \sqrt{\frac{2}{\lambda}}. \tag{4.35}$$

In practice, to avoid unacceptable computational expense and loss of resolution, we have have used lower values of η, for a given λ, than would satisfy (4.35). Adequate immunity to double edges is retained. Typical values used in earlier examples (figures 2.4 and 2.5, page 22) are $\lambda = 8$ pixels and $\eta = 15\%$, for a 256 pixel square image. Discontinuities in those two images, for a range of η and λ are shown in figures 4.19 and 4.20.

4.5 Sparse data

Stereoscopic depth data is sparse. At each point in cyclopean space, where a pair of features have been successfully matched, a spot-depth is obtained.

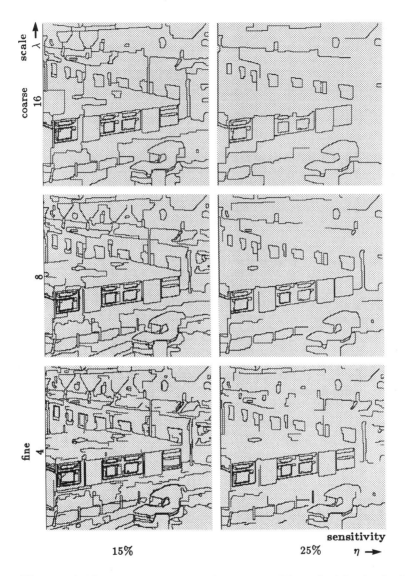

Figure 4.19: Adaptive edge detection. Discontinuities in the intensities of the image in figure 2.4 are shown, for various sensitivities (η) and scales (λ). (The image is 256×256 pixels square.)

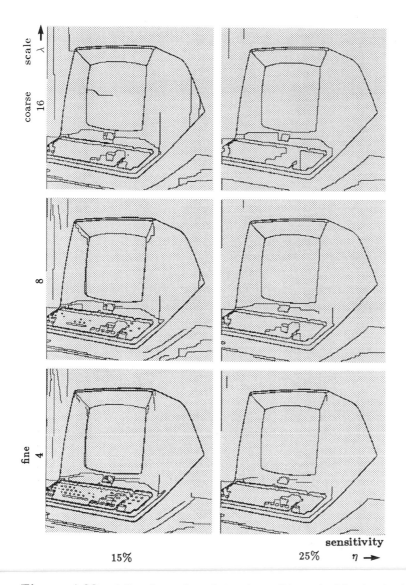

Figure 4.20: Adaptive edge detection. Discontinuities in the intensities of the image in figure 2.5 are shown, for various sensitivities (η) and scales (λ). (The image is 256×256 pixels square.)

The resulting pointilliste depth map can then be used to generate a dense surface map, complete with discontinuities. It was argued in chapter 2 that this is a useful thing to do over textured surfaces, whose discontinuities may not be visible monocularly.

The optimisation problem, which was given by (4.30) for dense data, becomes[3]

$$E = \frac{A}{K} \sum_{i=1}^{K} (u(x_i, y_i) - d_i)^2 + \int \{\lambda^2 (\nabla u)^2\} \, dA + \alpha \int dl \qquad (4.36)$$

where $A = \int dA$ is the total domain area. Note that α, λ here are "average" values. If (x_i, y_i) are laid out on a regular grid then scale and penalty are effectively homogeneous and equal to λ, α. But if the density s of the points (x_i, y_i), is not homogeneous then the "effective" scale is expected from (4.36) to vary as $1/\sqrt{s}$, and effective penalty as $1/s$. That would make the effective contrast threshold vary as $1/s^{1/4}$.

When data is sparse, discontinuity contours are not necessarily well defined, so that any contour lying in a certain band (figure 4.21) may be "acceptable". Indeed contours in sparse random-dot stereograms, as exhibited for example by Grimson (1981), do not appear to be sharply defined. Minimisation of (4.36) tends to find the shortest contour (figure 4.21b), as this produces the smallest penalty $\alpha \int dl$. In chapter 6 it is explained that the sparse problem as defined in (4.36) is harder to handle with the GNC algorithm. There is also an unfortunate tendency, if the "dots" in the data are small enough, for them to pull off the membrane altogether. This is because it becomes cheaper to pay the penalty αl for allowing a discontinuity around the circumference (length l) of the dot, than to allow the dot to deform the membrane. The problem could be obviated by penalising contour curvature as well as just length. But that is infeasible, for reasons given earlier.

So although reconstruction of sparse data *can* be done with GNC, it is probably preferable first to convert sparse data to dense, using a continuous membrane (i.e. minimising (4.36) with very large α) at small scale λ.

4.5.1   Hyperacuity

The problem of handling sparse data is closely related to the problem of hyperacuity (Fahle and Poggio 1984, Krotkov 1986) - that is, obtaining

---

[3]Actually this problem is ill-posed as it stands - it has no continuous solution. To be technically correct, $u(x)$ should be constrained to be constant along some short line segment passing through (x_i, y_i).

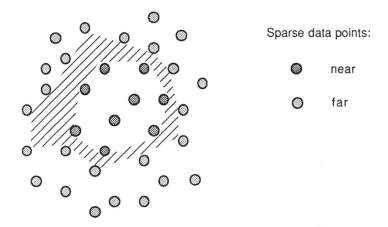

Sparse data points:

   ◉   near

   ◎   far

Figure 4.21: It would be reasonable to recover a discontinuity anywhere in the shaded band. Weak continuity constraints tend to produce the shortest contour.

subpixel accuracy in localisation of discontinuities in dense data. If reconstruction is done on a fine grid, finer than the grid over which data is quantised, then the data is effectively sparse with respect to the finer grid. As with sparse data in figure 4.21, the positions of discontinuities may be ambiguous if the energy in (4.36) is minimised. Figure 4.22 explains exactly why that is. The figure illustrates the 1D case, in which ambiguity always occurs. In an interval between data points, the string $u(x)$ can be shown to be piecewise linear (satisfying the Euler-Lagrange equation $u'' = 0$). Its boundary condition is that $u' = 0$ at free ends. In the gap in figure 4.22a,b that contains the discontinuity, $u' = 0$. Hence the energy $\lambda^2 \int u'^2 dx = 0$ over the gap, and the only remaining energy component is α, the penalty for 1 discontinuity. Thus the energy due to the gap is α, constant as the position of the discontinuity moves inside the gap. There is no unique minimum, and so no effective hyperacuity. This applies also, of course, in 2D to any data d that has translational symmetry. In other cases, for example a simple connected shape, the tendency to choose the shortest contour around the shape resolves the ambiguity, as in figure 4.21.

To achieve hyperacuity reliably, therefore, data must be subsampled onto the fine grid. Appropriate optical blurring before sampling and bandpass filtering before subsampling are required, in accordance with the sampling theorem, as described by Fahle and Poggio (1984). Then a weak

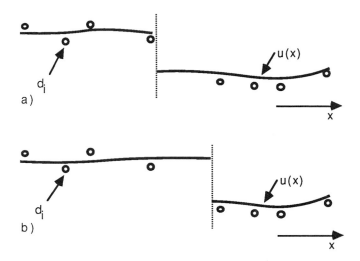

Figure 4.22: A weak string, used with sparse data, is of no help in achieving hyperacuity. The energies for 2 possible positions of a discontinuity as in (a), (b) are just the same. There is no unique, minimum energy position.

membrane can be fitted to that subsampled data, using a scale λ somewhat larger than one "coarse" pixel.

4.6 Hysteresis maintains unbroken edges

The purpose of this section is to demonstrate that the weak membrane incorporates edge-hysteresis. It is unnecessary to apply explicit hysteresis either by assigning energies to the line process (Geman and Geman 1984) that discourage edge termination, or by a two-threshold growing scheme (Canny 1983). Edge-hysteresis arises "naturally", because once a tear has started, it tends to propagate. Try tearing card, for instance: it is hard initially, but once the tear has started, it propagates more easily. In fact, we show that an energy penalty is already imposed for line terminations, as part of the natural operation of the membrane.

Consider 2D data

$$d(x, y) = \begin{cases} \frac{h}{2} & \text{if } y \geq 0 \\ -\frac{h}{2} & \text{otherwise,} \end{cases} \qquad x, y \in [-L, L].$$

A weak membrane represented by $u(x, y)$ is to be fitted to $d(x, y)$, using parameters λ, h_0, such that $\lambda \ll L$. Consider the case in which $h \geq h_0$ so that the globally minimal energy state of the weak membrane is $u \equiv d$, with energy $2\alpha L$. (There is zero energy from the membrane itself, so the only contribution is the penalty generated by the step edge in u, along $y = 0$, of length $2L$.) Now consider chopping out a small portion $x \in [-\epsilon/2, \epsilon/2]$ from the edge, as in figure 4.23. Of course this must raise the energy. The question is, how stable is the global minimum at $\epsilon = 0$?

The increase in the energy of the membrane itself (not including penalties) is ΔE. The total change, including penalties, is therefore $\Delta E - \alpha\epsilon$. For given ϵ, ΔE is the minimum of E subject to $u(x, 0) = 0$ for $x \in [-\epsilon/2, \epsilon/2]$, where

$$E = 2 \int_{y=0}^{L} \int_{x=-L}^{L} \left\{ (u - d)^2 + \lambda^2 (\nabla u)^2 \right\} \, dx \, dy$$

and since $L \gg \lambda$ this can be taken to be approximately

$$E = 2 \int_{y=0}^{\infty} \int_{x=-\infty}^{\infty} \left\{ (u - d)^2 + \lambda^2 (\nabla u)^2 \right\} \, dx \, dy. \qquad (4.37)$$

By substituting $X = x/\lambda, Y = y/\lambda, w = u/h$, it is easily shown that ΔE, the minimum value of E in (4.37), is

$$\Delta E(\epsilon) = h^2 \lambda^2 M(\epsilon/\lambda),$$

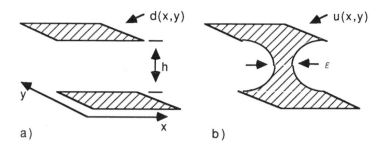

Figure 4.23: Hysteresis - step discontinuities in the weak membrane prefer to be unbroken. In the global minimum energy state, the membrane u fits data d exactly (a). But when a little piece is removed from the step edge, u is forced to be continuous - pinched together - across that piece (b).

where M is a dimensionless function. It has been obtained numerically, using a discrete implementation of the membrane and is plotted in figure 4.24a. It is straightforward to predict its asymptotic behaviour:

$$M(z) \to 0 \text{ as } z \to 0$$

and (it can be shown from (4.38) below)

$$M(z) \to \frac{1}{2}z \text{ as } z \to \infty$$

and the computed results agree with these limits.

The total increase in energy due to the gap is

$$M(\epsilon/\lambda)h^2\lambda^2 - \alpha\epsilon,$$

which, since $\alpha = \lambda h_0^2/2$,

$$= \lambda^2 h_0^2 \left\{ \left(\frac{h}{h_0}\right)^2 M(\epsilon/\lambda) - \frac{1}{2}(\epsilon/\lambda) \right\}. \tag{4.38}$$

This is plotted for the cases $h = h_0$ and $h > h_0$ in figure 4.24b,c respectively. Even at threshold, as in (b), there is a steep sided minimum at $\epsilon = 0$ which acts to discourage gaps of length ϵ much smaller than λ and this effect becomes even stronger above threshold. What is surprising is that, even near or at threshold, when the reconstructed membrane is least stable, gaps are still strongly inhibited. The inhibition is equivalent to the effect of an

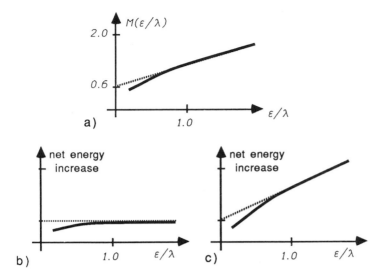

Figure 4.24: The function $M(\epsilon/\lambda)$ (a) determines the net increase in energy due to a break of length ϵ in an edge. Examples are for a step at contrast threshold (b) and above threshold (c). The intercept in (b) and in (c) represents the additional energy attributable to the pair of edge terminations introduced at the gap.

energy penalty directly attributable to edge terminations at each end of the gap. The increment appears as an intercept on the vertical axis in figure 4.24b,c. For a step at threshold, the increment is approximately $0.6h_0^2\lambda^2$ - this is effectively the additional cost charged for 2 edge terminations. For a step above threshold, the increment increases in proportion to h^2. This behaviour is intuitively appealing: the higher the contrast of the edge, the more strongly termination is inhibited.

4.7   Viewpoint invariance in surface reconstruction

The plate (see next chapter) and the membrane can be used for reconstruction of a visible surface, either from stereo, rangefinder, or other surface data. But simple first and second order energies are not entirely suitable for this purpose. This is because they are not fully invariant in 3D. They are, of course, invariant to rotation in the x, y plane (Brady and Horn 1983) but not to changes of viewpoint. This means that the optimal surface (the one that minimises such a non-invariant energy, subject to appropriate constraints) may wobble as the viewpoint varies (figure 4.25). It has been shown (Blake 1984) that, with sparse data, the wobble effect becomes appreciable when any normals of the reconstructed surface, in a particular viewer frame, are nearly orthogonal to the line of sight (within 20° or so). Thus contours that are extremal or nearly so cause the most trouble.

The effect of non-invariance on reconstruction varies considerably according to whether the data is dense or sparse. When data is dense, the reconstructed surface follows the data closely, so there is not much latitude for wobbling. But the detection of discontinuities is noticeably dependent on viewer frame. For example, when laser rangefinder data is reconstructed using a non-invariant weak membrane, multiple step discontinuities tend to appear near extremal boundaries, where surface energy is (in theory) unbounded (figure 4.26).

The cure is to use an invariant energy (Blake and Zisserman 1986c) based on surface area (membrane) or surface area and curvatures (plate). The simple, non-invariant membrane and plate are in fact approximations to these invariant energies. The approximations are close when all surface normals are nearly *parallel* to the line of sight. Hence wobble is most severe when some surface normals are nearly *orthogonal* to the line of sight. The invariant weak membrane has energy

$$E = \int \left\{ (u - d)^2 \cos^2 \phi + 2\lambda^2 \right\} \, dS \ + P \qquad (4.39)$$

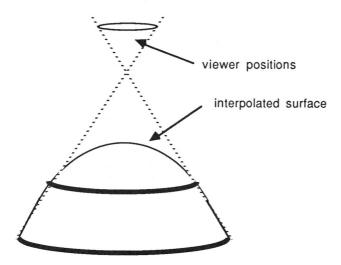

viewer positions

interpolated surface

Figure 4.25: Viewpoint invariant surface reconstruction. For viewer positions within the cone as shown, the lower ring is not obscured by the upper one. It is argued that, for viewer directions in that cone, the interpolated surface should remain static (invariant) in 3-D.

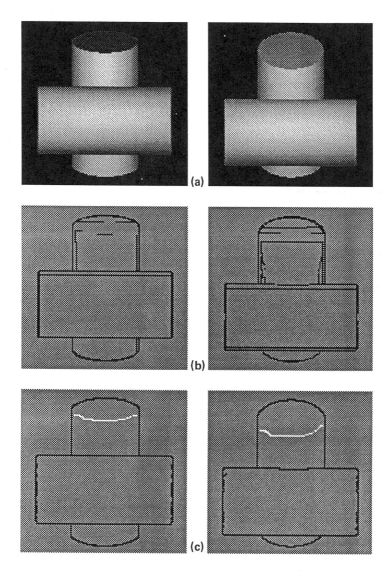

Figure 4.26: Surface reconstruction from range data, of the object pictured in (a), using a non-invariant weak membrane (b) and an invariant one (c). (Light lines mark creases, found by the weak plate - see next chapter).

where
$$P = \alpha \times (\text{total length of discontinuities}).$$

The surface element dS is given by

$$dS = \sec \phi \, dx \, dy \qquad (4.40)$$

where surface slant ϕ is a function of $u(x, y)$:

$$\sec \phi = \sqrt{1 + |\nabla u|^2}. \qquad (4.41)$$

So now
$$E = \int \left\{ (u - d)^2 \cos \phi + 2\lambda^2 \sec \phi \right\} dx \, dy + P. \qquad (4.42)$$

The invariant energy (4.39) is well approximated by the non-invariant one (up to an additive constant) provided $|u'|$ is small enough. Thus, for small signals, the invariant membrane acts like the non-invariant one, and smoothing occurs on a scale of λ. But for large signals, it behaves differently. If the contrast threshold h_0 for the equivalent non-invariant membrane is much greater than λ then the effective contrast threshold h_I for the invariant membrane is much larger than h_0. In fact

$$h_I = \frac{\alpha}{2\lambda^2} = \frac{h_0^2}{4\lambda} \qquad (4.43)$$

(figure 4.27) when $h_0 \gg \lambda$.

The $\cos^2 \phi$ term in (4.39) is included to render the error measure D invariant, as illustrated in figure 4.28. Such a correction is appropriate under the assumption that "noise" in the system derives from the surface, from surface texture for example. However it is inappropriate if the noise derives from the sensor itself, because the noise then "lives" in the viewer (sensor) frame. The energy in that case is

$$E = \int \left\{ (u - d)^2 + 2\lambda^2 \sec \phi \right\} dx \, dy + P. \qquad (4.44)$$

Of course there is a difficulty in applying the $\cos \phi$ correction, which is that ϕ is unknown. This can be dealt with by using $\phi = 0$ as an initial estimate, fitting the membrane once to obtain a new $u(x, y)$ and an improved estimate of ϕ from (4.41), and then fitting again.

Strictly, P above should also be made invariant (although in practice this is less important than using an invariant membrane energy). This could be done by incorporating slant and tilt dependent compensation, as Brady and Yuille (1984) did, for perimeter measurement under back-projection.

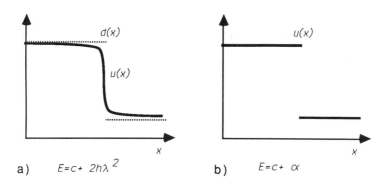

a) $E = c + 2h\lambda^2$ b) $E = c + \alpha$

Figure 4.27: Contrast threshold for the invariant weak membrane: compare energies (a) and (b), without and with a discontinuity respectively. (Energy of (a) is obtained by approximating $\sqrt{1 + u'^2} \approx |u'|$.)

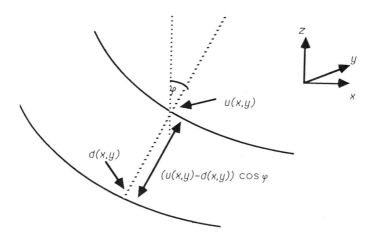

Figure 4.28: Invariant distance measurement. Under the assumption that the surface u, d are roughly parallel, a fair estimate of perpendicular distance between them at (x, y) is $(u - d)\cos\phi$.

Note that there is some remission of the gradient limit in the invariant weak membrane simply because, when the surface gradient $g = |\nabla u| \gg 1$, the surface area integrand above is proportional to $|g|$, rather than g^2 as for the non-invariant membrane. The improvement in behaviour is most noticeable near extremal boundaries. Quantitative estimates of the improvement can be made. For a given λ, h_0, g_l in the non-invariant membrane, the equivalent invariant membrane (the one with the same small scale smoothing parameter λ) has effective contrast threshold h_I and gradient limit g_I. It can be shown that the ratio

$$R_I = \frac{g_I/h_I}{g_l/h_0}$$

which can be regarded as a figure of merit for gradient limit effects, is a function only of h_0/λ. It can be computed by numerical methods, and is plotted in figure 4.29. The optimum occurs when $h_0 \approx 6\lambda$ giving an

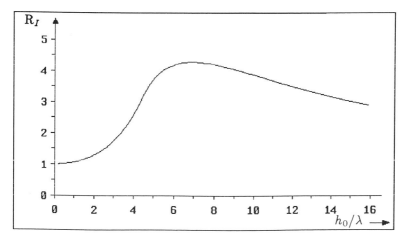

Figure 4.29: Gradient limit remission for the invariant membrane. The figure of merit R_I depends on h_0/λ for the equivalent non-invariant membrane. For $h_0 \ll \lambda$ $R_I = 1$, the non-invariant case, as expected.

improvement of a factor of $R_I \approx 4$. This suggests

$$h_0 = 6\lambda \tag{4.45}$$

as a natural depth/image-plane-distance scaling factor. At this optimum, the effective contrast threshold is

$$h_I \approx 1.8 h_0 \approx 11\lambda.$$

That concludes the discussion of variational properties of the weak string and membrane. The next chapter applies similar analysis in order to discover the properties of the weak rod and plate.

Chapter 5

Properties of the Weak Rod and Plate

The previous chapter dealt with the weak membrane and its 1D equivalent, the weak string. Variational analysis, applied to certain special cases, led to the notions of "scale", "contrast threshold" and "gradient limit". But the membrane and the string, with their 1st order energies, cannot detect crease discontinuities, because they have no intrinsic resistance to creasing. They can be creased without any associated energy increase.

In order to detect creases, a 2nd order surface must be used - one which has a high energy density where it is tightly curved. The thin plate (Landau and Lifschitz 1959, Grimson 1981, Terzopoulos 1983) has this property: intuitively it is easy to crease a sheet of elastic (a membrane) but hard to crease a sheet of steel. In this chapter, it is shown that the plate (and, in 1D, the rod) exhibits similar properties to the membrane - contrast threshold and characteristic scale - as well as its additional ability to detect steps and creases simultaneously.

Here is a summary of the main properties of the rod and plate:

- As with the string and membrane, there is a scale constant (μ for the rod and plate) and a contrast threshold. In addition, there is a "gradient difference threshold" which determines detectability of isolated creases. There is no gradient limit - one of the major benefits of using a higher order scheme. But just as the gradient limit expressed a limitation on performance of the membrane, so there is a higher order limit for the rod and plate - a "second derivative" limit.

- The performance of a mixed membrane and plate is considered. It is shown to have the worst of both schemes - the gradient limit of the membrane, as well as the additional computational load (see later chapters) of the plate. It is concluded that the pure plate is superior.

- The plate can be shown to exhibit hysteresis in edge formation, producing a tendency to maintain unbroken step edges, as the membrane did. Even in the presence of some noise, step discontinuities are more or less successfully detected and are unbroken.

- The weak plate is very expensive to compute, because of its 2nd order energy (see chapter 7). The practical alternative is the "1st order plate" in which plate fitting is decomposed into two 1st order processes. First, the usual weak membrane is fitted to obtain a piecewise continuous reconstruction $u(x, y)$, with step discontinuities explicitly labelled. Then $\nabla u(x, y)$ is used as gradient data for a weak plate, on which crease discontinuities are localised.

- In the previous chapter it was argued that the energy of a reconstructed 3D surface must be viewpoint invariant. It is shown that the plate can be modified to meet this requirement.

Supporting mathematical analysis for this chapter is given in appendix C. In a first reading of the book, it would be reasonable to skip the remainder of this chapter, if the reader prefers to go directly to the discrete implementation of the weak string and membrane.

5.1 Energy of the weak rod/plate

The energy of a weak rod is

$$E = \int \left\{ (u - d)^2 + \mu^4 u''^2 \right\} dx \ + P. \tag{5.1}$$

This differs from the energy of a weak elastic string (3.1) in that it includes the *second* derivative of u, rather than the first. Such an energy is termed "second order". Alternatively, a mixture of first and second order energies may be used, to give:

$$E = \int \left\{ (u - d)^2 + \lambda^2 u'^2 + \mu^4 u''^2 \right\} dx + P. \tag{5.2}$$

When u is continuous, this is somewhat akin to "splines under tension" (Barsky and Beatty 1983), and is used for reconstruction by Terzopoulos (1983, 1985).

Now that the energy is second order it is possible to include penalties both for steps and creases:

$$P = \alpha Z_{\text{step}} + \beta Z_{\text{crease}} \tag{5.3}$$

where, in 1D, $Z_{\text{step}}, Z_{\text{crease}}$ are simply the number of the respective discontinuities. To have included a crease penalty β in the string would have been pointless, for the following reason: a conventional (non-weak) string $u(x)$ merely conforms to any crease in the data. - it is restricted, in the variational problem, only to be continuous, not to be smooth. *Formally* incorporating a crease in $u(x)$ at $x = a$ would merely increase the energy E by β; The increased energy is obviously not the global minimum, so the weak string would never "choose" to invoke the crease penalty.

The energy E in (5.1) above has 3 parameters: μ, α, β, whereas E for a string had only two: λ, α. Two parameters λ (scale) and h_0 (contrast threshold) described the performance of the string. The performance of the rod is characterised by 3 measures: μ (scale), h_0 (contrast threshold) and g_0 (gradient difference threshold). The last of these three concerns sensitivity to the detection of creases. Just as for the string, and now for the rod too, an isolated step is detected if contrast exceeds h_0, so an isolated crease is detected if the gradient difference across the crease exceeds g_0. It transpires that α and β must obey the relation

$$\beta < \alpha < 2\beta$$

and it is shown in the next section that h_0 and g_0 are consequently related too.

The 2D equivalent of (5.1) for the plate comes in two varieties (Grimson 1981):

Quadratic variation:

$$E = \int \left\{ (u - d)^2 + \mu^4 (u_{xx}^2 + 2u_{xy}^2 + u_{yy}^2) \right\} \, dx \, dy \ + P \tag{5.4}$$

Square Laplacian:

$$E = \int \left\{ (u - d)^2 + \mu^4 (u_{xx} + u_{yy})^2 \right\} \, dx \, dy \ + P. \tag{5.5}$$

In fact any linear combination of these two is a feasible plate energy. The penalty P now includes costs α per unit length of step discontinuity, as with the membrane and, in addition, β per unit length of crease discontinuity.

5.2   Scale and sensitivity in discontinuity detection

To arrive at an interpretation of the parameters μ, h_0, g_0, similar variational analysis is followed as for the 1st order surfaces in chapter 4. As before, results obtained for ideal step data apply also to "effective step height" and "effective gradient difference" in non-ideal data. Results derived below in 1D apply, as in the previous chapter, to translationally symmetric and rotationally symmetric data in 2D. So analysis done for the rod will apply also to the plate. Details of energy calculations are given in appendix C.

5.2.1   Sensitivity to an isolated step

Consider data $d(x)$ in the form of an isolated, bi-infinite step of height h, as in chapter 4. Again, the minimal energy, with a step discontinuity in $u(x)$ at $x = 0$, is α. For a continuous u, the minimal energy is

$$E = \frac{1}{2\sqrt{2}}h^2\mu, \tag{5.6}$$

which is very similar to the equivalent for the string, except with μ in place of λ, and an additional factor of $1/\sqrt{2}$. As in (4.11) on page 58, for the membrane, comparing the two energies above gives a contrast threshold

$$h_0 = 2^{\frac{3}{4}}\sqrt{\alpha/\mu}. \tag{5.7}$$

The contrast threshold also applies to the plate, for translationally symmetric and for rotationally symmetric data (see end of appendix C).

5.2.2   Interaction of adjacent steps

Now consider data $d(x)$ in the form of a "top hat" of height h and width a, as in figure 4.5 on page 59. Again, sensitivity to step discontinuities is qualitatively the same as for the string. The minimal energy with two step discontinuities in $u(x)$ is 2α. With continuous u, minimal energy is

$$E = h^2\mu\left(\frac{1}{\sqrt{2}} - \exp\left(-\frac{a}{\sqrt{2}\mu}\right)\cos\left(\frac{a}{\sqrt{2}\mu} + \frac{\pi}{4}\right)\right). \tag{5.8}$$

Taking limits, as with the string, for $a \gg \mu$ the top hat is treated as two isolated steps. For $a \ll \mu$ there is an interaction: the detection threshold is $\sqrt{\alpha/a}$; so it varies as $1/\sqrt{a}$, just as for the string.

5.2.3 Sensitivity to an isolated crease

Bi-infinite data $d(x)$ with an isolated crease is the first case of behaviour beyond that of the string. The data consists of two semi-infinite, linear portions

$$d(x) = \begin{cases} g_1 x & \text{if } x < 0 \\ g_2 x & \text{otherwise,} \end{cases} \tag{5.9}$$

as in figure 5.1, with gradient difference $g = |g_2 - g_1|$. If u has a crease at

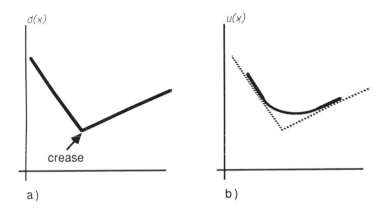

Figure 5.1: Bi-infinite data $d(x)$, with an isolated crease (a) may either be approximated by a continuous rod (b), or be fitted exactly by a rod with a crease coinciding with the crease in $d(x)$.

$x = 0$ then it fits $d(x)$ perfectly with energy β, the penalty for allowing the crease. But if there is no crease in u, the minimal energy is

$$E = \frac{1}{2\sqrt{2}} g^2 \mu^3. \tag{5.10}$$

Comparison of these two energies gives a threshold g_0 for detection of an isolated crease. It is detected if the gradient change g satisfies

$$g > g_0 = \left(\frac{\beta}{\alpha}\right)^{\frac{1}{2}} \frac{h_0}{\mu}. \tag{5.11}$$

5.2.4 Interaction of adjacent creases

A finite ramp (figure 4.8a on page 63) of gradient g and width a was used with the string to demonstrate and quantify the gradient limit - the effect whereby, when the gradient g exceeds g_l, a spurious step discontinuity may occur in u. There is no such effect with the rod because, unlike the string, a rod can conform to any constant gradient, incurring zero energy. But the finite ramp can be used, in a similar way to the top hat, to demonstrate the interaction between two creases. The energy of $u(x)$, when it has two creases coinciding with those of $d(x)$, is just 2β. The energy of the continuous rod is

$$E = g^2\mu^3 \left(\frac{1}{\sqrt{2}} - \exp\left(-\frac{a}{\sqrt{2}\mu} \right) \sin\left(\frac{a}{\sqrt{2}\mu} + \frac{\pi}{4} \right) \right). \tag{5.12}$$

When $a \gg \mu$ then, as for a pair of step discontinuities, the two crease discontinuities are treated independently - that is, detected if $g > g_0$. But when $a \ll \mu$ there is interaction, and of a qualitatively different form from that of two steps. The energy E above becomes

$$E \approx \frac{1}{2\sqrt{2}}(ga)^2\mu = \frac{1}{2\sqrt{2}}h^2\mu$$

and the (ga) term has the effect that the gradient difference threshold varies as $1/a$, compared with $1/\sqrt{a}$ for the contrast threshold.

Finally, it is important to observe that in addition to the two possibilities considered so far (continuous u and u with two creases), it is also possible to have one or more step discontinuities in u. Consider this third choice in the case when $a \ll \mu$. Now as a becomes smaller, it is plain that data $d(x)$ becomes more and more like a step of height $h = ga$. The three choices with corresponding energies can be shown to be:

Choice:	continuous	two creases	one step
Energy:	$\frac{1}{2\sqrt{2}}h^2\mu$	2β	$\alpha + \epsilon(a)$

where $\epsilon(a) \to 0$ as $a \to 0$. Notice first that, since a crease discontinuity represents a stronger constraint on $u(x)$ than a step discontinuity, we must have

$$\alpha > \beta.$$

Otherwise a step would incur a cheaper penalty, while imposing a weaker constraint on u. Energy would always be reduced by replacing all creases in u by steps, so that crease discontinuities would never occur. Now, inspecting the table above, it is also plain that if $\alpha \geq 2\beta$ then no matter how small a there would never be a step in u - two creases would always have lower total energy.

It seems therefore that α and β are tightly mutually constrained:

$$\beta < \alpha < 2\beta. \tag{5.13}$$

Referring back to (5.11), it is plain that h_0 and g_0, the contrast and gradient difference thresholds, are also tightly constrained:

$$\mu < \frac{h_0}{g_0} < \sqrt{2}\mu. \qquad (5.14)$$

So the parameters of the plate really have only two degrees of freedom, not three. In fact, in the discrete scheme, it is convenient to have $\alpha = 2\beta$, and formally cater only for creases. Then two adjacent creases (rod) or crease contours (plate) are interpreted as a step.

5.3   Mixed 1st and 2nd order energy performs poorly

For the mixed string and rod, whose energy was defined in (5.2), exact variational solutions are harder to obtain. The step is one case that can be analysed relatively easily, using the Fourier method described in appendix C. For a continuous u the minimal energy is

$$E = K^2 \mu h^2$$

where K is a function of λ/μ only. And, as before with the pure rod, when u has a step discontinuity at $x = 0$ (the position of the step in d), the minimal energy is $E = \alpha$. For example, in the "critically damped" case $(\lambda = \sqrt{2}\mu)$ $K^2 = 3/4$. (For this special combination of λ, μ, there is *just* sufficient damping influence from the 1st order energy to remove oscillatory terms in the Green's function.) So, comparing those two energies as usual, the contrast threshold for an isolated step is

$$h_0 = K^{-1}\sqrt{\frac{\alpha}{\mu}}.$$

Qualitatively (i.e. except for the constant K) this is the same as for the pure plate.

Ideally, one would like to analyse fully the response of the mixed rod and string to a finite ramp, and this is possible, but algebraically messy. Even without a full analysis, it is clear that the gradient limit behaviour of the string will persist, as long as $\lambda \neq 0$. Figure 5.2 shows what u looks like, with and without a discontinuity at $x = 0$. Qualitatively, the behaviour here is similar to the pure string in chapter 4, but the sagging effect, characteristic of the string, is reduced: as $\lambda/\mu \to \infty$, the gradients $u'(0+), u'(0-)$ in

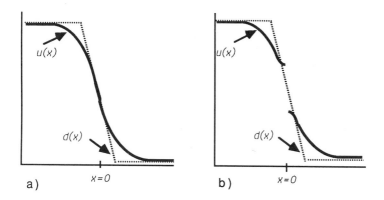

Figure 5.2: Gradient limit for the mixed rod and string. The continuous $u(x)$ (a) may have a higher energy than the discontinuous $u(x)$ (b), in which the surface is allowed to sag at $x = 0$, thus reducing energy.

figure 5.2b approach 0 - the behaviour of the pure string. So instead of a gradient limit

$$g_l = \sqrt{\frac{\alpha}{2\lambda^3}}$$

as for the string, one would expect that

$$g_l \to \sqrt{\frac{\alpha}{2\lambda^3}} \quad \text{as} \quad \mu \to 0, \text{ fixed } \lambda$$
$$g_l \to 0 \quad \text{as} \quad \lambda \to 0, \text{ fixed } \mu.$$

The conclusion is that by varying the proportion λ/μ of 1st order energy in the mix, the gradient limit can be controlled. But unfortunately, including even a small proportion of 2nd order energy can increase enormously the amount of computation required. The reason for this is explained in chapter 7. To achieve a significant improvement in the gradient limit over the pure weak string, one would expect to have $\mu \sim \lambda$. In that case, it will be shown that the computational cost is effectively the same as for a pure 2nd order energy, and much greater than a pure 1st order energy.

5.4   Hysteresis

The purpose of this section is to demonstrate that the weak plate incorporates hysteresis for step discontinuities, just as the weak membrane did. Recall that this property imparts a tendency for edges to be unbroken, because any small break causes an increase in energy. In fact, for the plate, the proof is somewhat easier than for the membrane because numerical integration is unnecessary. Hysteresis for crease discontinuities has yet to be investigated.

Consider 2D data

$$d(x,y) = \begin{cases} \frac{h}{2} & \text{if } y \geq 0 \\ -\frac{h}{2} & \text{otherwise} \end{cases} \quad x,y \in [-L, L].$$

A weak plate represented by $u(x, y)$ is to be fitted to $d(x, y)$, using parameters μ, h_0, such that $\mu \ll L$. Consider the case in which $h > h_0$ so that the globally minimal energy state of the weak plate is $u = d$, with energy $2\alpha L$. (There is zero energy from the plate itself, so the only contribution is the penalty generated by the step edge in u, along $y = 0$, of length $2L$.) Now consider chopping out a small portion $x \in [-\epsilon/2, \epsilon/2]$ from the edge, just as was done with the membrane. We seek to show that, however small ϵ is, there is an increase in total energy $\Delta E(\epsilon)$, which is bounded below by some bound greater than zero. It is sensible here to consider the limit $\epsilon \to 0$. This would have been useless for the membrane, because pinching the two sections of membrane together *at a point* generates an ill-defined problem.

For the plate, as $\epsilon \to 0$ the decrease in penalty $\alpha\epsilon \to 0$. But the plate u is forced to be continuous at $(x, y) = (0, 0)$, no matter how small ϵ is. The resulting u is "pinched together" at $(x, y) = (0, 0)$, as in figure 5.3. This causes an increase in the energy of the plate itself (not including penalties) of $\Delta E(0)$. The total change in energy for an edge gap of length ϵ, including penalties, is $\Delta E(\epsilon) - \alpha\epsilon$. It is clear that $\Delta E(\epsilon)$ is an increasing function of ϵ, because the continuity constraint on the plate becomes more and more extensive as the interval $[-\epsilon/2, \epsilon/2]$ lengthens. Consequently

$$\Delta E(\epsilon) - \alpha\epsilon > \Delta E(0) - \alpha\epsilon.$$

In the absence of any constraint on the plate, its energy $E = 0$, so the increment $\Delta E(0)$ is the minimum, subject to the constraint $u(0,0) = 0$, of

$$E = 2 \int_{y=0}^{L} \int_{x=-L}^{L} \left\{ (u - d)^2 + \mu^4 (u_{xx}^2 + 2u_{xy}^2 + u_{yy}^2) \right\} \, dx \, dy.$$

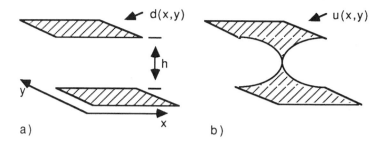

Figure 5.3: Hysteresis - step discontinuities in the weak plate prefer to be unbroken. In the global minimum energy state, the plate u fits data d exactly (a). This is compared with the energy when u is forced to be continuous - pinched together - at a point (b).

Since $L \gg \mu$ this can be taken to be approximately

$$E = 2 \int_{y=0}^{\infty} \int_{x=-\infty}^{\infty} \left\{ (u - d)^2 + \mu^4 (u_{xx}^2 + 2u_{xy}^2 + u_{yy}^2) \right\} \, dx \, dy. \quad (5.15)$$

By substituting $X = x/\mu, Y = y/\mu, w = u/h$, it is easily shown that

$$\Delta E(0) = Kh^2 \mu^2,$$

where K is a dimensionless constant.

Hence the total increase in energy due to the gap

$$\Delta E(\epsilon) - \alpha\epsilon > Kh^2 \mu^2 - \alpha\epsilon,$$

a net increase if $Kh^2\mu^2 > \alpha\epsilon$. So (using (5.7)), there is in-built resistance to forming small gaps of length

$$\epsilon < \epsilon_{max} = 2\sqrt{2}K \left(\frac{h}{h_0} \right)^2 \mu.$$

The minimum gap length is of order μ. The interpretation of this result is that, even in the presence of moderate noise, there will be a tendency to avoid gaps shorter than this minimum.

5.5   1st order plate

Because the plate has a 2nd order energy, it is expensive to compute (see chapter 7). Computation even of the continuous plate is made feasible only by the use of multilevel techniques (Terzopoulos 1983), and the indications are that multilevel computation could confer only a limited advantage when weak continuity constraints are in force (chapter 7). However, the weak plate problem can be reformulated as a sequence of two 1st order processes. The first is a weak membrane, applied to data d to produce a piecewise continuous reconstruction u in the usual way. Then a weak plate can be fitted to gradient data ∇u. (Gradient ∇u is well defined, because of the regularising effect of the membrane). The fitting is constrained not to cross step discontinuities already labelled. It is a 1st order process, minimising (in the case of quadratic variation)

$$E = \int \left\{ (p - p^0)^2 + (q - q^0)^2 + \mu^2 (p_x^2 + p_y^2 + q_x^2 + q_y^2) \, dx \, dy \right\} + P \quad (5.16)$$

where $(p^0, q^0) = \nabla u$. Results are shown in figure 5.4. Computational cost is that of two 1st order processes, which is very much less than that of one 2nd order process. There are of course two scale parameters in this scheme - λ_1 for the membrane fitting and λ_2 for the fitting of the plate to gradient data. Practical experience suggests that it is best to choose λ_2 somewhat greater than λ_1 so that the plate fitting is relatively immune to distortion created by the smoothing effect of the membrane.

The 1st order plate delivers step and crease discontinuities, as the true plate does. But it does not produce a fully filtered, smooth reconstruction. Instead, it generates a piecewise continuous reconstruction u, and piecewise continuous surface orientation (p, q).

In practice, for reasons that the authors do not understand very clearly, use of the square Laplacian produces unstable results (figure 5.5). This occurs regardless of whether the true plate or the 1st order plate is used. It may be similar to the puckering effect that Grimson (1981) observed at plate boundaries. It is uncertain whether its origin is a property of the energy itself, or simply of the discrete approximation.

5.6 Viewpoint invariance

In the previous chapter, it was argued that a scheme for reconstructing 3D surfaces should use a viewpoint invariant surface energy. For the membrane, this meant replacing the approximation $\frac{1}{2}(\nabla u)^2 \, dx \, dy$ by $dS = (1 + (\nabla u)^2)^{1/2} \, dx \, dy$, the area of a surface element. Then $\int dS$ is invariant because it is defined with respect to the visible surface, rather than the x, y coordinate frame.

Quadratic variation and square Laplacian are not viewpoint invariant. They are merely approximations to certain measures of intrinsic surface

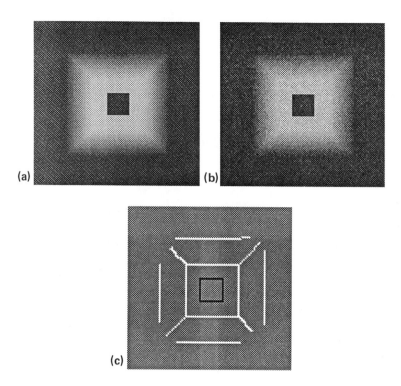

Figure 5.4: A synthetic image (a) with added noise (b) is fitted by a weak (quadratic variation) plate (c). Steps (black) and creases (white) are marked.

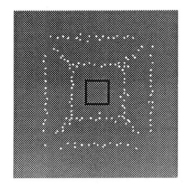

Figure 5.5: Instability results when square Laplacian is used in the plate (cf. figure 5.4).

properties.

The invariant equivalent of the square Laplacian (5.5) is

$$E = \int \left\{ (u - d)^2 \cos^2 \phi + \mu^4 (\kappa_1 + \kappa_2)^2 \right\} dS + P \qquad (5.17)$$

where κ_1, κ_2 are principal curvatures, dS is a surface element as before and ϕ is surface slant. The squared sum of curvatures is expressed in the viewers frame as

$$(\kappa_1 + \kappa_2)^2 = \frac{(Au_{xx} - 2Bu_{xy} + Cu_{yy})^2}{D^3}, \qquad (5.18)$$

where

$$A = 1 + u_y^2, \ B = u_x u_y, \ C = 1 + u_x^2 \text{ and } D = \sec^2 \phi,$$

(do Carmo 1976). Note that A, B, C, D are all functions of 1st derivatives of u only. If the sum of squared curvatures is to be used (the invariant form of quadratic variation) then

$$\kappa_1^2 + \kappa_2^2 = (\kappa_1 + \kappa_2)^2 - 2\kappa_1\kappa_2, \qquad (5.19)$$

where (do Carmo 1976) the Gaussian curvature

$$\kappa_1\kappa_2 = \frac{u_{xx}u_{yy} - u_{xy}^2}{D^2}.$$

As in the previous chapter, the $\cos^2 \phi$ term in (5.17), renders the $(u-d)^2$ term of (5.5) invariant. This correction is omitted if noise is thought to originate in the sensor frame rather than on the surface, to give

$$E = \int (u - d)^2 \, dx \, dy \; + \int \mu^4 (\kappa_1 + \kappa_2)^2 \, dS \; + P. \qquad (5.20)$$

Expressing the energy E as

$$E = \int \overline{E}(u_x, u_y, u_{xx}, u_{xy}, u_{yy}) \, dx \, dy \; + P,$$

it can be shown (Blake 1984) that the integrand $\overline{E}$ is a non-convex function of $u_x, \dots$. So even with a fixed set of discontinuities, it is not known whether there is a uniquely optimal u to be found (Troutman 1983).

This problem is dealt with, in an approximate way[1], by using a 1st order plate, as already proposed for the non-invariant case. First, estimates for $u_x(x, y)$, $u_y(x, y)$ are obtained by fitting an invariant weak membrane. This labels step discontinuities and yields estimates of u_x, u_y which can be inserted as constants into $\overline{E}$ which is then convex with respect to u_{xx}, u_{xy}, u_{yy}. Then $\overline{E}$ is minimised with respect to p_x, p_y, q_x, q_y, The integrability constraint $p_y = q_x$ is *not* imposed, as to do so costs a great deal of computation (chapter 7).

That concludes the topic of the last two chapters - the variational analysis of function fitting under weak continuity constraints. The next two chapters consider how the variational problems can be turned into discrete computations, and how appropriate algorithms can be constructed. The measure of success of the algorithms will be how far the results that they produce agree with the theoretical predictions of the last two chapters.

---

[1]The solution is still not truly invariant, but at least the severe variations at near-extremal boundaries are greatly reduced.

Chapter 6

The Discrete Problem

The previous two chapters concentrated on exact, variational solutions to problems with weak continuity constraints. That enabled performance to be predicted in terms of contrast threshold, scale parameter and so on. But in order to perform function fitting with arbitrary, discrete data, the energy E must of course be converted to a discrete form. Finite elements, first used for visual reconstruction problems by Terzopoulos (1983), are the appropriate formalism for this. They have the advantage that the accuracy of a discrete solution, as an approximation to a continuous one, is known (Zinkiewicz and Morgan 1983). Details are given, in this chapter, of discrete energies for string, membrane and plate.

The discrete form of E is a function both of real-valued variables u_i and of the boolean line-variables l_i that signal positions at which the continuity constraint is broken, as explained in chapter 3. The energy $E(u_i, l_i)$ is to be minimised with respect to u_i, l_i. But it was also mentioned that minimisation with respect to l_i can be done "in advance". Explicit reference to the line process is eliminated to yield a simplified cost function $F(u_i)$, depending only on real-valued variables u_i. The function F, we saw in chapter 3, is difficult to minimise, owing to its lack of convexity. A general discussion of algorithms for minimising non-convex functions is given in this chapter. Then in the following chapter, our GNC minimisation algorithm is described in some detail.

6.1   Discretisation and elimination of line variables

To solve a functional minimisation problem computationally, it must first be discretised. For the 1D elastic string of section 2, the simplest conceivable finite element was used to do this - a linear element (figure 3.2 on page 42). That produced a discrete expression for the energy E, as a function of nodal values u_i, and of the line variables l_i. Later, other finite elements will be given for the membrane and plate in 2D. But first we describe the procedure for elimination of line-variables from the energy for the weak string.

To eliminate the line-process $\{l_i\}$, E must first be expressed as:

$$E = D + \sum_{i=1}^{N} h_{\alpha,\lambda}(u_i - u_{i-1}, l_i) \tag{6.1}$$

where

$$h_{\alpha,\lambda}(t, l) = \lambda^2(t)^2(1 - l) + \alpha l. \tag{6.2}$$

and

$$D = \sum_{0}^{N}(u_i - d_i)^2 \tag{6.3}$$

as before. All dependence of E on the line-process $\{l_i\}$ is now contained in the N copies of $h_{\alpha,\lambda}$ that appear in the formula (6.1). The function $h_{\alpha,\lambda}$ (plotted in fig 6.1a) governs local interactions between the $\{u_i\}$. The problem is now (from (6.1)):

$$\min_{\{u_i, l_i\}} D + \sum_{1}^{N} h_{\alpha,\lambda}(u_i - u_{i-1}, l_i),$$

or

$$\min_{\{u_i\}} \left(D + \min_{\{l_i\}} \sum_{1}^{N} h_{\alpha,\lambda}(u_i - u_{i-1}, l_i) \right)$$

- since D does not involve the $\{l_i\}$. Now, immediately performing the minimisation over $\{l_i\}$, the remaining problem is to minimise F with respect to u_i, where

$$F = D + \sum_{1}^{N} g_{\alpha,\lambda}(u_i - u_{i-1}), \tag{6.4}$$

$$\text{and } g_{\alpha,\lambda}(t) = \min_{l \in \{0,1\}} h_{\alpha,\lambda}(t, l).$$

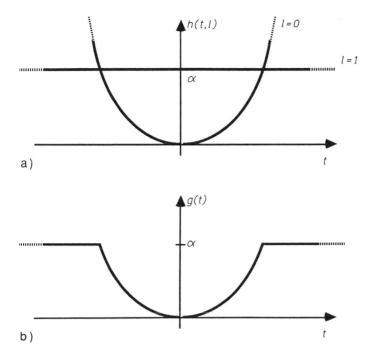

Figure 6.1: a) The energy function for local interaction between adjacent nodes. b) The line process l can be eliminated from a) by minimisation over $l \in \{0, 1\}$

(Often the function $g_{\alpha,\lambda}$ will be written simply g, when this is unambiguous, and similarly for $g^*, g^{(p)}$ as defined in the next chapter.) The function $g_{\alpha,\lambda}$ is shown in fig 6.1b and is simply the minimum of the 2 graphs in fig 6.1a. Explicitly, $g_{\alpha,\lambda}$ is

$$g_{\alpha,\lambda}(t) = \begin{cases} \lambda^2 t^2 & \text{if } |t| < \sqrt{\alpha}/\lambda \\ \alpha & \text{otherwise.} \end{cases} \tag{6.5}$$

The line process l can be explicitly recovered, at any time, from $g(t)$ by a simple formula:

$$l = \begin{cases} 1, & \text{if } |t| > \sqrt{\alpha}/\lambda \\ 0 & \text{otherwise.} \end{cases} \tag{6.6}$$

6.1.1   Extending 1D methods to 2D

The natural extension to 2D of the linear element used above, is a linear triangular element. Within each element, $u(x,y)$ is linear and determined by 3 nodal values as in fig 6.2. Line-variables on each triangle, as shown,

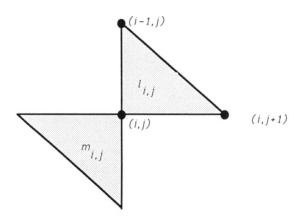

Figure 6.2: Linear triangular elements for the membrane. Line-variables $l_{i,j}, m_{i,j}$ are attached to each triangle. However, this arrangement of line-variables may prove inconvenient in practice (see text).

indicate ($l_{i,j} = 1$ or $m_{i,j} = 1$) when a discontinuity exists, disabling the energy of that triangle, and incurring a penalty α. Along a contour of discontinuity, a whole chain of triangles is disabled, each accruing a penalty α. The total penalty P, incorporated in energy E, is therefore equal to α

times the total length of all discontinuity contours, and that is just as required (chapter 4). The resulting energy, analogous to (6.1) above, is

$$E = D \;+\; \sum_{i,j} h_{\alpha,\lambda}\left(\sqrt{(u_{i,j} - u_{i-1,j})^2 + (u_{i,j} - u_{i,j+1})^2}, l_{i,j}\right) \quad (6.7)$$

$$+\; \sum_{i,j} h_{\alpha,\lambda}\left(\sqrt{(u_{i,j} - u_{i+1,j})^2 + (u_{i,j} - u_{i,j-1})^2}, m_{i,j}\right)$$

where now

$$D = \sum_{i,j}(u_{i,j} - d_{i,j})^2. \quad (6.8)$$

Line variables can be eliminated, replacing h with g as before, to obtain an energy $F(\mathbf{u})$. As in chapter 3, it is necessary to construct a convex approximation F^*. This proves to be particularly difficult for the arrangement of elements and line-variables in figure 6.2. It turns out that it is no longer feasible to guarantee, as we can for the string (see next chapter), that F^* is as close as possible to F whilst still being convex. Additional inefficiency arises because of the need to compute the square roots in (6.7).

Instead, a different arrangement of line-variables is adopted, whose physical role is perhaps a little less sympathetic to the spirit of finite elements, but which facilitates construction of a convex approximation. The new discrete energy is

$$E = D + \sum_{i,j} h_{\alpha,\lambda}\left(u_{i,j} - u_{i-1,j}, l_{i,j}\right) + \sum_{i,j} h_{\alpha,\lambda}\left(u_{i,j} - u_{i,j+1}, m_{i,j}\right). \quad (6.9)$$

Now $l_{i,j} = 1$ flags the collapse of two adjacent triangles in a Northerly direction, as in fig 6.3. And $m_{i,j} = 1$ flags the collapse of a pair of triangles, but in an Easterly direction. Line-variables in (6.9) can be eliminated to give the 2D equivalent of (6.4):

$$F = D + \sum_{i,j} g(u_{i,j} - u_{i-1,j}) + \sum_{i,j} g(u_{i,j} - u_{i,j+1}). \quad (6.10)$$

Line-variables are recovered as before, from (6.6).

The viewpoint invariant membrane, described earlier in chapter 4, must use the original triangulation scheme (figure 6.2). This is because the gradient term in the energy integrand is $\sqrt{1 + u_x^2 + u_y^2}$ so that the two components u_x^2, u_y^2 are not separable. But, as before, the convex approximation is less satisfactory.

From the point of view of 2D rotational invariance, equilateral triangular elements would actually be preferable. Of course they may be inconvenient

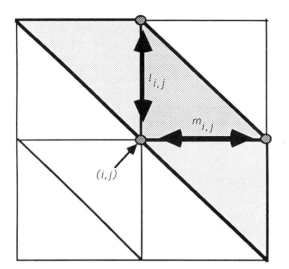

Figure 6.3: When line-variable $l_{i,j} = 1$, this signifies that the "Northerly" component of the energy of the membrane, over the 2 triangles shown, is disabled. Similarly for $m_{i,j} = 1$, but acting in an Easterly direction.

for use with the usual rectangularly formatted images, but are in keeping with the hexagonal tesselation of retinal mosaics. They are better because they enable more precise measurement of contour lengths (in the term P), as shown in figure 6.4. Imagine Manhattan built with hexagonal blocks - distances by road would be reduced, and would be much closer to distance as the crow flies. Hexagonal tesselation would make sensitivity to contrast, in the weak membrane, vary far less with varying orientation of contours. In fact variations are reduced by a factor of almost 3, from about $\pm 18\%$ to about $\pm 7\%$. In practice, however, an approximately square grid is used.

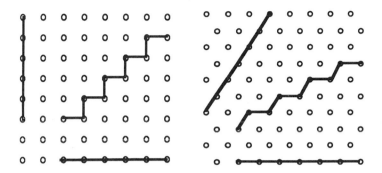

Figure 6.4: Rotational invariance of length measurement is greatly improved on a hexagonal grid.

As expected, sensitivity is greatest for horizontal and vertical lines, and least for diagonal ones. (See, for example, some of the images in figure 4.1 on page 53.

6.1.2　Higher order energies: weak rod and plate

Since energies for the rod (1D) and the plate (2D) include 2nd derivatives of the fitted function u, linear elements are inadequate (having zero 2nd derivative). The 1D case is an obvious specialisation of the 2D one, so the following discussion is restricted to the plate. The simplest element, though somewhat unorthodox, is the non-conforming quadratic element of Terzopoulos (1983), developed for the smooth, thin plate. It is unorthodox in having nodes which lie outside the element itself - see fig 6.5. Values of 2nd derivatives within the (i, j)th element are simple functions of nodal

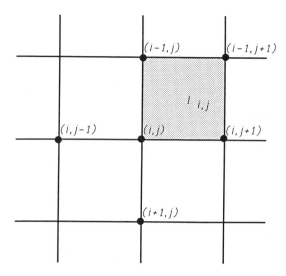

Figure 6.5: The non-conforming, square, quadratic element of Terzopoulos has 6 nodes, 2 of which lie outside the square. For the weak plate, a line-variable $l_{i,j}$ is associated with each element.

values:

$$
\begin{aligned}
u_{xx} &= u_{i,j-1} + u_{i,j+1} - 2u_{i,j}, && (6.11) \\
u_{yy} &= u_{i-1,j} + u_{i+1,j} - 2u_{i,j}, \\
u_{xy} &= -u_{i,j} - u_{i+1,j+1} + u_{i,j+1} + u_{i-1,j}.
\end{aligned}
$$

As mentioned in chapter 5, there is in fact a one parameter family of suitable (rotationally invariant) 2nd order energy functions (Grimson 1981, Brady and Horn 1983). They are the linear combinations of the square Laplacian (5.5) and the quadratic variation (5.4). Quadratic variation proves more awkward to handle, because line-variable elimination generates the following energy:

$$
F = D + \sum_{i,j} g_{\beta,\mu^2} \left(\sqrt{V_{i,j}} \right) \tag{6.12}
$$

where $V_{i,j}$ is the discrete form of quadratic variation

$$
u_{xx}^2 + 2u_{xy}^2 + u_{yy}^2,
$$

in which u_{xx}, u_{xy}, u_{yy} are each represented discretely as in (6.11). This is inefficient for much the same reasons that the ideal membrane scheme with triangular elements (see above) is inefficient: the convex approximation F^* is not as good, and square roots must be computed. The square Laplacian energy gives a simpler computational scheme, with just one line-variable per element. After elimination of line-variables, the energy of the weak plate is

$$
F = D + \sum_{i,j} g_{\beta,\mu^2} (u_{i,j-1} + u_{i,j+1} + u_{i-1,j} + u_{i+1,j} - 4u_{i,j}) \tag{6.13}
$$

similar to (6.4) for the membrane, but with parameters μ^2, β in place of λ, α, and the argument of g_{β,μ^2} being a discrete Laplacian of u rather than a first derivative. In practice, the Laplacian scheme exhibits instability on boundaries (figure 5.5, page 109).

As before (6.6), after F has been minimised, line-variables $l_{i,j}$ can be recovered. But now the interpretation of line-variables is a little different than for the membrane. In 1D (the rod), for example, a single line-variable with the value $l_i = 1$ indicates a gradient discontinuity (a crease). Two adjacent line-variables with values $l_i = 1$, $l_{i+1} = 1$ indicate a step. In 2D, a crease appears as a contour along which the line-variables are set. A step appears as a thick contour of set line-variables, two elements wide. And a wide step (as occurs in intensity data, at shadow boundaries) is labelled as a tramline - a pair of parallel contours.

6.1.3 First order plate

Since the computational cost of schemes employing 2nd order energies will prove to be high a more economical way of achieving a similar effect is needed. In the previous chapter, it was shown that the weak plate computation can be split into two 1st order computations. The first is the ordinary membrane, already discussed, which produces step discontinuities and a surface $u(x, y)$. The surface can be differentiated to give

$$\mathbf{p}^0(x, y) = (p^0(x, y), q^0(x, y)) = \nabla u(x, y)$$

whose discrete form

$$\mathbf{p}^0_{i,j} = (u_{i,j} - u_{i,j+1}, u_{i,j} - u_{i-1,j})$$

can be used as data for a second 1st order process to reconstruct gradient $\mathbf{p}_{i,j}$, complete with discontinuities. These represent 1st order (crease) discontinuities in the original data $d_{i,j}$.

The gradient reconstruction operates by minimising

$$F = \sum_{i,j} \left\{ \|\mathbf{p}_{i,j} - \mathbf{p}^0_{i,j}\|^2 + g\left(\sqrt{V_{i,j}}\right) \right\} \tag{6.14}$$

where $V_{i,j}$ is quadratic variation, as before, but now expressed in terms of $\mathbf{p}_{i,j}$:

$$V_{i,j} = (p_{i,j} - p_{i-1,j})^2 + (p_{i,j} - p_{i,j-1})^2 + (q_{i,j} - q_{i-1,j})^2 + (q_{i,j} - q_{i,j-1})^2$$

Note that there is no attempt to impose the integrability constraint that $p_y = q_x$, although we have a perfect right to do so. The reason is that computation time to minimise F would be severely increased, as shown in the next chapter.

6.1.4 Sparse data

So far, energies have been given for the case in which data is dense. Stereoscopic depths, remember, are not dense but are sparsely and irregularly distributed in the image planes. A simple modification to the energy takes care of this. Suppose that data d_k is available at points $(i_k, j_k), k = 1, .., K$. The "faithfulness to data" component D of energy (6.8) must be replaced by

$$D = \frac{A}{K} \sum_{k=1}^{K} (u_{i_k, j_k} - d_k)^2 \tag{6.15}$$

Other energy terms are unchanged.

6.2 Minimising convex energies

What makes the discrete problems difficult to solve is the fact that discontinuities are incorporated into the reconstructed functions. In this section a little time is taken out to discuss the simpler problem of reconstructing surfaces which are entirely continuous, before proceeding to consider how to solve the main problem.

This class of problem was extensively examined by Grimson (1981) and Terzopoulos (1983). In chapter 2 it was concluded that continuous reconstruction has limited application. That was because the most compelling reason for going to the computational expense of explicit surface reconstruction is to pick out discontinuities masked by texture. A surface fitting scheme to do this *must* be able to recover discontinuities which are *a priori* unknown, and localise them accurately.

However, there are one or possibly two ways in which continuous reconstruction of depth data can be useful. The first is in converting sparse data to dense, using a continuous membrane to do the "filling-in" (McLauchlan et al. 1987). The data is then in a more convenient form for reconstruction with discontinuities, for reasons that were given in chapter 4. The second use is that, as was pointed out in chapter 2, it *might* be convenient to have a depth map available for path planning and collision avoidance. Again, a membrane is quite adequate; there is no reason to go to the expense of reconstructing a smooth surface by means of a plate.

6.2.1 Algorithms based on gradient descent

Energies for continuous surfaces can be obtained by "disabling" the line processes in the energies defined earlier. Since the membrane with sparse data is the process that is of most interest, that is the one considered here. Line variables in (6.9) are switched off -

$$l_{i,j} = m_{i,j} = 0$$

- to give the energy for the continuous membrane:

$$
\begin{aligned}
E &= D + \sum_{i,j} h_{\alpha,\lambda}\left(u_{i,j} - u_{i-1,j}, 0\right) + \sum_{i,j} h_{\alpha,\lambda}\left(u_{i,j} - u_{i,j+1}, 0\right) \\
&= D + \lambda^2\left(\sum_{i,j}(u_{i,j} - u_{u-1,j})^2 + \sum_{i,j}(u_{i,j} - u_{i,j+1})^2\right).
\end{aligned}
\tag{6.16}
$$

The error term D for sparse data was defined in (6.15). If, for some reason, it is known that the surface u is discontinuous along some contour, then the energy is modified simply by clamping the line variables "on" ($l_{i,j} = 1, m_{i,j} = 1$) at all points along the contour. Similarly, if the fitting process is restricted to some irregularly shaped region, such as a region already found to contain image texture, line variables are clamped on along the region boundary.

With all line variables *fixed*, minimisation of E is an entirely classical problem. The condition for **u** to be the desired minimum is that

$$\partial E/\partial u_{i,j} = 0, \ \forall i \qquad (6.17)$$

- the gradient of E (with respect to **u**) vanishes. Energy E is a quadratic function of **u**, so this is a system of linear simultaneous equations. What is more, the fact that E is "strictly convex" (see next chapter for discussion of convexity) guarantees that there is one and only one solution.

There are numerous ways to solve such an equation, most of which involve successive adjustments of the $u_{i,j}$ to reduce E, until it can be reduced no further. The crudest way to do that is simply to try small changes to each of the $u_{i,j}$ in turn, and to accept changes which reduce E. (That was the method described, at the end of chapter 3, to find a minimum of the function $F^{(p)}$.) It does work, but can be inefficient. A better strategy is to use the gradient $\partial E/\partial u_{i,j}$ as a guide to how $u_{i,j}$ should be changed, in order to reduce E fastest. Grimson (1981) used the "conjugate gradient" algorithm to minimise the energy of a plate. Terzopoulos (1983) used the "Gauss-Seidel" algorithm, which is a special case of the "Successive Over-relaxation" (SOR) algorithm.

SOR works as follows. For each site (i, j), gradient $\partial E/\partial u_{i,j}$ is computed, and the the quantity

$$\frac{w}{T} \left(\partial E/\partial u_{i,j} \right)$$

is subtracted from $u_{i,j}$. The constant T is carefully chosen to ensure convergence whenever $w \in (0, 2)$. The whole process is repeated many times (the next chapter tells just how many) until the solution is reached. This algorithm (SOR) is laid out explicitly, in the case of a membrane with sparse data, in figure 6.6. Note that the "Gauss-Seidel" algorithm is the special case of SOR in which $w = 1$. As it stands, the algorithm is serial, because the $u_{i,j}$ are updated in strict sequence. Parallel versions do, however, exist: "simultaneous over-relaxation" and "chequerboard SOR".

6.2.2   Multi-grid algorithms

Terzopoulos greatly enhanced the basic SOR algorithm by making use of multi-grid techniques (Brandt 1977), in which relaxation takes place simultaneously, on coarse and fine arrays. Use of four arrays, with density in

Nodes: $i \in \{0, ..., N\}$, $j \in \{0, ..., N\}$.
Iterate $n = 1, 2, ...$

For $i = 1, ..., N - 1$, $j = 1, ..., N - 1$:
  If there is data at node $\{i, j\}$:

$$u_{i,j}^{(n+1)} = u_{i,j}^{(n)} - \omega \left\{ \left(1 + 4\lambda^2\right) u_{i,j}^{(n)} - d_{i,j} - \lambda^2 \left(u_{i-1,j}^{(n+1)} + u_{i,j-1}^{(n+1)} \right.\right.$$
$$\left.\left. + u_{i+1,j}^{(n)} + u_{i,j+1}^{(n)} \right)\right\} / \left(1 + 4\lambda^2\right)$$

  otherwise:

$$u_{i,j}^{(n+1)} = u_{i,j}^{(n)} - \omega \left\{ 4u_{i,j}^{(n)} - \left(u_{i-1,j}^{(n+1)} + u_{i,j-1}^{(n+1)} \right.\right.$$
$$\left.\left. + u_{i+1,j}^{(n)} + u_{i,j+1}^{(n)} \right)\right\} / 4$$

Modification is necessary at corners, for example:
  If there is data at node $\{0, 0\}$:

$$u_{0,0}^{(n+1)} = u_{0,0}^{(n)} - \omega \left\{ \left(1 + 2\lambda^2\right) u_{0,0}^{(n)} - d_{0,0} - \lambda^2 \left(u_{1,0}^{(n)} + u_{0,1}^{(n)}\right)\right\}$$
$$/ \left(1 + 2\lambda^2\right)$$

  otherwise:

$$u_{0,0}^{(n+1)} = u_{0,0}^{(n)} - \omega \left\{ 2u_{0,0}^{(n)} - \left(u_{1,0}^{(n)} + u_{0,1}^{(n)}\right)\right\} / 2.$$

Modification is also necessary on array edges, for example:
  If there is data at node $\{0, j\}$, $1 \le j \le N - 1$:

$$u_{0,j}^{(n+1)} = u_{0,j}^{(n)} - \omega \left\{ \left(1 + 3\lambda^2\right) u_{0,j}^{(n)} - d_{0,j} - \lambda^2 \left(+u_{0,j-1}^{(n+1)} \right.\right.$$
$$\left.\left. + u_{1,j}^{(n)} + u_{0,j+1}^{(n)} \right)\right\} / \left(1 + 3\lambda^2\right)$$

  otherwise:

$$u_{0,j}^{(n+1)} = u_{0,j}^{(n)} - \omega \left\{ 3u_{0,j}^{(n)} - \left(u_{0,j-1}^{(n+1)} + u_{0+1,j}^{(n)} + u_{0,j+1}^{(n)}\right)\right\} / 3.$$

Figure 6.6: An SOR algorithm for the membrane, with sparse data.

the ratios 8:4:2:1, achieved a speed-up in excess of 100:1, for the continuous plate. In our case, speed-up for the membrane (McLauchlan et al. 1987) is typically 10:1 (somewhat dependent on the scale λ and the sparsity of the data).

The principle of multigrid operation is illustrated in figure 6.7. The

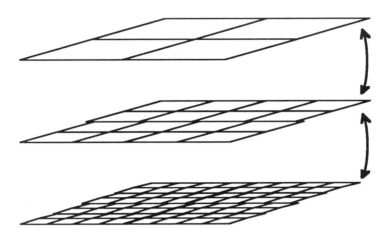

Figure 6.7: Multigrid relaxation. In this illustration, grids are shown at three levels. Relaxation takes place on coarse and fine grids, moving both upwards and downwards in order to achieve fastest convergence.

problem is that standard SOR, at a single level, rapidly smooths away error signals of high spatial frequency, leaving a persistent low frequency error that decays slowly. This happens because each iteration of relaxation is a local process; high frequencies are removed locally, but low frequencies require long distance propagation, taking many iterations. That is where coarse grids help. Low spatial frequencies, projected onto a coarse grid, become high frequencies with respect to the new grid. To put it another way, neighbour to neighbour communication on a coarse grid covers more ground per iteration than on a fine grid. An adaptive scheme switches the relaxation process between levels (both coarse to fine and fine to coarse). Switching occurs according to the spectral composition of the error signal, as measured by local Fourier transformation. For the membrane, "chequerboard Gauss-Seidel" was found to be most effective. Imagining the grid at each level to be a chessboard, all the black squares are updated in one iteration, and all the white ones in the next. This means that, in any one iteration, each square that is updated has four nearest neighbours that are left alone. There is no interaction, therefore, between any pair of squares being updated. Thus the order of updating does not matter, and therefore computation is truly parallel within each iteration.

6.3 Overcoming non-convexity

Let us now return to the main problem - dealing with weak continuity constraints. The energy functions F for weak continuity problems are non-convex. Convexity is a sufficient condition for all local minima to be global minima. Since F is non-convex it may have many local minima, many of which are not global. We showed in section 2 that F *does* in fact have many local minima - possibly as many as 2^N, for a weak elastic string with data vector $d_0, .., d_N$. This means that naive gradient descent will almost certainly stick at a local minimum that is of higher cost than the global minimum. What is more, which local minimum is reached will depend strongly on the starting point of the descent. For this reason, it was argued in chapter 3 (where our myopic fly remained trapped at altitude), an algorithm is needed that has some ability to "look ahead".

6.3.1 The GNC algorithm

This book proposes the GNC algorithm, already described briefly in chapter 3, and due to be explained fully in the next chapter. The algorithm given in chapter 3 (figure 3.7, page 49) worked by direct descent, trying small changes in each of the u_i in turn, and accepting them if they reduce the energy function $F^{(p)}$. More sophisticated gradient following methods (SOR) are described in the next chapter. For now, recall the central step of the earlier algorithm: to test a small increment (or a decrement) δ in u_i and compute the energy change

$$\Delta F^{(p)} = F^{(p)}(u_1, .., u_i + \delta, .., u_N) - F^{(p)}(u_1, .., u_i, .., u_N). \quad (6.18)$$

If $\Delta F^{(p)} < 0$ then the change is accepted. This operation is applied in sequence to the u_i, to comprise one iteration. Iterations are repeated, for a given p, until convergence. Non-convexity parameter p is decreased from 1 (convex) towards 0 (true energy function).

There are three main alternatives to GNC, each somewhat different in nature. All three are algorithms of general applicability, whereas GNC is somewhat special to problems involving weak continuity constraints - which is both its weakness and its strength.

The first of the alternatives is simulated annealing. Kirpatrick et al. (1982) described its application to the minimisation of non-convex energies.

Smith et al. (1983) used it for image restoration. Geman and Geman (1984) also applied it to image restoration, using a cost function that incorporates weak continuity constraints.

The second is Hopfield's neural network computation (Hopfield 1984). It involves constructing a *single* energy function which is a compromise between the true F and a convex approximation to F. This compromise function is somewhat like $F^{(p)}$ in the GNC algorithm, for some intermediate value of $p \in [0, 1]$. His method of obtaining the convex F^* is generally applicable to integer programming problems, but at the price of being a rather poor approximation compared with the F^* used in GNC.

Finally dynamic programming (Bellman and Dreyfus 1962), previously used for curve detection by Montanari (1971), has been successfully applied to the weak string by Papoulias (1985).

6.3.2   Simulated annealing

Simulated annealing is a powerful, general method for finding global optima of functions which have many local optima. It is based on the algorithm of Metropolis et al. (1953) for simulating statistical mechanical systems. Instead of direct descent, some randomness is introduced into the descent path. This avoids sticking in local minima. The degree of randomness is controlled by a temperature parameter, which is initially high. As the system approaches the global minimum, it is allowed to cool.

The structure of the algorithm is superficially similar to GNC. Instead of sweeping parameter p from 1 to 0, a temperature T is reduced from some starting value towards 0. And in place of the deterministic updating rule, increments δ in each u_i are tested according to a random rule. The energy change is defined, similarly to (6.18), but for the actual cost function F, rather than for $F^{(p)}$:

$$\Delta F \;=\; F(u_1, .., u_i + \delta, .., u_N) - F(u_1, .., u_i, .., u_N). \qquad (6.19)$$

The following rule is then applied: if $\Delta F < 0$ then the change is accepted as before, but if $\Delta F \geq 0$ then it is accepted randomly, with probability

$$\exp\left(-\Delta F / T\right),$$

and otherwise rejected. The schedule for reduction of temperature is given (Geman and Geman 1984) by

$$T = C / \log(1 + k)$$

at the kth iteration, where C is an appropriate energy constant, related to a characteristic energy of the system. When T is large, energy increases are often accepted, enabling the system to jump out of local minima. As $T \to 0$, the system "freezes", becoming almost deterministic in its descent towards a minimum of energy.

The generality of simulated annealing is a great attraction. Simulated annealing can, in a sense, be regarded as a general engine for non-convex problems. It can be argued however that the additional freedom to choose a cost function for simulated annealing is not of great benefit for visual reconstruction problems. For example, a more complex line process (Geman and Geman 1984) can be used to penalise breaks and endings of edges. But the hysteresis effect, intrinsic to the membrane and plate, already do that very satisfactorily. In any case, computational requirements can escalate alarmingly if an "arbitrary" energy is designed at will. This is illustrated in the next chapter, where it is shown that energies of second or greater order necessarily demand much more computation than first order ones.

Comparison of efficiency is difficult, since execution times are strongly dependent on data and on precise choice of energy function. Execution time of GNC, for instance, increases markedly when the data is very noisy (see later), and this may also be the case with simulated annealing. Typical reported runtimes for simulated annealing with energies most closely comparable to ours are around 1000 iterations (Marroquin 1984). Equivalent runtime for GNC can be as low as 50 iterations, tending to be higher at large spatial scale λ, μ. Another significant advantage of GNC over simulated annealing is the potential for implementation in conventional analogue hardware, without the need to use noise generators.

6.3.3 Hopfield's neural model

Hopfield's neural model (Hopfield 1984) solves certain boolean programming problems. It can be expressed[1] as the minimisation of an energy $F^{(0)}$, where

$$F^{(p)} = -\frac{1}{2} \sum_{i,j} T_{i,j} V_i V_j + \sum_i I_i V_i + \sum_i Z_i^{(p)}(V_i), \qquad (6.20)$$

with respect to $V_i \in [0,1]$. Constants $T_{i,j}$ and I_i between them encode problem constraints and data. The function $Z^{(p)}$, plotted in figure 6.8, controls convexity, just as in GNC. The final configuration of the V_i represents the solution. Variables V_i are allowed to take real values in the range [0,1], but as $p \to 0$ they are forced naturally towards boolean values[2] 0,1.

---

[1]The notation here is slightly altered from Hopfield's original, so as to make the analogy with GNC clear.

[2]In Hopfield's formulation, the V_i take values $-1, 1$, but that is a minor detail.

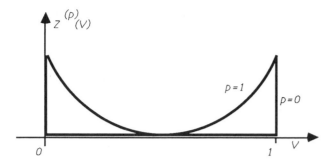

Figure 6.8: Control of convexity in Hopfield's system. When $p = 0$, the rectangular energy function forces solutions to be boolean-valued.

It is desired to minimise the energy for $p = 0$; unfortunately $F^{(0)}$ is non-convex. In the limit $p \to 1$, $F^{(p)}$ becomes convex, but of course with totally different extrema. Hopfield's procedure uses $F^{(p)}$ with an intermediate value of p. Recent work suggests that, as in GNC, sweeping p from 1 to 0 may be useful in the neural model (Hopfield and Tank 1985). Whereas such a strategy will be proven, in the next chapter, to be effective in GNC, there are as yet no corresponding proofs for neural networks.

The main difference from GNC is that the convex approximation $F^{(1)}$ in (6.20) is by no means a close one, though general for a certain class of integer problems. If only one value of parameter p is used, rather than sweeping p, the solution is not necessarily an extremum of the original function F. Moreover, optimisation of a convex $F^{(p)}$ in Hopfield's method need not yield the solution for $F^{(0)}$, because the extrema of such $F^{(p)}$ are not generally integer solutions $V_i \in \{0, 1\}$. In GNC, however, $F^{(1)}$ is often a sufficiently good approximation to $F^{(0)}$ to yield a correct solution.

In any case, an exact comparison of the methods is difficult because they solve different problems. The Hopfield scheme might be made to implement a weak string, for example, by extending it to deal with mixed real and boolean variables (Yuille 1985). The energy (6.20) would become a cubic polynomial in u_i, l_i (taking the place of the V_i above), as in (3.3) on page 42.

6.3.4   Dynamic programming

Dynamic programming is a technique for optimising functions of discrete variables, applicable when the function F can be decomposed as a sum of many functions, each with just a few arguments. Since dynamic programming requires discrete valued variables, the variables u_i must be quantised into M discrete levels.

A dynamic programming algorithm to minimise the energy F of the weak string runs as follows. First "return functions" ϕ_k are defined and computed by a recurrence relation:

$$\phi_0(u_1) = \min_{u_0} \left\{ (u_0 - d_0)^2 + g(u_1 - u_0) \right\}$$

$$\phi_k(u_{k+1}) = \min_{u_k} \left\{ (u_k - d_k)^2 + g(u_{k+1} - u_k) + \phi_{k-1}(u_k) \right\}, \quad 1 \leq 1 < N.$$

The minimisation here must be done by brute force, testing for each possible value of u_k in succession. As they are computed, the minimising value u_k, in the definition of ϕ_k above, defines the value of "policy functions" $\psi_k(u_{k+1})$. Each policy function is stored as an M-element table. Now, as a starting condition, set u_N to the value that minimises

$$(u_N - d_N)^2 + \phi_{N-1}(u_N).$$

The bulk of the work has been done; all that remains, in order to determine the optimal u_i, is a single reverse scan. For $k = N-1, ..., 0$ perform a single table lookup to compute

$$u_k = \psi_k(u_{k+1}).$$

The method has the great advantage of being exact, regardless of convexity. This is because it is essentially an ordered search over all possible values of all variables. Unlike direct descent, it makes no use of the local smoothness of the function F. Papoulias (1985) implemented a dynamic programming algorithm for the weak string. He showed that, for data elements of length N, the time complexity of the algorithm is $O(NM^2)$. Storage requirement is $O(NM)$.

Papoulias pointed out that the use of dynamic programming is impractical for the weak rod, for which the functions f above have not two but three variables. Time complexity rises to $O(NM^3)$ and storage to $O(NM^2)$. Since typical values are $N = M = 100$, runtime on a microcomputer increases from about 1 minute to about 1 hour. For 2D problems, the membrane and the plate, dynamic programming is quite unusable. This is because, although the energy function F partitions much as in 1D, there is no natural ordering of the variables in a 2D array.

Chapter 7

The Graduated Non-Convexity Algorithm

At the end of the last chapter, the various methods available for solving non-convex problems were reviewed. Now, the method proposed in this book - the GNC algorithm - will be described in some detail. In chapter 3 we saw that there are two main steps. The first is to construct a convex approximation to the non-convex function, and then proceed to find its minimum. The way in which such a function can be constructed will be explained - for the weak string, and then for a more general case. The second step is to define a sequence of functions, ending with the true cost function, and to descend on each in turn. Descent on each of these functions starts from the position reached by descent on the previous one.

Such a procedure is certainly intuitively appealing. It is unlikely that very strong general statements can be made about its effectiveness for an arbitrary non-convex cost function. But, in the case of the energy functions that describe the weak string and membrane, the algorithm can be shown to be correct (section 7.3) for a significant class of signals. Performance of the computer implementation also reflects faithfully the variational truths of chapter 4. It will become apparent that this is a consequence of the particular convex approximation F^* that has been defined. Other plausible convex approximations, when used in a GNC procedure, fail to find global minima.

Convergence properties of the algorithm are derived. It is this that leads to the conclusion that 2nd order schemes must require far more computation than 1st order ones. Moreover, imposing an integrability constraint in the second stage of the 1st order plate - natural though it would be to do so - would result in very slow convergence. Optimal values for relaxation parameters are computed. Relaxation algorithms are summarised in a way that would, hopefully, enable the reader to implement them.

7.1   Convex approximation

7.1.1   Weak string

Recall that the energy

$$F = D + \sum_{i=1}^{N} g(u_i - u_{i-1})$$

is to be approximated by a convex function

$$F^* = D + \sum_{i=1}^{N} g^*(u_i - u_{i-1})$$

by constructing an appropriate neighbour interaction function g^*. This is done by "balancing" the positive second derivatives in the first term $D = \sum_i (u_i - d_i)^2$ against the negative second derivatives in the g^* terms. The balancing procedure is to test the *Hessian matrix* H (Roberts and Varberg 1976) of F^*: if H is positive definite then $F^*(\mathbf{u})$ is a convex function[1] of $\mathbf{u}$.
   The Hessian H of F^* is

$$H_{ij} = \frac{\partial^2 F^*}{\partial u_i \partial u_j} = 2I_{i,j} + \sum_k g^{*\prime\prime}(u_k - u_{k-1}) Q_{k,i} Q_{k,j}, \qquad (7.1)$$

where I is the identity matrix and Q is defined as follows:

$$Q_{k,i} = \partial(u_k - u_{k-1})/\partial u_i = \begin{cases} 1 & \text{if } i = k \\ -1 & \text{if } i = k-1 \\ 0 & \text{otherwise.} \end{cases}$$

Now suppose g^* were designed to satisfy

$$\forall t \; g^{*\prime\prime}(t) \geq -c^* \qquad (7.2)$$

where $c^* > 0$. Then the "worst case" of H occurs when

$$\forall k \; g^{*\prime\prime}(u_k - u_{k-1}) = -c^*,$$

---

[1]In appendix D.2 it is shown that positive definite H means F^* is convex, even when the 2nd derivative of g^*, and hence the 2nd partial derivatives of F^*, are discontinuous, as they are for the g^* defined below in (7.7).

so that

$$H_{i,j} = 2I_{i,j} + \sum_k (-c^*)Q_{k,i}Q_{k,j} \qquad (7.3)$$

or

$$H = 2I - c^* Q^T Q. \qquad (7.4)$$

To prove that H is positive definite, it is necessary simply to show that the largest eigenvalue v_{max} of $Q^T Q$ satisfies

$$v_{max} \leq 2/c^*. \qquad (7.5)$$

In appendix D.1 it is shown that this really is a worst case: convexity of H in (7.3) does guarantee convexity of H in the general case (7.1).

Construction of a function g^* with a given bound $-c^*$ as in (7.2) is relatively simple. Suppose the extra condition is imposed that

$$\forall t \; g^*(t) \leq g(t), \qquad (7.6)$$

then the best such g^* (closest, pointwise, to g) is obtained by fitting a quadratic arc of the form $-\frac{1}{2}c^* t^2 + bt + a$ to the function $g(t)$, as shown in fig 7.1. The definition of $g^* \equiv g_{\alpha,\lambda}^*$ is now:

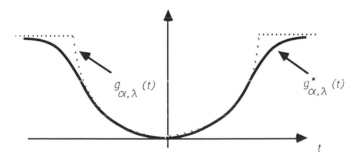

Figure 7.1: The local interaction energy function g of fig 6.1 is modified to function g^*, in order to produce a cost function F^* that is convex, and approximates F.

$$g_{\alpha,\lambda}^*(t) = \begin{cases} \lambda^2(t)^2, & \text{if } |t| < q \\ \alpha - c^*(|t| - r)^2/2, & \text{if } q \leq |t| < r \\ \alpha, & \text{if } |t| \geq r \end{cases} \qquad (7.7)$$

where

$$r^2 = \alpha \left(\frac{2}{c^*} + \frac{1}{\lambda^2} \right), \quad \text{and } q = \frac{\alpha}{\lambda^2 r}. \qquad (7.8)$$

All that remains now is to choose a value c^* by determining the largest eigenvalue v_{max} of $Q^T Q$. Then, to satisfy (7.5) while keeping c^* as small as possible (so that g^* is as close as possible to g), we choose

$$c^* = 2/v_{max}. \tag{7.9}$$

For example, for the string, it is shown in appendix D that the largest eigenvalue $v_{max} = 4$, so from (7.9) $c^* = \frac{1}{2}$.

7.1.2   General method

In general, for all 1D and 2D problems, our function F has the form:

$$F(\mathbf{u}) = D + \sum_k g_k(\mathbf{u}) \tag{7.10}$$

$$\text{where } g_k(\mathbf{u}) = g\left(\sum_l Q_{k,l} u_l\right) \tag{7.11}$$

with g as before[2] and Q is a "circulant" matrix, representing a convolution operation defined by an array C. For example, for the 1D weak string, the circulant matrix Q would be

$$Q = \begin{pmatrix} \cdots & \cdots & \cdots & \cdots & \cdots & \cdots \\ \cdots & -1 & 1 & 0 & 0 & \cdots \\ \cdots & 0 & -1 & 1 & 0 & \cdots \\ \cdots & 0 & 0 & -1 & 1 & \cdots \\ \cdots & \cdots & \cdots & \cdots & \cdots & \cdots \end{pmatrix} \tag{7.12}$$

and the corresponding convolution is

$$C = (\ \cdots \ \ 0 \ \ -1 \ \ 1 \ \ 0 \ \ 0 \ \ \cdots \ ),$$

which means

$$C_k = \begin{cases} -1 & \text{for } k = -1 \\ 1 & \text{for } k = 0 \\ 0 & \text{otherwise.} \end{cases}$$

It can be seen that matrix Q is simply made up of rows which are successively displaced copies of C. That is the definition of a circulant Q. For 2D problems like the membrane, index k in (7.10) is a double index. The convolution C is therefore a two dimensional array, so the circulant Q is

---

[2]Note that the functions g, g^*, as defined above, do not quite apply to quadratic variation, or to the invariant membrane. They can be suitably modified however.

four-dimensional! Strictly, Q is a circulant only if the computational array is considered to be circular (or toroidal in 2D). To account for boundary conditions on array borders, Q is slightly modified. But this doesn't really affect the computation of eigenvalues, as is shown in appendix D.4.

Now, replacing g by g^* in (7.10), to obtain

$$F^*(\mathbf{u}) = D + \sum_k g_k^*(\mathbf{u}) \qquad (7.13)$$

$$\text{where } g_k^*(\mathbf{u}) = g^* \left(\sum_l Q_{k,l} u_l \right)$$

its Hessian can be computed.

$$H_{ij} = \frac{\partial^2 F^*}{\partial u_i \partial u_j} = 2 + \sum_k g^{*\prime\prime} \left(\sum_l Q_{k,l} u_l \right) Q_{k,i} Q_{k,j}. \qquad (7.14)$$

In the worst case

$$H = 2I - c^* Q^T Q,$$

which is positive definite if the largest eigenvalue of $Q^T Q$ satisfies

$$v_{max} \leq 2/c^*.$$

So g^* is as defined in (7.7) with

$$c^* = 2/v_{max}.$$

The calculation of v_{max}, for the weak string, rod, membrane and plate appears in appendix D.3. The task is made relatively easy by the fact that Q is (almost) a circulant, so that there is a formula (Davies 1979) which gives all its eigenvalues. The results are summarised in the following table.

	c^*
string	$1/2$
membrane	$1/4$
rod	$1/8$
plate (Laplacian)	$1/32$

The value given for the plate is for the square Laplacian, since an exact value cannot readily be obtained for quadratic variation. Similarly, exact values cannot conveniently be computed for the invariant membrane. It is almost as useful to have a lower bound on c^* since that can also be used to construct a convex function, though not necessarily the closest one. In the GNC algorithm, to be described next, this simply has the effect of wasting some computation on "more than convex" approximations, before the "closest" convex approximation is reached.

7.1.3   Convex approximation for sparse data

The foregoing discussion of convexity does not apply to reconstruction directly from sparse data. This is because the component D that describes adherence to data, as we saw in the previous chapter, is

$$D = \frac{A}{K} \sum_{k=1}^{K} (u_{i_k, j_k} - d_k)^2$$

rather than

$$D = \sum_{i,j} (u_{i,j} - d_{i,j})^2.$$

Since it is not known *a priori* at which points (i_k, j_k) there is a data element d_k, no component of D can be "relied upon" to be present. It is necessary to be able to construct an approximation F^* that is convex even when (data of unlimited sparsity!) the D term is altogether absent. From (7.13), if the D term is absent,

$$F^*(\mathbf{u}) = \sum_k g_k^*(\mathbf{u}) \tag{7.15}$$

$$\text{with } g_k^*(\mathbf{u}) = g^* \left(\sum_l Q_{k,l} u_l \right), \tag{7.16}$$

so it is clear that $g^*(t)$ itself must now be convex. This can be done for t lying in some finite range, as shown in figure 7.2. But the resulting g^* is not nearly such a close approximation to g as for the dense case. Anyway, because of the ambiguity problem discussed in chapter 4, direct reconstruction from sparse data is not recommended. Instead, sparse data is first converted to dense using a continuous membrane, using small spatial scale λ to avoid distortion.

    This discussion of sparse data also underlines a general principle. The more carefully the specific structure of energy F is taken into account, the closer the convex approximation F^* can be made. In the case of sparse data, a rather general approach had to be used for construction of F^*, so the approximation cannot be as good as it was for dense data. Even so,

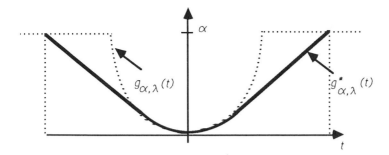

Figure 7.2: With sparse data, a convex cost function F^* is constructed by replacing g by g^*, over some finite interval. But the approximation is much poorer than for dense data (fig 7.1).

specific structure was taken into account insofar as line variable elimination was still incorporated, so that the energy has the form $F(\mathbf{u})$. Without that, the energy would have had the form $E(\mathbf{u}, \mathbf{l})$, for which it is difficult to obtain a convex approximation at all, even by the most general methods (for example Hopfield's method as in the previous chapter).

7.2   Performance of the convex approximation

Minimisation of the convex approximation F^* is only the first of two steps of the GNC algorithm. But before proceeding to define the second step, it is worth looking at the performance of the first step, in its own right. After all, having constructed an approximation to the cost function F, might it not be sufficient to minimise that? The answer is "sometimes" - if the spatial scale constant λ is small enough. But for larger λ, we shall see that it is essential to proceed to the second step of GNC.

When is the global minimum of F^*, which can be found by gradient descent, also the global minimum of F? A completely general answer, that applies for any data $\mathbf{d}$, cannot be given. But certain strong results can be obtained for a class of data comprising "isolated" steps and including noise.

The conclusion of the analysis turns out to be that F^* behaves exactly like F except when the step height h is close to the contrast sensitivity threshold h_0. Just how close depends on λ. If $\lambda \approx 1$ then h must be quite close to h_0 before F^* starts to behave badly. But if $\lambda \gg 1$ then F^* behaves badly almost all the time. Intuitively, the result that F^* works well only for small λ is plausible when one considers $g^*_{\alpha,\lambda}$ which approximates $g_{\alpha,\lambda}$ well only for small λ, as figure 7.3 shows. Hence F^* is a much closer

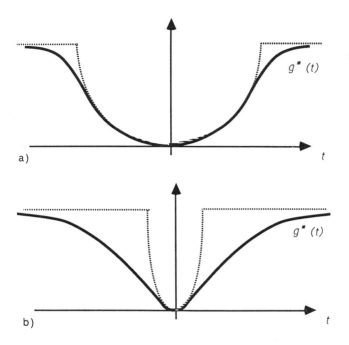

Figure 7.3: Neighbour interaction function $g^*_{\alpha,\lambda}$ is a much better approximation to $\acute{g}_{\alpha,\lambda}$ for $\lambda \approx 1$ (a) than for $\lambda \gg 1$ (b).

approximation to F when λ is small. These observations apply also to the membrane, and (substituting μ^2 for λ) to the rod and plate.

A test for success in optimising F^* (in the sense that the minimum $\mathbf{u}^*$ of F^* is also the global minimum of F) is that:

$$F^*(\mathbf{u}^*) = F(\mathbf{u}^*). \tag{7.17}$$

Graphical justification of this was given in figure 3.6 on page 48. The algebraic justification is also simple: g^* is defined (7.6,7.7) in such a way that

$$\forall t, \; g^*(t) \leq g(t)$$

(with equality for $|t| \leq q$ and $|t| \geq r$). This means, from (7.10) and (7.13),

that
$$\forall \mathbf{u}, \ F^*(\mathbf{u}) \leq F(\mathbf{u})$$

Combining this with the definition of $\mathbf{u}^*$, that

$$\forall \mathbf{u}, \ F^*(\mathbf{u}^*) \leq F^*(\mathbf{u}),$$

and with (7.17) gives
$$\forall \mathbf{u}, \ F(\mathbf{u}^*) \leq F(\mathbf{u}). \tag{7.18}$$

So when (7.17) holds $\mathbf{u}^*$ is the global minimum of F.

Once $\mathbf{u}^*$ has been computed, a formula like (6.6) on page 114 that is used with F, is needed to recover the line variables. It is obtained from the definition (7.7) of g^*:

$$l_i = \begin{cases} 1, & \text{if } |u_i - u_{i-1}| > r \\ 0, & \text{if } |u_i - u_{i-1}| < q \\ \text{ambiguous} & \text{otherwise.} \end{cases} \tag{7.19}$$

It is easily seen that if and only if no line variables come up ambiguous then condition (7.17) is satisfied, and the convex optimisation has been successful. Otherwise the ambiguity must be resolved by the second step of the GNC algorithm. An example of how this works in practice is given in figure 7.4.

In appendix E the minimisation of F^* for the weak string applied to an ideal step of height h, is solved. A recurrence relation is obtained for the components u_i^* of $\mathbf{u}^*$. It is shown that if the effective height h of the step is large enough, or small enough, the test (7.17) succeeds. For intermediate step heights, however, it fails because at least one of the line variables is ambiguous in (7.19). The range $[h_-, h_+]$ of intermediate step heights, which increases as λ increases, is

$$[h_-, h_+] = [h_0/\sqrt{2\lambda}, h_0\sqrt{2\lambda}] \tag{7.20}$$

(for $\lambda \gg 1$). For small λ, the range in which ambiguity occurs is small; this reemphasises that minimising F^* is most effective, as a means of finding the global minimum of F, when λ is small.

This ambiguity result can be shown to apply also to quite general data (appendix E) provided that potential discontinuities are "isolated", that is, separated by a distance somewhat greater than λ. The generalisation, which works for much the same reasons that it worked in the variational analysis in chapter 4, applies as follows:

First of all, appealing to the notion of an isolated discontinuity, the interpretation of line variables can be extended in the following way. Instead

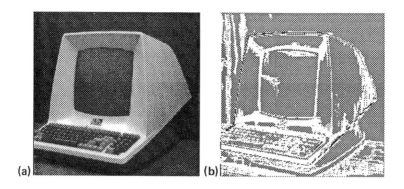

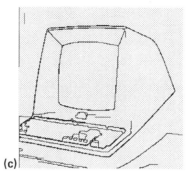

Figure 7.4: The convex approximation to the weak membrane is applied to the intensities of image (a). (b) White areas show line-variables that are in the ambiguous state after optimisation. The second step of the GNC algorithm is necessary to produce well-defined discontinuities (c). (Scale: $\lambda = 4$ pixels; sensitivity: $\eta = 25\%$.)

of requiring all l_i to be recovered unambiguously, it is enough that they are recovered unambiguously in an interval $[i_1, i_2]$ of length several times λ. In that case the minimisation of F^* has succeeded over a central portion of that interval. (The central portion is constructed by chopping about λ off each end). The values of u_i^* over that portion agree with the true global minimum u_i of F.

Secondly, for a potential discontinuity in non-ideal data, the range of effective step height h over which the convex minimisation produces an ambiguous result, is $h_- < h < h_+$ as in (7.20). (Effective step height was defined in figure 4.4 on page 57.) The result holds provided noise and other variations in d_i are not too violent - to be specific, provided the gradient in the fitted membrane everywhere satisfies:

$$|u_{i+1} - u_i| < M \tag{7.21}$$

where (appendix E)

$$M \approx \frac{\sqrt{\alpha}}{4\lambda^3}.$$

7.3 Graduated non-convexity

The previous sections showed that F^* is a useful approximation to F, for the weak elastic string, for small λ. But for large λ the second step of the GNC algorithm must be performed.

A one-parameter family of cost functions $F^{(p)}$ is defined, replacing g^* in the definition (7.13) of F^* by $g^{(p)}$. Now g^* was defined in (7.7) and $g^{(p)}$ is similar, except that c^* is replaced by a variable c, that varies with p. For the string

$$F^{(p)} = D + \sum_1^N g^{(p)}(u_i - u_{i-1}) \tag{7.22}$$

with

$$g_{\alpha,\lambda}^{(p)}(t) = \begin{cases} \lambda^2(t)^2, & \text{if } |t| < q \\ \alpha - c(|t| - r)^2/2, & \text{if } q \le |t| < r \\ \alpha, & \text{if } |t| \ge r \end{cases} \tag{7.23}$$

$$\text{where } c = \frac{c^*}{p}, \quad r^2 = \alpha \left(\frac{2}{c} + \frac{1}{\lambda^2} \right), \quad \text{and } q = \frac{\alpha}{\lambda^2 r}. \tag{7.24}$$

At the start of the algorithm, $p = 1$ and $c = c^*$, so $g^{(1)} \equiv g^*$. As p decreases from 1 to 0, $g^{(p)}$ changes steadily from g^* to g. Consequently $F^{(p)}$ starts as F^*, when $p = 1$, and changes steadily towards F, as p decreases towards 0.

The GNC algorithm begins by minimising $F^{(1)}$ (which is the same as F^* and hence convex, with a unique minimum). Then, from that minimum, the local minimum of $F^{(p)}$ is tracked continuously as p varies from 1 to 0. In principle p should be decreased continuously. In practice, of course, a sequence of discrete values of p is used. Each $F^{(p)}$ is minimised, using the minimum of the previous $F^{(p)}$ as a starting point.

The claim is that following such a progression is more effective, especially when λ is large, than simply optimising F^*, or than optimising F^* and then F. Figure 3.6c on page 48 attempted to give an intuitive feel for why this might be so.

An analytical explanation can also be given. We will see that the negative quadratic portion of $g^{(p)}$ is, in effect, "titrated" with the other positive quadratic terms in $F^{(p)}$ to make certain structures within the emerging reconstruction unstable. The instability causes them to home onto their own minimal energy configuration. It is as if the function $F^{(p)}$ were the true convex envelope (multidimensional!) of F, with respect to just those structures. Furthermore this behaviour is selective for structure size. That is, associated with each value of p, there is a characteristic size of structure in u_i. Only structures of that size are unstable, at a given p. Initially, when $p = 1$, the characteristic size is as small as it can be - one pixel. Then as $p \to 0$ it becomes larger until it attains its maximum size which is, one might have guessed, λ (neglecting discretisation error). In this way F is optimised "with respect to" all structures, in turn, in increasing order of size.

The notion of instability being selective of structure size can be derived by a development of the earlier argument that $F^* \equiv F^{(1)}$ is finely set up to be *just* convex. When $p = 1$ $F^{(p)}$ is unstable with respect to the very smallest structures. Calling also on the idea (section 4.1.2) that constraining one end of a piece of elastic string is like pulling on a spring whose spring rate increases with the length of the piece, the dependence of structure size on p can be demonstrated.

7.4   Why GNC works

Correctness can be demonstrated for important special cases: the isolated discontinuity, and a pair of interacting discontinuities. It is shown that, in these cases, the GNC algorithm reproduces the behaviour predicted by variational analysis. The second case is particularly significant because its behaviour (sensitivity varies as $1/\sqrt{a}$, where a is the separation between discontinuities) is a distinctive feature of weak continuity constraints; linear filters followed by thresholding cannot behave in this way. In fact there is a special condition under which the GNC algorithm fails with interacting steps. Practically, it is unimportant, but it has a theoretical significance because it indicates that GNC can fail, and that there is therefore no point in looking for a *general* proof of correctness. Finally, GNC can be shown to have the ability to filter noise. In practice, noise filtering performance approaches variational limits (chapter 4), far exceeding theoretical predictions of performance of the algorithm itself.

7.4.1   Isolated discontinuity

What is meant here by "isolated"? That after optimisation of the convex F^*, all i for which

$$g^*(\Delta_i) \neq g(\Delta_i)$$

(where $\Delta_i = u_{i+1} - u_i$) are separated by distances that are large compared with λ. Line variables for these i are in the ambiguous "as-yet-undecided" state[3]. The separations prevent interaction between them (see appendix E). All other line variables remain in the continuous state $l_i = 0$.

The minimum energy state can be tracked as p varies from 1 to 0 - a simulation of the GNC algorithm. This is shown in fig 7.5. The outcome - $l_0 = 0$ or $l_0 = 1$ - depends on whether h exceeds a certain threshold, and that threshold can be shown to agree with the variationally predicted h_0 to within the $O(1/\lambda^2)$ error caused by discretisation (appendix E). Perhaps more surprisingly, the resulting u_i is an *exact* solution to the discrete problem of minimising F.

The reason is as follows: the energy $F^{(p)}(u_i)$ can be regarded as a function solely of Δ_0, because the movements of u_i on either side of the discontinuity are entirely determined by continuous elastic string behaviour. All the u_i therefore depend linearly on Δ_0. (This is just what happened in the variational case.) It is shown in appendix E (E.18) that (up to an additive constant):

$$F^{(p)}(\Delta_0) = \frac{1}{2}\mathcal{F}(h - \Delta_0)^2 + g^{(p)}(\Delta_0). \qquad (7.25)$$

where $\mathcal{F}$ is a constant. Now (appendix E) $F^{(p)}(\Delta_0)$ is convex if

$$c \leq \mathcal{F}$$

and when $c = \mathcal{F}$, $F^{(p)}$ becomes linear for $q \leq \Delta_0 \leq r$, causing an instability which forces $F^{(p)}$ to the global minimum of F (figure 7.6). Thus, (from

---

[3]This can be shown to hold, for example, for an ideal step in noise, provided the amplitude of the noise is not too great (appendix E).

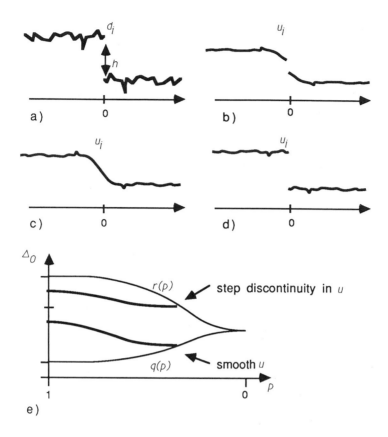

Figure 7.5: Progress of graduated non-convexity. A step (a) of (effective) height h may be "pulled" together (b) as the algorithm progresses and finally, either becomes smooth (c) or snaps back (d). Tracking $\Delta_0 = |u_1 - u_0|$ as the algorithm progresses ($p : 1 \to 0$) determines the outcome. (e) If Δ_0 hits the line labelled q before hitting r then the resulting u_i is smooth as in (c) - $l_0 = 0$. But if the Δ_0 line hits r before hitting q, then u_i has a step discontinuity as in (d) - $l_0 = 1$.

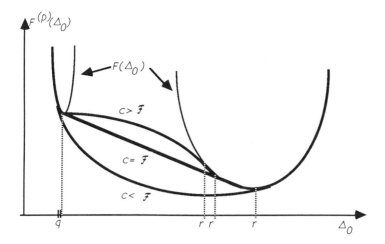

Figure 7.6: GNC is correct for an isolated discontinuity. The GNC energy function $F^{(p)}$ is effectively dependent on one variable only. As $p \rightarrow 0$ c reaches a critical value $\mathcal{F}$ at which the minimum of $F^{(p)}$ must also be the desired minimum of F.

(7.24)), when p reaches the value $c^*/\mathcal{F}$ the algorithm has reached its final state - further reduction in p has no effect. Since $\mathcal{F} \leq \Lambda \approx \lambda$ for the isolated step (appendix E), there is no point in reducing p below about c^*/λ. This can be shown to be true, not only for an isolated step, but for the weak string in general. A similar result should hold for the membrane. Figure 7.7 shows how true energy $F(\mathbf{u})$ varies for the weak string, in successive iterations, as p decreases. As predicted, the final state is reached by the time $p = c^*/\lambda$. It is reached exactly at $p = c^*/\lambda$ when $h \approx h_0$, or sooner when h and h_0 differ substantially (in agreement with results in appendix E.5). It is reassuring to see that, as expected, energy does not decrease monotonically as GNC progresses. First it increases, then it decreases again - the fly's problem (figure 3.4, page 45) has been solved.

7.4.2 Interacting discontinuities

Having shown that the GNC algorithm solves the isolated discontinuity problem exactly, it is natural to examine the case of interacting discontinuities. It can be shown that GNC almost always solves the problem correctly, but errs when both the effective step heights h_1, h_2 are close to their detection threshold. Of course, when the discontinuities are separated by $a \gg \lambda$, they do not interact. They just behave as two isolated discontinuities. The worst case is for discontinuities separated by width $a \ll \lambda$ (figure 7.8). Energy $F^{(p)}$ can be regarded as a function of the two variables Δ_0, Δ_a, controlling the size of each discontinuity in $u(x)$:

$$F^{(p)}(\Delta_0, \Delta_a) = \frac{\lambda}{2}(\Delta_0 - h_1)^2 + \frac{\lambda}{2}(\Delta_a - h_2)^2$$
$$- \lambda \exp\left(-\frac{a}{\lambda}\right)(\Delta_0 - h_1)(\Delta_a - h_2) + g^{(p)}(\Delta_0) + g^{(p)}(\Delta_a). \tag{7.26}$$

In the special case $h_1 = h_2$, it reduces still further, to be a function of one variable since $\Delta_0 = \Delta_a$ by symmetry:

$$F^{(p)} = 2\left(\frac{a}{2}(\Delta_0 - h_1)^2 + g^{(p)}(\Delta_0)\right). \tag{7.27}$$

(This is an approximation for the case $a \ll \lambda$.) Formally, this is just the same as for the isolated discontinuity (7.25) and so $F^{(p)}$ is again correctly minimised by GNC. The critical value of c at which instability occurs is $c = a$. This is an instance of structure size selection in GNC: as $p \to 0$, interacting discontinuity pairs of progressively increasing separation $a = c$ (still assuming $a \ll \lambda$) become unstable and reach their minimal energy configuration. Finally, as $c \to \lambda$, structures of all sizes have been dealt with.

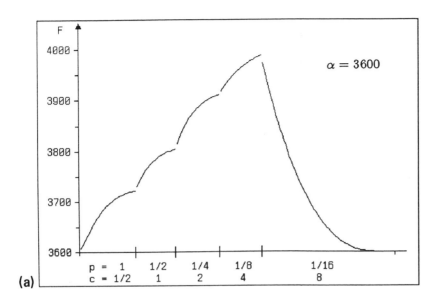

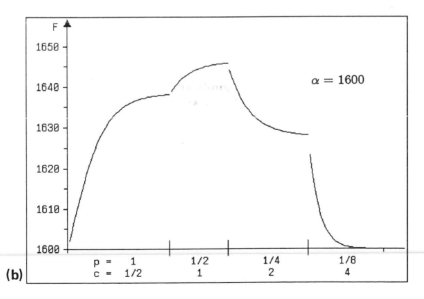

Figure 7.7: Convergence to final energy in GNC. The final state of GNC is reached when $p = c^*/\lambda$ (a) ($h \approx h_0$), or sooner (b) ($h_0 \approx 0.6h$). (Weak string ($c^* = 1/2$), ideal step, $\lambda = 8$, free of noise.)

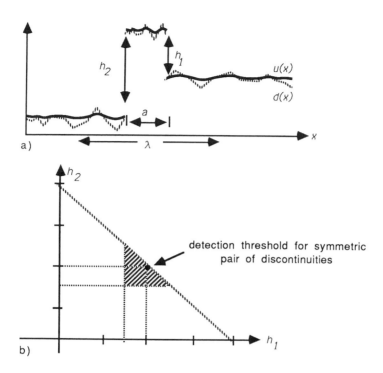

Figure 7.8: Interacting discontinuities (a). GNC is exact except for a small range of effective step heights h_1, h_2, close to the detection threshold (b).

Analysis of the general case involves more algebra, which is not reproduced here. It is assumed that $h_1, h_2 \geq 0$. As $p \to 0$, $F^{(p)}$ (7.26) passes through 2 unstable states, one for each variable. The first (when the Hessian of $F^{(p)}$ becomes singular) occurs at

$$c = \lambda \left(1 - \exp\left(-\frac{a}{\lambda} \right) \right)$$

or, when $a \ll \lambda$, at $c \approx a$. At this point one of the following conditions must be met:

$$|\Delta_0| \leq q \text{ or } |\Delta_0| \geq r \text{ or } |\Delta_a| \leq q \text{ or } |\Delta_a| \geq r.$$

Then c is increased up to the next unstable value and a second of those conditions is satisfied. Comparing the outcome with the variational prediction (4.18) on page 61, it turns out to be correct, except for a small range of values of h_1, h_2 close to threshold (figure 7.8).

7.4.3 Noise

Variational analysis predicted that the weak string should be more or less immune to "false alarms" in noise for which $\sqrt{\alpha/2}$ exceeds σ. In practice, the GNC algorithm gives agreement with that prediction.

It can be shown that the GNC algorithm must reject noise up to about $\sigma = \frac{1}{2}\sqrt{\alpha/\lambda}$, which falls short of the above limit by a factor of $\sqrt{2\lambda}$. Consider data $d(x) = 0$ with additive noise $n(x)$. If the continuous string $u(x)$ satisfies

$$\left\langle u'^2(x) \right\rangle^{\frac{1}{2}} < \frac{q}{2} \tag{7.28}$$

then, in its discretised form,

$$|\Delta_i| < q$$

for each i, with probability of 95% or so (because of the factor of 2 in $q/2$). In that case, the continuous string solution is a local minimum of F^* and hence must be its global minimum. There are no discontinuities in the problem, or perhaps (with low probability) a few isolated ones, and GNC correctly minimises F.

To establish (7.28), the Green's function (A.6) and the definition of σ (B.2) are used to show that, for data in a bi-infinite interval,

$$\left\langle u'^2(x) \right\rangle^{\frac{1}{2}} = \left(\frac{\sigma^2}{4\lambda^3} \right)^{\frac{1}{2}}.$$

Now, on the convex function $(p = 1)$, $c = c^* = 1/2$ so that

$$q \approx \frac{1}{\lambda^2} \left(\frac{\alpha c^*}{2} \right)^{\frac{1}{2}} = \frac{\sqrt{\alpha}}{2\lambda^2}$$

(assuming $\lambda \gg 1$). So condition (7.28) is met provided

$$\sigma \leq \frac{1}{2} \sqrt{\alpha/\lambda}.$$

As for the remaining factor of $\sqrt{2\lambda}$ in the limit of noise resistance, here is what probably happens. Over an interval of length $a \ll \lambda$ it can be shown that

$$\left\langle u'^2(x) \right\rangle^{\frac{1}{2}} \approx \left(\frac{a\sigma^2}{3\lambda^4} \right)^{\frac{1}{2}} \tag{7.29}$$

so that (7.28) is satisfied if $\sigma < \frac{1}{4}\sqrt{3\alpha/a}$. Of course the shortest possible interval in the discrete problem is $a = 1$ for which the condition becomes $\sigma < \frac{1}{4}\sqrt{3\alpha}$. This is close to the variational limit of performance $\sigma < \sqrt{\alpha/2}$. What this suggests is that, after descent on $F^{(p)}$ at $p = 1$, large amplitude noise in the data will appear as a sequence of short segments of length $a = 1$ or so. As $p \to 0$ and q increases, (7.28) permits larger values of $\left\langle u'^2(x) \right\rangle^{\frac{1}{2}}$ and hence, from (7.29), longer segment length a. This agrees with behaviour of GNC observed in figure 3.8 on page 50, in which noise is progressively grouped into longer and longer segments as p decreases.

The addition of noise to, say, an isolated step dominates the progress of the GNC algorithm. The change in energy $F(\mathbf{u})$ as the algorithm progresses (figure 7.9) looks entirely different from the noise-free case (figure 7.7). The most obvious difference is that the final energy is very much less than the initial energy, and this is due to filtering of the noise. Another difference is that the fastest energy decrease happens at large p (small c); this is in accordance with the earlier conjecture that filtering of small scale structure generated by noise would occur at small c. The removal of noise causes a rapid decrease in energy, due to remission of penalties for discontinuities.

7.4.4   Summary

It is worth attempting to state, at this point, what is the *general* property of the function sequence $F^{(p)}$ that leads to the correctness of GNC as above. It can be summarised as follows. First of all, the reconstruction problem itself was expressed in terms of a one-parameter system, with a cost function $F(u_i(z))$, in which the $u_i(z)$ are known to be linear functions.

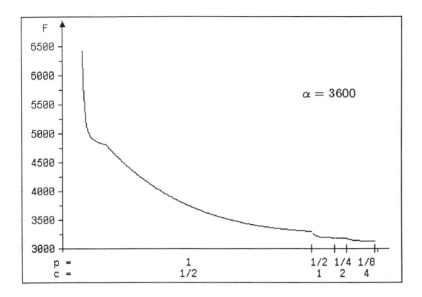

Figure 7.9: Convergence of GNC in the presence of noise. (Weak string and data as for figure 7.7a, but with noise added.)

For the isolated step, for instance, the parameter z was Δ_0; all the u_i vary as linear functions of Δ_0. Secondly, the family of functions $F^{(p)}$ applied to any such system, satisfies the following condition: there exists a p such that, for all z,

$$\text{either}: \quad F^{(p)''}(z) = 0 \qquad (7.30)$$
$$\text{or}: \quad F^{(p)}(z) = F(z).$$

What that means is that, for this one parameter system, *either* $F^{(p)}$ agrees with F, *or* it is unstable (as in figure (7.6).

For example, imagine a scheme that involved sweeping the scale parameter λ in F from small to large scale, instead of sweeping the parameter p. Such a scheme would have the advantage of generating a multi-scale reconstruction in one sweep. It would not satisfy the condition (7.30) above. In practice too, it is found not to work: sweeping λ at constant α consistently supresses discontinuities at coarser scales; sweeping at constant h_0 generates too many discontinuities.

7.5   Descent algorithms

A simple algorithm for GNC was given in figure 3.7 on page 49. This algorithm has been implemented for the string and the membrane. Its use (at large values of λ) is reported in (Blake 1983b). It is a *direct* descent algorithm and hence provably convergent - energy is monotonic decreasing and bounded below.

However, it is arguably more effective to do gradient descent, using local quadratic approximation to determine optimal step sizes. In fact this is a form of non-linear successive over-relaxation (SOR). For the iterative minimisation of $F^{(p)}$ (in its general form (7.10)) the nth iteration is

$$u_l^{(n+1)} = u_l^{(n)} - \omega \frac{1}{T_l} \frac{\partial F^{(p)}}{\partial u_l}, \tag{7.31}$$

where $0 < \omega < 2$ is the "SOR parameter", governing speed of convergence, and T_l is an upper bound on the second derivative:

$$T_l \geq \frac{\partial^2 F^{(p)}}{\partial u_l^2} \quad \forall \mathbf{u}. \tag{7.32}$$

A simultaneous version for parallel implementation could easily be obtained by applying a "chequer-board" updating scheme, as described in the previous chapter.

Convergence   Both successive and simultaneous schemes are convergent for $\omega \in (0, 2)$. This is easily proved by observing that each application of (7.31) is a movement along a piecewise quadratic function of *one* variable (u_l), towards its minimum. In other words, temporarily regarding $F^{(p)}$ as a function $F^{(p)}(u_l)$ of u_l only, it is piecewise quadratic. The proof of convergence is illustrated graphically in figures 7.10 and 7.11. If $w \leq 1$ then the step from $u_l^{(n)}$ to $u_l^{(n+1)}$ is guaranteed to be downhill all the way - there is no change of the sign of the gradient. This is because the change in the gradient is bounded. Suppose, without loss of generality, that initially, at $u_l = u_l^{(n)}$, the gradient is negative, that is:

$$\frac{\partial F^{(p)}}{\partial u_l} \left(u_l^{(n)} \right) \leq 0. \tag{7.33}$$

It can easily be shown from (7.32) and the mean value theorem that for any u_l such that

$$u_l^{(n)} \leq u_l \leq u_l^{(n+1)},$$

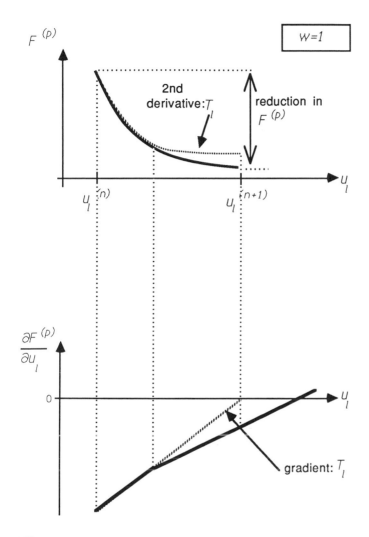

Figure 7.10: Proof of convergence for non-linear SOR. The case $w = 1$.

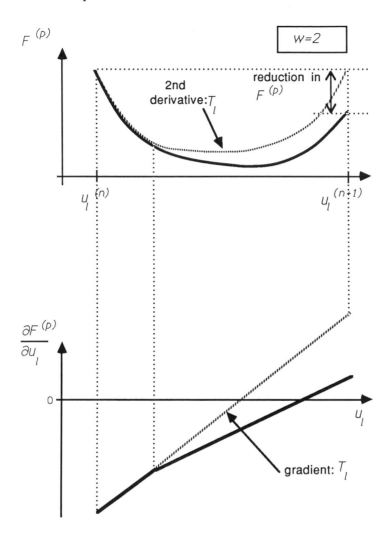

Figure 7.11: Proof of convergence for non-linear SOR. The case $w = 2$.

the inequality

$$\frac{\partial F^{(p)}}{\partial u_l}(u_l) - \frac{\partial F^{(p)}}{\partial u_l}(u_l^{(n)}) \le T_l(u_l^{(n+1)} - u_l^{(n)})$$

holds. Now, from (7.31),

$$\frac{\partial F^{(p)}}{\partial u_l}(u_l) - \frac{\partial F^{(p)}}{\partial u_l}(u_l^{(n)}) \le -w\frac{\partial F^{(p)}}{\partial u_l}(u_l^{(n)}).$$

So throughout the descent,

$$\frac{\partial F^{(p)}}{\partial u_l}(u_l) \le (1-w)\frac{\partial F^{(p)}}{\partial u_l}(u_l^{(n)})$$

which, by hypothesis (7.33), remains negative, provided $w \le 1$.

When $w > 1$ the gradient $\partial F^{(p)}/\partial u_l$ may change sign on the way to $u_l^{(n)}$, but only if $w \ge 2$ (it can easily be shown) can the overshoot be sufficiently severe that there is no net *decrease* in cost. Hence for $w \in (0, 2)$, cost is monotonically decreasing and bounded below. The algorithm must converge. It might appear from figures 7.10 and 7.11 that $w = 1$ should give fastest convergence since, for any given step (n, l), $w = 1$ produces the largest reduction in the value of $F^{(p)}$. The cumulative effect of many steps, however, is somewhat different. It turns out that values of w in the range $(1, 2)$ give fastest overall convergence (see next section).

The terms in (7.31) are computed as follows. The gradient term is

$$\partial F^{(p)}/\partial u_l = 2(u_l - d_l) + \sum_k g_{\alpha,\lambda}^{(p)'}\left(\sum_s Q_{k,s}u_s\right)Q_{k,l} \qquad (7.34)$$

where

$$g^{(p)'}_{\alpha,\lambda}(t) = \begin{cases} 2\lambda^2 t, & \text{if } |t| < q \\ -c(|t| - r)\text{sign}(t), & \text{if } q \le |t| < r \\ 0, & \text{if } |t| \ge r \end{cases} \qquad (7.35)$$

(and Q was defined in (7.10) and (7.11)). The bound T_l on the second derivative is obtained by differentiating (7.34) and observing that $g^{(p)''} \le 2\lambda^2$:

$$T_l = 2 + 2\lambda^2 \sum_k Q_{k,l}^2.$$

For the rod/plate, of course, λ is replaced by μ^2. An iterative (SOR) scheme for the weak string is summarised in figure 7.12 and one for the weak membrane in figure 7.13.

Choose λ, h_0 (scale and sensitivity).
Set $\alpha = h_0^2 \lambda / 2$.
SOR parameter: $w = 2(1 - 1/\lambda)$.
Function sequence: $p \in \{1, 0.5, 0.25, ..., 1/\lambda, 1/2\lambda\}$.
Nodes: $i \in \{0, ..., N\}$.

For each p, iterate $n = 1, 2, ...$

For $i = 1, ..., N - 1$:

$$u_i^{(n+1)} = u_i^{(n)} - \omega \left\{ 2 \left(u_i^{(n)} - d_i \right) + g_{\alpha,\lambda}^{(p)'} \left(u_i^{(n)} - u_{i-1}^{(n+1)} \right) \right. $$
$$\left. + g_{\alpha,\lambda}^{(p)'} \left(u_i^{(n)} - u_{i+1}^{(n)} \right) \right\} / \left(2 + 4\lambda^2 \right)$$

Appropriate modification is necessary at boundaries:

$$u_0^{(n+1)} = u_0^{(n)} - \omega \left\{ 2 \left(u_0^{(n)} - d_0 \right) + g_{\alpha,\lambda}^{(p)'} \left(u_0^{(n)} - u_1^{(n)} \right) \right\} / \left(2 + 2\lambda^2 \right)$$

and similarly at $i = N$.

Figure 7.12: An SOR algorithm for the weak string.

Choose λ, h_0 (scale and sensitivity).

Set $\alpha = h_0^2 \lambda / 2$.

SOR parameter: $w = 2(1 - 1/(\sqrt{2}\lambda))$.

Function sequence: $p \in \{1, 0.5, 0.25, ..., 1/\lambda\}$.

Nodes: $i \in \{0, ..., N\}$, $j \in \{0, ..., N\}$.

For each p, iterate $n = 1, 2, ...$

For $i = 1, ..., N - 1$, $j = 1, ..., N - 1$:

$$
\begin{aligned}
u_{i,j}^{(n+1)} = u_{i,j}^{(n)} \quad &- \quad w \left\{ 2(u_{i,j}^{(n)} - d_{i,j}) + g_{\alpha,\lambda}^{(p)'} \left(u_{i,j}^{(n)} - u_{i-1,j}^{(n+1)} \right) \right. \\
&+ g_{\alpha,\lambda}^{(p)'} \left(u_{i,j}^{(n)} - u_{i,j-1}^{(n+1)} \right) + g_{\alpha,\lambda}^{(p)'} \left(u_{i,j}^{(n)} - u_{i+1,j}^{(n)} \right) \\
&\left. + g_{\alpha,\lambda}^{(p)'} \left(u_{i,j}^{(n)} - u_{i,j+1}^{(n)} \right) \right\} / (2 + 8\lambda^2)
\end{aligned}
$$

Appropriate modification is necessary at boundaries:

For $i = 0$, $j = 0$:

$$
\begin{aligned}
u_{0,0}^{(n+1)} = u_{0,0}^{(n)} \quad &- \quad w \left\{ 2(u_{0,0}^{(n)} - d_{0,0}) + g_{\alpha,\lambda}^{(p)'} \left(u_{0,0}^{(n)} - u_{1,0}^{(n)} \right) \right. \\
&\left. + g_{\alpha,\lambda}^{(p)'} \left(u_{0,0}^{(n)} - u_{0,1}^{(n)} \right) \right\} / (2 + 4\lambda^2)
\end{aligned}
$$

and similarly at the other corners.

For $i = 0$, $j = 1, ..., N - 1$:

$$
\begin{aligned}
u_{0,j}^{(n+1)} = u_{0,j}^{(n)} \quad &- \quad w \left\{ 2(u_{0,j}^{(n)} - d_{0,j}) \right. \\
&+ g_{\alpha,\lambda}^{(p)'} \left(u_{0,j}^{(n)} - u_{0,j-1}^{(n+1)} \right) + g_{\alpha,\lambda}^{(p)'} \left(u_{0,j}^{(n)} - u_{1,j}^{(n)} \right) \\
&\left. + g_{\alpha,\lambda}^{(p)'} \left(u_{0,j}^{(n)} - u_{0,j+1}^{(n)} \right) \right\} / (2 + 6\lambda^2)
\end{aligned}
$$

and similarly at the other sides.

Figure 7.13: An SOR algorithm for the weak membrane.

7.6   Convergence properties

Analysis of the convergence rate of GNC is difficult. It is possible however, to obtain exact results for equivalent continuous problems, without weak constraints (or, to put it another way, in the limit that the penalty constant α is large). Experimental results have been obtained to show just how far these results apply also under weak continuity constraints.

7.6.1   Continuous problems

For "Jacobi" relaxation (simultaneous updating of $u_i^{(n)} \rightarrow u_i^{(n+1)}$ using relaxation parameter $w = 1$), the largest eigenvalue of the iteration matrix gives a lower bound on the rate of convergence[4]. This can also be used to derive convergence rates for successive over-relaxation (SOR), which is a serial algorithm, and converges in far fewer iterations.

Convergence results are summarised as follows:

Convergence norm: a convenient norm to use as a measure of convergence is the "infinity norm"

$$\|\mathbf{u}\|_\infty = \max_i |u_i|. \qquad (7.36)$$

At successive iterations, the dynamic norm

$$\|\mathbf{u}^{(n+1)} - \mathbf{u}^{(n)}\|_\infty \qquad (7.37)$$

is measured as an indication of progress towards convergence. Of course the quantity of real interest is the absolute norm

$$\|\mathbf{u}^{(n)} - \mathbf{u}^{(\infty)}\|_\infty \qquad (7.38)$$

which is a measure of accuracy of the current $\mathbf{u}^{(n)}$ compared with the true solution. Happily, absolute and dynamic norms are related, in theory, by

$$\|\mathbf{u}^{(n)} - \mathbf{u}^{(\infty)}\| \approx \gamma \|\mathbf{u}^{(n+1)} - \mathbf{u}^{(n)})\|, \qquad (7.39)$$

where γ is the decay-time for the algorithm, measured in iterations (see below). This result is borne out by experiments.

string/membrane: decay time for Jacobi relaxation (number of iterations for an appropriately defined error measure to fall by a factor of $1/e$) is of order λ^2. This clearly indicates that convergence is slower for larger scale constant λ.

---

[4]Eigenvalues can be found by a circulant analysis similar to that used for convexity proofs in appendix D.

rod/plate: Jacobi decay time is of order μ^4. This is born out in practice - the plate tends to converge slowly. For this reason Terzopoulos found it essential to use multilevel relaxation for the plate (Terzopoulos 1983), as described in the previous chapter. This may not be effective when weak continuity constraints are applied, the problem being non-linear. The reason will be apparent from figures 7.15 and 7.16, which make it plain (in the case of the string) that convergence *without* weak constraints is already fast enough. Multigrid algorithms could be used but, on this type of process (dense data, scale λ not too large) would give only modest benefit. For the rod or plate the potential gain is greater, but still limited compared with Terzopoulos' experiments when the data is dense. What does take time in GNC is the treatment of discontinuities. This is what makes the problem non-linear and takes it outside the scope of classical multigrid algorithms. (Fourier analysis, for instance, can no longer altogether characterise the progress of the algorithm.)

2D compared with 1D: decay time (in iterations) is of much the same order in 2D as in 1D (e.g. the same for membrane as for string).

Successive over-relaxation (SOR): SOR can be made to converge much faster than Jacobi. If the decay time for Jacobi is γ then that for SOR is reduced to $\sqrt{\gamma/8}$ - provided the following optimal SOR parameter is used (Smith 1978):

$$w = 2 \left(1 + \frac{\sqrt{1 + 2\gamma}}{1 + \gamma} \right)^{-1}. \tag{7.40}$$

Assuming λ (μ^2) to be somewhat greater than 1, this is approximated by

$$w = 2 \left(1 + \sqrt{2/\gamma} \right)^{-1}. \tag{7.41}$$

Experiments confirm that this value of w does indeed produce fastest convergence (figure 7.15). If the optimal parameter is not used, however, the speed increase is comparatively small. For instance Gauss-Seidel relaxation (the special case of SOR in which $w = 1$) produces an increase of a factor of 2 only - the decay time is $\gamma/2$. This is illustrated graphically in figure 7.14. Decay times for Jacobi and SOR algorithms are summarised in the following table.

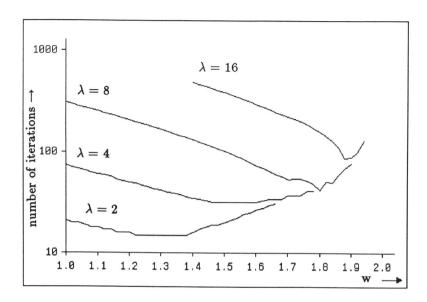

Figure 7.14: The theoretically optimal relaxation parameter w does indeed give fastest convergence. Continuous string, iterated to fixed accuracy.

	Decay time		
	Jacobi	SOR	optimal w
String	$2\lambda^2$	$\lambda/2$	$2/(1+1/\lambda)$
Membrane	$4\lambda^2$	$\lambda/\sqrt{2}$	$2/(1+1/\sqrt{2}\lambda)$
Rod	$6\mu^4$	$\sqrt{3}\mu^2/2$	$2/(1+1/\sqrt{3}\mu^2)$
Plate	$20\mu^4$	$\sqrt{5/2}\mu^2$	$2/(1+1/\sqrt{10}\mu^2)$

mixed 1st and 2nd order: as might be expected, the 2nd order term dominates, so that convergence of a mixed plate/membrane is essentially as slow as the "equivalent" plate.

gradient data for the plate: suppose that, gradient data $\mathbf{p}^{(0)}$ is given, so that the reconstruction problem is to minimise

$$E = D + P, \text{ where } D = \int (\nabla u - \mathbf{p}^{(0)})^2 \, dx \qquad (7.42)$$

and P is energy density for a plate. This is like the first order plate problem (previous chapter) except that there is an implied integrability constraint because the reconstructed signal is represented as $u(x, y)$, rather than as $p(x, y), q(x, y)$. Decay time for the corresponding discrete problem becomes very long - $O(N)$ for data in an $N \times N$ array. This is essentially because integrability of u must be maintained. The associated Green's function extends over the entire domain because, effectively, the data is being "integrated" over the entire array. But if integrability is not enforced, as in the scheme of (5.16) on page 107, then decay time is only $O(\mu)$. That is the situation for the 1st order plate, described earlier.

7.6.2   Adding weak constraints

When weak continuity constraints are imposed, exact analysis is difficult. Examination of g in (6.5) on page 114 indicates just how narrow the minima in F are. Narrow minima are likely to be difficult for any algorithm to find. Width is $O(1/\lambda)$ for string/membrane, but $O(1/\mu^2)$ for the rod/plate. Again the problem becomes harder for increasing scale, and is much harder for rod/plate than for string/membrane (at similar scales).

Experiments indicate that decay-rates are initially slower than for the continuous problems, but catch up again as convergence is reached. Figure 7.16a illustrates this. Initially, optimal SOR is no better than Gauss-Seidel,

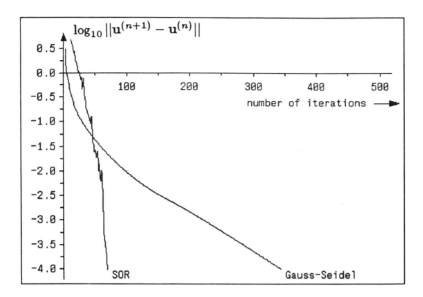

Figure 7.15: Decay rates for SOR algorithm. Optimal SOR decays much faster than Gauss-Seidel, in agreement with theoretical predictions (see text). (Continuous string, $\lambda = 8$, applied to a step of height h in Gaussian noise with $\sigma \approx 0.2h$.)

but then its decay rate increases, although it never becomes as rapid as for the continuous case (figure 7.15). The degree of this degradation depends strongly on the presence of noise. Without any noise there is virtually no degradation (figure 7.16b). The actual value of w that gives optimal convergence is much as in the continuous case, although slightly increased under some circumstances. The ratio between absolute and dynamic norms also agrees experimentally with the value γ predicted theoretically for the continous case (7.39). Total convergence time for the algorithm is roughly $O(\lambda)$ (figure 7.17).

7.6.3 Granularity of the $F^{(p)}$ sequence

In practice p has to decrease in discrete steps, as the GNC algorithm progresses. What effect does this have on the accuracy of the solution? The answer is given in appendix E.5, for the case of an isolated step. When p is decreased continuously, the GNC algorithm minimises F exactly. If instead successive reductions $p \to p/P$ are used then the algorithm continues to be correct, except when the effective step height h lies in a certain interval (E.22):

$$h \in [h_q, h_r] \text{ where } \frac{h_r}{h_q} \leq P.$$

So the reduction ratio P is also a bound on the proportionate error in the "effective" contrast threshold, compared with the true contrast threshold h_0. In practice P is a rather generous bound on the error in h_0, and since it is not usually important to be very accurate about fixing h_0, even $P = 2$ is found to be quite acceptable. Using a value of P that is not too small saves some computation time, as figure 7.18 shows.

7.6.4 Activity flags

In our serial implementations, *activity flags* are used to speed convergence (typically by a factor of 2-10). If no activity occurs in iteration n at node l, its activity flag a_l is switched off. (For direct descent, "no activity" means that $u_l^{(n+1)} = u_l^{(n)}$; but this is inappropriate for gradient descent, where instead the condition is that $|u_l^{(n+1)} - u_l^{(n)}|$ is below some fixed limit.) But if there is activity at node l then a_l is switched on, *and* so are all neighbouring nodes a_m. (Nodes m, l are defined to be neighbours if, for some s, $Q_{s,l} \neq 0$ and $Q_{s,m} \neq 0$.) When, in a given iteration, it is time to update the lth node, a_l is first examined. If it is off, the node can be ignored. This saves time particularly on the exponential tail of the convergence, at which point most u_i have reached their steady state.

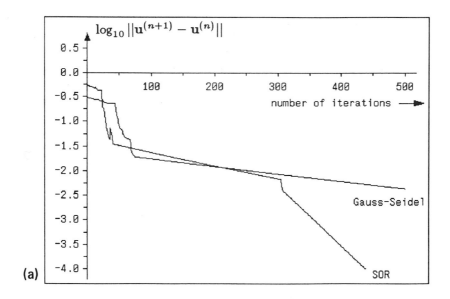

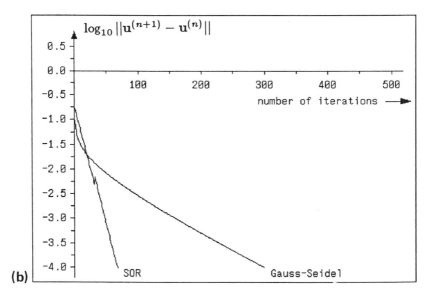

Figure 7.16: Decay rates under weak continuity constraints (a) As figure 7.15, but with weak continuity constraints ($h_0 \approx 0.6h$) - decay is much slower. (b) As (a) but without noise - decay is more or less as rapid as for the continuous case (figure 7.15). (Decay rates for optimisation of F^*.)

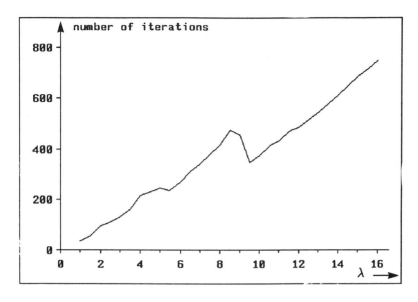

Figure 7.17: Convergence of GNC, as a function of spatial scale.

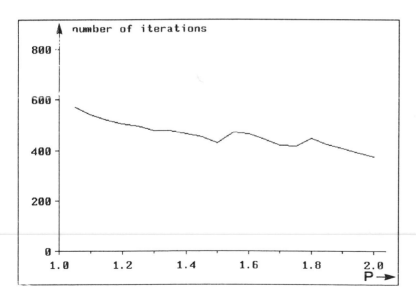

Figure 7.18: Convergence time decreases somewhat as the "reduction ratio" P increases (but to the detriment of accuracy). ($\lambda = 8$.)

The discussion of the GNC algorithm and its convergence properties is now complete. It remains to stand back a little, discuss some of the problems that remain to be solved in modelling piecewise continuity, and consider how application of weak continuity constraints might be extended to new aspects of Visual Reconstruction. This is done in the next and final chapter.

Chapter 8

Conclusion

We conclude by mentioning briefly some interesting questions and directions for further research.

8.1 Further applications in vision

Four visual reconstruction tasks have been discussed in the course of the book: edge detection, reconstruction of sparse and dense data, and curve description. But there are others that may be susceptible to treatment by weak constraints of some kind. Computation of lightness might seem to be an obvious candidate but in fact it calls for no further application of weak continuity constraints beyond what is already included in segmentation of intensity data. Discontinuities in intensity data must be supplied, but the computation of lightness *given* the intensity distribution and its discontinuities is a classical, quadratic minimisation problem (Horn 1974, Blake 1985c). Shape from shading (Ikeuchi and Horn 1981) is similar - discontinuities in intensity must be supplied, but beyond that there seems to be little further use for weak continuity constraints. This is because most if not all evidence for surface discontinuities is contained in the discontinuities of intensity. Texture segmentation, however, seems to be a potential application of weak continuity constraints. Promising experiments have been done by Derin and Cole (1986). So far, they assume known MRF texture models, and *a priori* fixed numbers of regions. These assumptions need to be relaxed. Furthermore, analysis of texture in real 3D images would demand viewpoint invariance, to take care of perspective foreshortening. Segmentation of optical flow is another promising area, calling for some kind of weak rigidity constraint - preferring fewer independent motions without insisting on absolute rigidity (Buxton and Murray 1985). And in stereoscopic vision a similar problem arises when several surfaces at different depths are overlaid, as when looking out of the window through net curtains. Weak continuity constraints may be appropriate, but extended to deal with multiple visible surfaces. It might even be feasible to integrate the process into the stereo algorithm itself, so that a subset of the "ghost field" of potential stereo matches is grouped directly into surfaces. Indeed this is somewhat related to the disparity gradient limit (Burt and Julesz 1980) already used by Pollard et al. (1985) for elimination of ghost matches. There is little doubt that energy functions with appropriate weak constraints could be set up for these problems. The real question is whether stochastic or deterministic minimisation algorithms that are computationally feasible can be designed for them. Furthermore, how far can energy functions be built or refined by inductive learning, as exhibited to some degree in neural networks (Hinton and Sejnowski 1983, Hopfield 1982, Wallace 1985).

8.2   Hardware Implementation

It is clear from the parallel nature of the GNC algorithm (when simultaneous updating is used) that it maps efficiently onto massively parallel machines, whether with cellular (Duff 1978, Marks 1980) or a less regularly structured "MIMD" architecture. The latter, it can be argued (Blake 1983a) is a more efficient use of computing power. The former might lend itself more naturally to VLSI implementation.

Another intriguing possibility is that of parallel analogue hardware. Classical quadratic schemes can of course be realised with analogue components (Horn 1986, Poggio et al. 1985). Is this still true when weak continuity constraints are in force? We have done some simulations that strongly suggest feasibility. The benefits in terms of simplicity and speed are tempting, and the limited accuracy available from analogue hardware should not be a problem in reconstruction tasks.

8.3   Mechanical or probabilistic models?

In the introduction, we promised that this chapter would contain a more detailed justification of our preference for mechanical, rather than probabilistic, models of piecewise continuity. Of course the probabilistic viewpoint has afforded crucial insights, but the mechanical viewpoint seems more appropriate to Visual Reconstruction. The principal reasons are these:

- MRF parameters (in the form of conditional probabilities) must be specified, in the probabilistic view of things. It is highly unlikely however that these would be known in advance, say in the case of surface models. (Interestingly enough, though, Geman (1987) has recently proposed a means - "reparametrization" - of learning these parameters, inductively.)

- The mechanical viewpoint also requires parameters to be specified, but they are far more natural ones. They depend on: the magnitude of the Gaussian noise, desired sensitivity to contrast, and spatial scale. A trade-off between these performance characteristics must be chosen. And it is probably unreasonable to expect there to be a single, correct spatial scale - rather, the truth lies in multiple scales (Marr and Hildreth 1980, Koenderinck 1984, Witkin 1983). Nelson's column (in Trafalgar Square, London) is a cylinder at coarse scale (when seen from a considerable distance), but at fine scale it is a corrugated polyhedral prism.

- The model should, fundamentally, be continuous (as opposed to discrete). Surfaces and intensity distributions in the world are, after all, continuous. It is only the visual data that is discrete, as a result of image sampling. The mechanical model is continuous (energy is a function of surface derivatives), as required, whereas the MRF used by Geman and Geman is discrete (defined, from the start, in terms of cells on a grid).

- Availability of a continuous model facilitates variational analysis - a powerful theoretical tool that predicts properties of function estimation by energy minimisation, for example: contrast sensitivity, natural scale and resistance to noise. It even provides useful predictions when the signals being estimated are two-dimensional.

- Implementation of viewpoint invariance (Blake 1984), essential for veridical reconstruction of 3D surfaces from range data, is made possible by the explicit presence of differential geometric quantities in the continuous model.

- The probabilistic view encourages the idea that reconstruction schemes are limited only by the requirement to find the right probability distribution. We argue that this is unduly optimistic. The limitations of MRFs and the constraint of computational tractability severely curtail freedom to specify a distribution.

- The probabilistic view has lead to elegant statistical optimisation procedures, for performing the function estimation. Even so, the mechanical viewpoint leads naturally to the Graduated Non-Convexity algorithm which, whilst less general, is deterministic and efficient.

8.4   Improving the model of continuity

Back in the first chapter, it was pointed out that the first order energy model of continuity was clearly inadequate. It is attractive because it is tractable, but it suffers from the "gradient limit". Second order quadratic energies do not remove the problem, they just move it to a higher derivative. Even forgetting problems of computational feasibility, is there a better model? One promising line of investigation is to try and define an appropriate function space, rather than a surface energy, and then apply weak continuity constraints in that space. The fact that gradient maxima are good *detectors* of discontinuities (though bad localisers) suggests using spaces of convex or concave functions. The weak continuity constraint would become a weak constraint on sign of curvature. The problem, in 1D, is then to minimise

$$E = \int (u - d)^2 \, dx + \alpha K \tag{8.1}$$

where u is piecewise convex/concave, with changes of curvature sign at $x = x_i$, $i = 1..K$. Minimisation is with respect to u and to the x_i. Initial experiments are quite promising. Fitting monotonic functions (i.e. constant sign of gradient, rather than of curvature) has an impressive noise smoothing effect (figure 8.1 below). There are of course a number of questions here: how would the function class be extended to 2D (preserving viewpoint invariance for surfaces), and could a deterministic algorithm be used? Good localisation properties of the weak string would be preserved, because that is intrinsic to least squares regression. Note that the form of (8.1) does not suggest any fixed, natural scale - presumably effective scales would be determined by the data.

8.4.1   Psychophysical models

The literature on Gaussian multi-channel models of contrast sensitivity is well-established (Campbell and Robson 1968, Wilson and Bergen 1979, Watt and Morgan 1985). It would be interesting to know however, whether such models successfully predict systematic localisation error for asymmetric stimuli (figure 4.10). A pair of such stimuli, positioned appropriately, should show a differential error in apparent edge location, of the order of

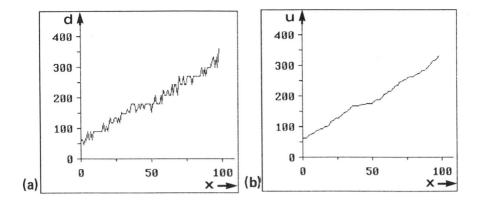

Figure 8.1: The noisy signal (a) is effectively filtered by optimally fitting a monotonic function (b).

twice the size of the finest channel (0.7 minutes of arc in the MIRAGE model of Watt and Morgan (1985)). Similarly, significant though smaller errors, random ones this time, should be observed with noisy stimuli. If such errors were not observed, this would question the validity of current multichannel linear-filtering models.

8.4.2 The role of visual reconstruction

In conclusion, an important class of reconstruction processes has been investigated, and proves to have attractive properties not found in methods based on linear filtering. They are a promising basis for a variety of visual tasks. They do not, contrary to some speculations, seem to have the capacity to drive an immense, cooperative, data-fusion machine. Instead, well defined, self-contained reconstruction processes call for subtle integration, ensuring graceful failure and intelligent, opportunistic control.

References

Ambler,A.P., Barrow,H.G., Brown,C.M., Burstall,R.M. and Popplestone,R.J. (1975). A versatile system for computer controlled assembly. *Artificial Intelligence, 6*, 129 - 156.

Asada,H. and Brady,M. (1986). The Curvature Primal Sketch. *IEEE PAMI*, 8, 1, 2-14.

Baker,H.H. (1981). Depth from edge and intensity based stereo. *IJCAI conf. 1981*, 583-588.

Barsky,B.A. and Beatty,J.C (1983). Local control of bias and tension in Beta-splines. *ACM trans. Graphics*, 2, 2, 27-52.

Bellman,R. and Dreyfus,S. (1962). *Applied dynamic programming*. Princeton Univ. Press, Princeton, U.S..

Besag,J. (1974). Spatial interaction and statistical analysis of lattice systems. *J Roy. Stat. Soc. Lond. B*, 36, 192-225.

Blake,A. (1983a). The least disturbance principle and weak constraints. *Pattern Recognition Letters, 1, 393-399.*

Blake,A. (1983b). *Parallel computation in low-level vision*. Ph.D. Thesis, University of Edinburgh.

Blake,A. (1984). Reconstructing a visible surface. *Proc AAAI conf. 1984*, 23-26.

Blake,A. and Zisserman,A. (1985a). Using weak continuity constraints. Report CSR-186-85, Dept. Computer Science, Edinburgh University, Edinburgh, Scotland. Also Pattern recognition letters, in press.

Blake,A. (1985c). Boundary conditions for lightness computation in Mondrian World. *Computer vision graphics and image processing*, 32, 314-327.

Blake,A., Zisserman,A. and Knowles,G. (1985d). Surface descriptions from stereo and shading. *Image and Vision Computing*, 3, 4, 183-191.

Blake,A., Zisserman,A. and Papoulias,A.V. (1986a). Weak continuity constraints generate uniform scale-space descriptions of plane curves. *Proc. ECAI, Brighton, England.*

Blake,A. and Zisserman,A. (1986b). Some properties of weak continuity constraints and the GNC algorithm. *Proc. CVPR Miami*, 656-661.

Blake,A. and Zisserman,A. (1986c). Invariant surface reconstruction using weak continuity constraints. *Proc. CVPR Miami*, 62-67.

Boissonat,J.D. (1984). Representing solids with the Delaunay triangulation. *Proc. ICPR*, 745-748.

Braddick,O., Campbell, F.W. and Atkinson,J. (1978). Channels in vision: basic aspects. In *Handbook of sensory physiology*, 8, 3-38, Springer-Verlag.

Brady,J.M. and Horn,B.K.P. (1983). Rotationally symmetric operators for surface interpolation. *Comp. Vis. Graph. Image Proc.*, 22, 70-94.

Brady,J.M and Yuille,A. (1984). An extremum principle for shape from contour. *IEEE trans. PAMI*, 6, 3, 288-301.

Brandt (1977). Multi-level adaptive solutions to boundary value problems. *Math. Comput.*, 31, 333-390.

Brookes,S., Hoare,C. and Roscoe,A. (1984). A theory of communicating sequential processes. J. ACM, 560-599.

Brooks,R.A. (1981). Symbolic reasoning among 3-D models and 2-D images. *AI Journal*, 17,285-348.

Bruss,A.R. (1983). Is what you see what you get? *Proc. IJCAI conf. 1983*, 1053-1056.

Burch,S.F., Gull,S.F. and Skilling,J. (1983). Image restoration by a powerful maximum entropy method. *Computer Vision Graphics and Image Processing.*

Burt,P. and Julesz,B. (1980). Modifications of the classical notion of Panum's fusional area. *Perception*, 9, 671-682.

Buxton,B.F. and Buxton,H. (1983). Monocular depth perception from optical flow by space-time signal processing. *Proc. Roy. Soc. Lond. B*, 218, 22-47.

Buxton,B.F. and Murray,D.W. (1985). Optic flow segmentation as an ill-posed and maximum likelihood problem. *Image and Vis. Comp.*, 3, 4, 163-169.

Campbell,F.W. and Robson,J.G. (1968). Application of Fourier analysis to the visibility of gratings. *J. Physiol. Lond.*, 197, 551-566.

Canny,J.F. (1983). *Finding edges and lines in images.* S.M. thesis, MIT, Cambridge, USA.

Davies,P.J. (1979). *Circulant Matrices.* John Wiley and Sons, New York.

de Boor,C. (1978). *A practical guide to splines.* Springer-Verlag, New York.

Derin,H. and Cole,W.S. (1986). Segmentation of textured images using Gibbs random fields. *CVGIP,* 35, 1, 72-98.

do Carmo,M.P. (1976). *Differential geometry of curves and surfaces.* Prentice-Hall, Englewood Cliffs, New Jersey.

Duff,M.J.B. (1978). Review of the CLIP image processing system, *National Computer Conference 1978,* 1011 - 1060.

Fahle,M. and Poggio,T. (1984). Visual hyperacuity: spatiotemporal interpolation in human vision. In *Image Understanding 1984*, Ullman,S. and Richards,W. eds., Ablex, Norwood, USA.

Geman,S. and Geman,D. (1984). Stochastic Relaxation, Gibbs distribution, and Bayesian restoration of images. *IEEE PAMI, Nov 1984.*

Geman,D. (1987). A stochastic model for boundary detection. *Image and vision computing,* in press.

Gennert,M.A. (1986). Detecting half edges and vertices in images. *Proc. IEEE CVPR, Miami,* 552-557.

Grimson,W.E.L. (1981). *From images to surfaces.* MIT Press, Cambridge, USA.

Grimson,W.E.L and Pavlidis,T. (1985). Discontinuity detection for visual surface recognition. *Computer Vision Graphics and Image Processing,* 30, 316-330.

Haralick,R.M. (1980). Edge and region analysis for digital image data. *Computer Graphics and Image Processing, 12, 1,* 60 - 73.

Hildreth,E.C. (1984). Computations underlying the measurement of visual motion. *Art. Int. J.*, 23, 3, 309-354.

Hinton,G.E. (1978). *Relaxation and its role in vision*, Ph.D. thesis, University of Edinburgh.

Hinton,G.E. and Sejnowski,T.J. (1983). Analysing cooperative computation. *Proc. 5th conf. Cognitive Science*, Rochester, New York.

Hopfield,J.J. (1982). Neural networks and physical systems with emergent collective computational abilities. *Proc. Natl. Acad. Sci. USA*, 79, 2554-2558.

Hopfield,J.J. (1984). Neurons with graded response have collective computational properties like those of two-state neurons. *Proc. Nat. Acad. Sci. USA*, 81, 3088-3092.

Hopfield,J.J. and Tank,D.W. (1985). "Neural" computation of decisions in optimization problems. *Biol. Cybern.*, 52, 141-152.

Horn,B.K.P. (1974). Determining lightness from an image. *Computer Graphics and Image Processing*, 3, 277-299.

Horn,B.K.P and Schunk,B.G. (1981). Determining optical flow. *Computer Vision*, ed. Brady,J.M.

Horn,B.K.P. (1986). *Robot Vision*. MIT Press, Cambridge, USA.

Hubel,D.H. and Wiesel,T.N. (1968). Receptive fields and functional architecture of monkey striate cortex. *J. Physiol. Lond.*, 195, 215-244.

Hueckel,M.H. (1971). An operator which locates edges in digitized pictures. *Journal of the Association for Computing Machinery*, 18, 1, 113 - 125.

Ikeuchi,K. and Horn,B.K.P. (1981), Numerical shape from shading and occluding boundaries, *Computer Vision*, ed. Brady,J.M., 141-184.

Ikeuchi,K. (1983). Constructing a depth map from images. *AI Lab. Memo.* 744. MIT, Cambridge, USA.

Jameson,D. and Hurvich,L.M. (1961). Opponent chromatic induction: experimental evaluation and theoretical approach. *J. Opt. Soc. Am.*, 51, 46-53.

Julesz,B (1971). *Foundations of cyclopean perception*. University of Chicago Press.

Kirkpatrick,S., Gellatt,C.D. and Vecchi,M.P. (1982). Optimisation by simulated annealing. IBM Thomas J. Watson Research Centre, Yorktown Heights, NY, USA.

Koenderinck,J.J. and van Doorn,A.J. (1976). The singularities of the visual mapping. *Biol. Cybernetics,* 24, 51-59.

Koenderinck,J.J.(1984). The structure of images. *Biol. Cybernetics,* 50, 363-370.

Krotkov,E.P. (1986). Visual hyperacuity: representation and computation of very high precision position information. *CVGIP,* 33, 99-115.

Land,E.H. (1983). Recent advances in retinex theory and some implications for cortical computations: color vision and the natural image. *Proc. Natl. Acad. Sci. USA.,* 80, 5163-5169.

Landau,L.D. and Lifschitz,E.M. (1959). *Theory of elasticity.* Pergamon.

Leclerc,Y. (1985). The local structure of image discontinuities. Research report, Computer Vision and Robotics Laboratory, McGill University, Montreal, Canada.

Livingstone,M.S. and Hubel,D.H. (1984). Anatomy and physiology of a color system in the primate visual cortex. *J. Neurosci.,* 4, 309-356.

Longuet-Higgins,H.C. and Prazdny,K. (1980). The interpretation of moving retinal images. *Proc. Roy. Soc. Lond. B,* 208, 385-397.

Longuet-Higgins,H.C. (1984). The visual ambiguity of a moving plane. *Proc. Roy. Soc. Lond. B.,* 223, 165-175.

Luke,Y. L. (1962). *Integrals of Bessel functions.* McGraw-Hill, U.S.A.

McLachlan,N. W. (1961). *Bessel functions for engineers.* Oxford.

McLauchlan,P. Zisserman,A. and Blake,A. (1987). A knowledge source for describing stereoscopicaly viewed textured surfaces. Submitted to *Image and Vision Computing.*

Marks,P. (1980). Low-level vision using an array processor *Computer Graphics and Image Processing, 14,* 281 - 292.

Marks,W.B., Dobelle,W.H. and MacNichol,E.F. (1964). Visual pigments of single primate cones. *Science,* 143, 1181-1183.

Marr,D. (1976a). Early processing of visual information. *Phil. Trans. Roy. Soc. Lond.*, 275, 483-524.

Marr,D. (1976b). Cooperative computation of stereo disparity. *Science*, 194, 283-287.

Marr,D. and Poggio,T. (1979). A computational theory of human stereo vision. *Proc. Roy. Soc. Lond. B*, 204, 301-328.

Marr,D. and Hildreth,E. (1980). Theory of edge detection. *Proc. Roy. Soc. Lond. B*, 207, 187-217.

Marr,D. (1982). *Vision*. Freeman, San Francisco.

Marroquin,J. (1984). Surface reconstruction preserving discontinuities. Memo 792, AI Laboratory, MIT, Cambridge, USA.

Mayhew,J.E.W and Frisby,J.P. (1981). Towards a computational and psychophysical theory of stereopsis. *AI Journal*, 17, 349-385.

Mayhew,J.E.W. (1982). The interpretation of stereo-disparity information: the computation of surface orientation and depth. *Perception*, 11, 387-403.

Metropolis,N., Rosenbluth,A.W., Rosenbluth,M.N., Teller,A.H. and Teller,E. (1953). Equation of state calculations by fast computing machines. *Journal of Chemical Physics*, 6, 1087.

Milner,R. (1980). *A calculus of communicating systems*. Springer-Verlag.

Minsky,M. and Papert,S. (1969). *Perceptrons*. MIT Press, Cambridge, USA.

Montanari,U. (1971). On the optimal detection of curves in noisy pictures. *Commun. ACM* 14, 5, 335-345.

Mumford,D. and Shah,J. (1985). Boundary detection by minimising functionals. *Proc. IEEE CVPR conf.*, 22.

O'Gorman,F. (1978). Edge detection using walsh functions. *Artificial Intelligence*, *10*, 215 - 223.

Papoulias,A. (1985). *Curve segmentation using weak continuity constraints*. M.Sc. thesis, Dept. Computer Science, University of Edinburgh.

Pavlidis,T. (1977). *Structural Pattern Recognition*. Springer-Verlag, New York.

Perkins,W.A. (1978). A model-based system for industrial parts. *IEEE Trans. Comp.*, 27, 2, 126 - 143.

Plass,M. and Stone,M. (1983). Curve-fitting with piecewise parametric cubics. *Computer graphics, 17, 3,* 229-239.

Poggio,T. and Reichardt,W. (1976). Visual control of orientation behaviour in the fly. Part 2. Towards the underlying neural interactions. *Quart. Rev. Biophys.*, 9, 3, 377-438.

Poggio,T., Voorhees,H. and Yuille,A. (1984). A regularised solution to edge detection. MIT AI Lab memo 776, MIT, Cambridge, USA.

Poggio,T., Torre,V. and Koch,C. (1985). Computational vision and regularization theory. *Nature*, 317, 314-319.

Pollard,S.P., Mayhew,J.E.W. and Frisby,J.P. (1985). PMF: a stereo correspondence algorithm using a disparity gradient limit. *Perception*, 14, 449-470.

Pollard, S.B., Pridmore,T.P., Porrill,J., Mayhew,J.E.W. and Frisby,J.P. (1987). Geometrical modelling from multiple stereo views. *AI Journal*, in press.

Poston,T. and Stewart,I. (1978). *Catastrophe theory and its applications.* Pitman, London.

Ramer,E.U. (1975). The transformation of photographic images into stroke arrays *IEEE Trans. CAS*, 22, 4, 363 - 374.

Roberts,L.G. (1965). Machine perception of three-dimensional solids. In *Optical and Electro-optical Information Processing*, J.P Tippett et al. eds, MIT Press, Cambridge, USA.

Roberts,A.W. and Varberg,D.E. (1976). *Convex functions.* Academic Press, New York.

Rosenblatt, F. (1962). *Principles of Neurodynamics.* Spartan Books, New York.

Rosenfeld,A., Hummel,R.A. and Zucker,S.W. (1976). Scene labelling by relaxation operations. *IEEE Trans. SMC*, 6, 6, 420 - 433.

Smith,G.D. (1978). *Numerical solutions of partial differential equations: finite difference methods*, Oxford University Press.

Smith,W.E., Barrett,H.H. and Paxman,R.G. (1983). Reconstruction of objects from coded images by simulated annealing. *Optics letters*,8, 4, 199-201.

Strang,G. and Fix,G.J. (1973). *An analysis of the finite element method.* Prentice-Hall, Englewood Cliffs, USA.

Terzopoulos,D. (1983). Multilevel computational processes for visual surface reconstruction, *Computer Vision Graphics and Image Processing*, 24, 52-96.

Terzopoulos,D. (1985). Computing visible surface representations. AI memo 800, AI Lab., MIT, Cambridge, USA.

Terzopoulos,D. (1986). Regularization of inverse problems involving discontinuities. *IEEE PAMI*, 8, 4, 413-424.

Troutman,J.L. (1983). *Variational calculus with elementary convexity.* Springer-Verlag, New York.

Ullman,S. (1979a). Relaxed and constrained optimisation by local processes. *Computer Graphics and Image Processing*, 10, 115-125.

Ullman, S. (1979b). *The interpretation of visual motion.* MIT Press, Cambridge, USA.

Uttal,W.R. (1981). *A taxonomy of visual processes.* Erlbaum, Hillsdale NJ, USA.

Wallace,D.J. (1985). Spin glass models of neural networks; size dependence of memory properties. *Proc. Conf. Advances in Lattice Gauge Theory, Tallahassee,* World Scientific.

Watson,G.N. (1952). *A treatise on the theory of Bessel functions.* Cambridge University Press.

Watt,R.J. and Morgan,M.J. (1985). A theory of the primitive spatial code of human vision. *Vision Res.*, 11, 1661-1674.

Wilson,H.R. and Bergen,J.R. (1979). A four mechanism model for threshold spatial vision. *Vision Research*, 19, 19-32.

Witkin,A.P. (1983). Scale-space filtering. *Proc. IJCAI 1983,* 1019-1022.

Woodham,R.J. (1977). A cooperative algorithm for determining surface orientation from a single view. *Proc IJCAI 1977,* 635-641.

Yuille,A.L. and Poggio,T. (1984). Fingerprints theorems. *Proc. AAAI 1984,* 362-365.

Yuille,A.L. (1985). Personal communication.

Zeki,S. (1983). The distribution of wavelength and orientation selective cells in different areas of monkey visual cortex. *Proc. R. Soc. Lond. (Biol.)*, 217, 449-470.

Zinkiewicz,O.C. and Morgan,K. (1983). *Finite elements and approximation*. Wiley, New York.

Zucker,S.W., Hummel,R.A. and Rosenfeld,A (1977). An application of relaxation labelling to line and curve enhancement. *IEEE trans. comp.*, 26, 4,394-403.

Zucker,S.W. (1982). Early orientation selection and grouping. Tech. rep. 82-6, McGill University, Montreal.

Appendix A

Energy Calculations for the String and Membrane

A.1 Energy calculations for the string

Methods for calculating extremal energies

Using the of Calculus of Variations on the energy functional

$$E = \int_{-a}^{b} \left\{ (u(x) - d(x))^2 + \lambda^2 (u')^2 \right\} \, dx \tag{A.1}$$

gives the Euler Lagrange equation

$$u - \lambda^2 \frac{d^2 u}{dx^2} = d \tag{A.2}$$

with the boundary conditions

$$u'|_{x=-a,b} = 0 \tag{A.3}$$

Green's function: The solution of (A.2) which satisfies (A.3) is given by

$$u(x) = \int_{-a}^{b} G(x, x') d(x') \, dx' \tag{A.4}$$

where $G(x, x')$ is the Green's function for the system. It is straightforward to show that

$$G(x, x') = \frac{1}{\lambda \sinh(\frac{a+b}{\lambda})} \cosh\left(\frac{x_< + a}{\lambda}\right) \cosh\left(\frac{x_> - b}{\lambda}\right) \tag{A.5}$$

where $x_>$ ($x_<$) is the greater (lesser) of x and x'.

If the domain is bi-infinite then, letting $a, b \to \infty$, gives

$$G(x, x') = \frac{1}{2\lambda} e^{-|x-x'|/\lambda} \tag{A.6}$$

and $u(x)$ is obtained from (A.4) with infinite limits.

Extremal energy: having obtained $u(x)$ for a finite or bi-infinite region the extremal energy can be found from

$$E = \int_{-a}^{b} d(x)(d(x) - u(x))\, dx \tag{A.7}$$

where again the limits are infinite for a bi-infinite domain.

Derivation of energy formula (A.7): In the following the integration limits can be either finite or infinite.

$$E = \int \{(u - d)^2 + \lambda^2(u')^2\}\, dx. \tag{A.8}$$

Integrating the second term by parts gives

$$E = \lambda^2[uu'] + \int \{(u - d)^2 - \lambda^2 uu''\}\, dx$$

The first term is zero by the boundary conditions (A.3), and rearranging

$$E = \int \{d(d - u) + u[u - d - \lambda^2 u'']\}\, dx$$

The expression in square brackets is zero by the Euler Lagrange equation (A.2). Hence

$$E = \int d(x)(d(x) - u(x))\, dx$$

Calculating extremal energy by fourier transform: this is applicable only to a bi-infinite domain. The energy is given by

$$E = \lambda^2 \int_{-\infty}^{\infty} \frac{\omega^2|\hat{d}(\omega)|^2}{1 + \lambda^2\omega^2}\, d\omega \tag{A.9}$$

where $\hat{d}(\omega)$ is the Fourier transform of $d(x)$ namely

$$\hat{d}(\omega) = \frac{1}{\sqrt{2\pi}} \int_{-\infty}^{\infty} d(x)e^{-ix\omega}\, dx$$

Derivation of energy formula (A.9):   Taking the Fourier transform of
the Euler Lagrange equation (A.2) and rearranging:

$$\hat{u} = \frac{\hat{d}}{1 + \lambda^2 \omega^2}$$

Applying Parseval's Theorem to (A.8) gives

$$E = \int_{-\infty}^{\infty} \left[\frac{\lambda^4 \omega^4}{(1 + \lambda^2 \omega^2)^2} + \frac{\lambda^2 \omega^2}{(1 + \lambda^2 \omega^2)^2} \right] |\hat{d}|^2 \, d\omega$$

which simplifies to (A.9) as required.

Extremal energy for the top hat

As an example, the methods of the previous section, are used to calculate
the energy of the top hat data shown in figure 4.5a on page 59.

Green's function method   The form of (A.7) means that we only need
to find $u(x)$ in the region where $d(x)$ is non-zero - i.e. inside the top hat.
For this region (using equations (A.4) and (A.6))

$$\begin{aligned}
u(x) &= \frac{h}{2\lambda} \left\{ e^{-\frac{x}{\lambda}} \int_{-\frac{a}{2}}^{x} e^{\frac{x'}{\lambda}} \, dx' + e^{\frac{x}{\lambda}} \int_{x}^{\frac{a}{2}} e^{-\frac{x'}{\lambda}} \, dx' \right\} \\
&= h \left(1 - e^{-\frac{a}{2\lambda}} \cosh \frac{x}{\lambda} \right) \qquad -\frac{a}{2} \le x \le \frac{a}{2}.
\end{aligned}$$

Using (A.7)

$$\begin{aligned}
E &= h^2 \int_{-\frac{a}{2}}^{\frac{a}{2}} e^{-\frac{a}{2\lambda}} \cosh \frac{x}{\lambda} \, dx \\
&= h^2 \lambda (1 - e^{-\frac{a}{\lambda}}) \qquad\qquad\qquad\qquad \text{(A.10)}
\end{aligned}$$

Fourier transform method   The Fourier transform of $d(x)$ is

$$\hat{d}(\omega) = \frac{2h}{\sqrt{2\pi}} \frac{\sin \frac{a\omega}{2}}{\omega}$$

Using this in (A.9) for the energy gives

$$E = \frac{4h^2 \lambda^2}{2\pi} \int_{-\infty}^{\infty} \frac{\sin^2 \frac{a\omega}{2}}{1 + \lambda^2 \omega^2} \, d\omega$$

which, using complex contour integration,

$$= h^2 \lambda (1 - e^{-\frac{a}{\lambda}}),$$

agreeing with (A.10) above.

Extremal energy for the finite ramp

Here the data $d(x)$ consists of a bi-infinite anti-symmetric step of height h, whose central portion is a (steep) ramp of width a and gradient $g = h/a$, as shown in the 4th and 5th rows of figure 4.9 on page 64:

$$d(x) = \begin{cases} -h/2 & \text{if } x < -a/2 \\ gx & \text{if } |x| < a/2 \\ h/2 & \text{if } x > a/2 \end{cases} . \tag{A.11}$$

Using either of the methods above, the energy E for the continuous string can be shown to be:

$$E = g^2\lambda^2 \left(a - \lambda\left(1 - e^{-a/\lambda}\right)\right). \tag{A.12}$$

In the limit that $a \to 0$, $d(x)$ becomes an ideal step of height h, and the string energy is simply

$$E = \frac{1}{2}h^2\lambda(1 + O(a/\lambda)). \tag{A.13}$$

Extremal energy for the step and ramp

Data $d(x)$ is defined over the finite interval $[-a, b]$ as:

$$d(x) = \begin{cases} h & \text{for } -a \le x < 0 \\ gx & \text{for } 0 \le x \le b \end{cases} . \tag{A.14}$$

Using the Green's function and equation (A.7), it can be shown that the energy of the $u(x)$ that extremises (A.1) is:

$$E_{h,g}(a,b) = h^2\lambda \frac{\sinh\left(\frac{a}{\lambda}\right)\sinh\left(\frac{b}{\lambda}\right)}{\sinh\left(\frac{a+b}{\lambda}\right)} + 2g\lambda^2 h \frac{\sinh\left(\frac{a}{\lambda}\right)\left(1 - \cosh\left(\frac{b}{\lambda}\right)\right)}{\sinh\left(\frac{a+b}{\lambda}\right)} \tag{A.15}$$

$$+ g^2\lambda^2 b - g^2\lambda^3 \frac{\cosh\left(\frac{a+b}{\lambda}\right) + \cosh\left(\frac{a}{\lambda}\right)\left(\cosh\left(\frac{b}{\lambda}\right) - 2\right)}{\sinh\left(\frac{a+b}{\lambda}\right)}$$

Note that, as expected, when $g = 0$ and $a, b \gg \lambda$ this approximates to $h^2\lambda/2$ as for the bi-infinite simple step (A.13).

This result is used in chapter 4 to determine the variation in extremal energy $E(\epsilon)$ as a function of localisation error ϵ, for the asymmetric step in fig 4.12 on page 67:

$$E(\epsilon) = \begin{cases} E_{h,g}(L - \epsilon, 0) + E_{h,g}(\epsilon, b) & \text{for } \epsilon < 0 \\ E_{h,g}(L, \epsilon) + E_{h,g}(0, b - \epsilon) & \text{for } \epsilon > 0. \end{cases} \tag{A.16}$$

Energy increase under constraint

It is extremely useful to know how extremal energy increases when one end of a weak string is constrained. It enables increase of energy under continuity constraints to be computed.

Suppose the optimal configuration of $u(x), x \in [0, L]$, under the constraint $u(0) = z$, has energy $E(z)$. Clearly the minimum of $E(z)$, with respect to z, must be the unconstrained case. Say this case is $u = \bar{u}$ occurring when $z = \bar{z}$. Now u satisfies (A.2) with $u(0) = z, u'(L) = 0$. Suppose also $w(x)$ is the solution of

$$w - \lambda^2 \frac{d^2 w}{dx^2} = 0 \ \text{ with } w(0) = 1, \ w'(L) = 0,$$

then u is given by

$$u = (z - \bar{z})w + \bar{u} \tag{A.17}$$

so that $u_z = w$ and $u_{zz} = 0$. Then from (A.1) (with $a = 0, b = L$), differentiating twice with respect to z:

$$E_{zz} = \int_0^L \left\{ 2w^2 + 2\lambda^2 w_x^2 \right\} dx \tag{A.18}$$

- a function of L, λ only. What is more, higher derivatives of E w.r.t. z are zero. So, defining $\mathcal{E} = E_{zz}/2$,

$$E(z) = \mathcal{E}(z - \bar{z})^2 + \text{ const.} \tag{A.19}$$

- depending on data d only insofar as it is needed to compute $\bar{z}$. The actual value of $\mathcal{E}$ can be "calibrated" on any convenient data d. An antisymmetric step of height h has energy $E_{h,0}(L, L) = 2E(z)$, where $E_{h,g}(a, b)$ is given in (A.15) and $z = h/2$ since, by symmetry, $u(0) = h/2$. This gives

$$\mathcal{E} = \lambda \tanh \left(\frac{L}{\lambda} \right). \tag{A.20}$$

Energy increase due to a continuity constraint

When u is forced to be continuous at the join of two intervals, it is fixed, at the ends of both intervals, to a value z. The z is unknown *a priori* but it is determined by the requirement to minimize the total increase in energy, due to both intervals, which is

$$\Delta E = \mathcal{E}_1(z - \bar{z}_1)^2 + \mathcal{E}_2(z - \bar{z}_2)^2.$$

Increase ΔE is minimized when

$$z = \frac{\mathcal{E}_1 \bar{z}_1 + \mathcal{E}_2 \bar{z}_2}{\mathcal{E}_1 + \mathcal{E}_2} \tag{A.21}$$

so that

$$\Delta E = h^2 \left(\frac{1}{\mathcal{E}_1} + \frac{1}{\mathcal{E}_2} \right)^{-1}. \tag{A.22}$$

Fixing both ends of a string

If both ends of a string, in a finite interval of length L, are fixed at values $\bar{z}_1, \bar{z}_2$ then the total energy is:

$$E = E_0 + \mathcal{E}_- \left((z_1 - \bar{z}_1) - (z_2 - \bar{z}_2) \right)^2 + \mathcal{E}_+ \left((z_1 - \bar{z}_1) + (z_2 - \bar{z}_2) \right)^2 \tag{A.23}$$

where

$$\mathcal{E}_- = \frac{\lambda}{2} \coth \left(\frac{L}{2\lambda} \right) \text{ and } \mathcal{E}_+ = \frac{\lambda}{2} \tanh \left(\frac{L}{2\lambda} \right). \tag{A.24}$$

As expected, when $L \gg \lambda$ the two ends become decoupled and (A.23) is simply the sum of energies for 2 isolated ends as in (A.19). But when $L \ll \lambda$, $\mathcal{E}_+ \approx 0$ and the system is tightly coupled.

A.2   Energy calculations for the membrane

Using the method of Calculus of Variations on the energy functional

$$E = \int \{(u-d)^2 + \lambda^2 (\nabla u)^2\} \, dA \qquad (A.25)$$

gives the Euler Lagrange equation

$$u - \lambda^2 \nabla^2 u = d \qquad (A.26)$$

with the boundary condition

$$\mathbf{n}.\nabla u = 0 \quad \text{on } C \qquad (A.27)$$

where C is the boundary of the domain and $\mathbf{n}$ its normal.

As in 1D $u(\mathbf{x})$ can be obtained from $d(\mathbf{x})$ by using an infinite or finite Green's function - this is described in the following sections. First it is shown that the 1D energy expression (A.7) generalises to 2D. This can be used for infinite or finite regions.

Derivation of the 2D energy expression

Using the identity

$$\nabla.(u \nabla u) = \nabla u \, \nabla u + u \, \nabla^2 u$$

in the energy functional (A.25), we obtain

$$E = \int \{(u-d)^2 + \lambda^2 [\nabla.(u \nabla u) - u \, \nabla^2 u]\} \, dA.$$

Using the divergence theorem,

$$E = \lambda^2 \int_C u \nabla u.\mathbf{n} \, dl + \lambda^2 \int u(u - d - \nabla^2 u) \, dA + \int d(d - u) \, dA$$

where the line integral is around the boundary C. The first integral is zero because of the boundary conditions (A.27). The second is zero because of the Euler Lagrange equation (A.26), leaving

$$E = \int d(\mathbf{x})(d(\mathbf{x}) - u(\mathbf{x})) \, dA. \qquad (A.28)$$

A.3   Infinite domain calculations for the membrane

Derivation of the infinite Green's function

The Green's function for (A.26) satisfies the equation

$$G - \lambda^2 \, \nabla^2 \, G = \delta(\mathbf{x} - \mathbf{x}').$$

Taking the Fourier transform and inverting,

$$G(\mathbf{x}, \mathbf{x}') = \frac{1}{(2\pi)^2} \int \frac{e^{i\mathbf{k}.(\mathbf{x} - \mathbf{x}')}}{(1 + \lambda^2 k^2)} \, d^2 k$$

where $k = |\mathbf{k}|$. Changing to polar coordinates with the $\theta = 0$ axis along $\mathbf{x} - \mathbf{x}'$, this becomes

$$G(\mathbf{x}, \mathbf{x}') = \frac{1}{(2\pi)^2} \int_0^\infty k \, dk \int_0^{2\pi} d\theta \, \frac{e^{ikr \cos \theta}}{1 + \lambda^2 k^2}$$

where $r = |\mathbf{x} - \mathbf{x}'|$. Since (Watson 1952)

$$J_0(x) = \frac{1}{2\pi} \int_0^{2\pi} e^{ix \cos \theta} \, d\theta,$$

$$G(\mathbf{x}, \mathbf{x}') = \frac{1}{2\pi} \int_0^\infty \frac{k J_0(kr)}{1 + \lambda^2 k^2} \, dk$$

and using the integral representation (Luke 1962)

$$K_0(ax) = \int_0^\infty \frac{t J_0(xt)}{a^2 + t^2} \, dt,$$

we obtain

$$G(\mathbf{x}, \mathbf{x}') = \frac{1}{2\pi\lambda^2} K_0 \left(\frac{r}{\lambda} \right) \tag{A.29}$$

For a translationally symmetric problem, one in which $d(x, y)$ is a function of x only, it can be shown that, as expected, the Green's function (A.29) reduces to the 1D Green's function (A.6).

Fourier transform energy calculation

For an infinite domain the energy is given by

$$E = \lambda^2 \int_{-\infty}^\infty \int_{-\infty}^\infty \frac{k^2 |\hat{d}(\mathbf{k})|^2}{1 + \lambda^2 k^2} \, d^2 k \tag{A.30}$$

where $\hat{d}(\mathbf{k})$ is the 2D Fourier transform of $d(\mathbf{x})$ namely

$$\hat{d}(\mathbf{k}) = \frac{1}{2\pi} \int_{-\infty}^{\infty} \int_{-\infty}^{\infty} d(\mathbf{x}) e^{-i\mathbf{k}\cdot\mathbf{x}} \, d^2x \qquad (\text{A.31})$$

and $k = |\mathbf{k}|$. Derivation of (A.30) is exactly the 2D analogue of the equivalent 1D result (A.9).

Circular symmetry

If the data has circular symmetry then it is more convenient to use expressions which incorporate the symmetry explicitly - since these are essentially one dimensional. The Green's function for this case can either be obtained from the general Green's function (A.29) directly (using the addition theorem (Watson 1952) or by constructing the Green's function from the Euler Lagrange equation (A.26) expressed in cylindrical polar coordinates (ρ, θ). The result is

$$u(\rho) = \int_0^{\infty} G(\rho, \rho') d(\rho') \rho' \, d\rho' \qquad (\text{A.32})$$

where

$$G(\rho, \rho') = \frac{1}{\lambda^2} I_0 \left(\frac{\rho_<}{\lambda} \right) K_0 \left(\frac{\rho_>}{\lambda} \right). \qquad (\text{A.33})$$

For circular symmetry (A.28) for the energy becomes

$$E = 2\pi \int_0^{\infty} d(\rho)(d(\rho) - u(\rho))\rho \, d\rho \qquad (\text{A.34})$$

The other method of calculating the energy, via the Fourier transform (A.30), yields

$$E = 2\pi\lambda^2 \int_0^{\infty} \frac{k^3 |\hat{d}(k)|^2}{1 + \lambda^2 k^2} \, dk \qquad (\text{A.35})$$

where

$$\hat{d}(k) = \int_0^{\infty} J_0(k\rho) d(\rho)\rho \, d\rho. \qquad (\text{A.36})$$

Derivation. For circular symmetry $d(\mathbf{x}) = d(\rho)$ (where $\rho = |\mathbf{x}|$), and changing to polar coordinates with the $\theta = 0$ axis along $\mathbf{x}$ the double Fourier transform (A.31) becomes

$$\hat{d}(k) = \frac{1}{2\pi} \int_0^{\infty} \int_0^{2\pi} d\theta \, e^{-ik\rho\cos\theta} d(\rho)\rho \, d\rho.$$

Since (Watson 1952)

$$J_0(x) = \frac{1}{2\pi} \int_0^{2\pi} e^{-ix \cos\theta} \, d\theta,$$

this can be expressed as

$$\hat{d}(k) = \int_0^{\infty} J_0(k\rho) d(\rho) \rho \, d\rho.$$

Similarly, changing to polar coordinates, the energy (A.30) is

$$E = \lambda^2 \int_0^{\infty} k \, dk \int_0^{2\pi} d\theta \frac{k^2 |\hat{d}(k)|^2}{1 + \lambda^2 k^2}$$

which gives (A.35).

Extremal energy for the top hat

In this section we use each of the methods of the previous section to calculate the energy of a cylindrical top hat function. The top hat has height h and radius a, and in cylindrical polars it is

$$d(\rho) = \begin{cases} h & \text{if } \rho \le a \\ 0 & \text{otherwise.} \end{cases} \tag{A.37}$$

Green's function method   Because of the form of the energy expression (A.34) we need only find $u(\rho)$ inside the hat - i.e. $\rho \le a$.

Using equations (A.33) and (A.32) for $u(\rho)$ and identities from (McLachlan 1961) we obtain

$$u(\rho) = h \left\{ 1 - \frac{a}{\lambda} I_0 \left(\frac{\rho}{\lambda}\right) K_1 \left(\frac{a}{\lambda}\right) \right\}.$$

Then, from (A.34),

$$E = 2\pi a^2 h^2 K_1 \left(\frac{a}{\lambda}\right) I_1 \left(\frac{a}{\lambda}\right). \tag{A.38}$$

The modified Bessel functions in this expression have the following asymptotic limits

$$K_1(z) \sim \frac{1}{z} \qquad I_1(z) \sim \frac{z}{2} \qquad z \ll 1$$

$$K_1(z) \sim \sqrt{\frac{\pi}{2z}} e^{-z} \qquad I_1(z) \sim \frac{e^z}{\sqrt{2\pi z}} \qquad z \gg 1$$

Fourier transform method   Using equation (A.36)

$$\hat{d}(k) = h \int_0^a J_0(\rho)\rho \, d\rho$$

which, from (McLachlan 1961),

$$= \frac{ha J_1(ka)}{k}.$$

Using equation (A.35) for the energy gives

$$E = 2\pi\lambda^2 h^2 a^2 \int_0^\infty \frac{k J_1^2(ka)}{1 + \lambda^2 k^2} \, dk,$$

and from the following identity (Watson 1952)

$$\int_0^\infty \frac{k J_\nu^2(ka)}{x^2 + k^2} \, dk = I_\nu(ax) K_\nu(ax)$$

the energy is

$$E = 2\pi a^2 h^2 K_1\left(\frac{a}{\lambda}\right) I_1\left(\frac{a}{\lambda}\right)$$

as in (A.38) above.

Appendix B

Noise Performance of the Weak Elastic String

The purpose of following sections is to set out the supporting mathematics for two claims about noise performance.

The first is that noise-induced error in localisation of discontinuities is very low. For conventional linear smoothing operators followed by non-maximum suppression, the standard deviation δx of the error satisfies $\delta x \propto (h/n_0)^{-1}$, where h/n_0 is the signal-to-noise ratio (Canny 1983). But for the weak elastic string, δx is actually zero, provided signal-to-noise ratio is not too small.

The second is that the penalty constant α is a direct measure of immunity to noise. If standard deviation of *mean* noise is σ then "false alarms" (spurious discontinuities) do not occur if $\alpha \gg \sigma^2$. This condition is independent of λ.

B.1   Localisation

Consider a weak elastic string with data

$$d(x) = \begin{cases} 0 & \text{for } x \in [-L, 0) \\ h & \text{for } x \in [0, L] \end{cases}$$

and added noise $n(x)$, which has zero mean, and is homogeneous with standard deviation n_0:

$$n_0^2 = \frac{1}{l} \left\langle \int_y^{y+l} n^2(x)\, dx \right\rangle, \ \forall y, l > 0, \ y \in [-L, L-l] \qquad \text{(B.1)}$$

and the standard deviation of mean (spatially averaged) noise σ is defined by:

$$\left\langle \left(\int_y^{y+l} f(x)n(x) \, dx \right)^2 \right\rangle = \sigma^2 \int_y^{y+l} f^2(x) \, dx \qquad \text{(B.2)}$$

for $y, l > 0$, $y \in [-L, L - l]$ and an arbitrary function $f(x)$. (The brackets $\langle \rangle$ denote expected value.) The quantities σ, n_0 are related by

$$\sigma^2 = \rho n_0^2,$$

where ρ is a measure of the coherence length of the noise ($\rho \to 0$ for uncorrelated noise) and $1/\rho$ is a measure of noise bandwidth. Typically, $\rho = 1$, measured in pixel-diameters, so n_0 and σ are numerically equal.

We seek to compute the cost $E(u_\epsilon)$ of the extremal $u_\epsilon(x)$, given that it has a discontinuity at $x = \epsilon$. Assume $\epsilon \geq 0$. The situation is sketched in figure 4.15 on page 70. Because of the linearity of the problem, the solution is $u_\epsilon(x) = u_{\epsilon,d}(x) + u_{\epsilon,n}(x)$, the sum of the solutions for data alone, and noise alone, respectively. If the Green's function is $G_\epsilon(x, y)$ then

$$u_{\epsilon,d} = \int_{-L}^{L} G_\epsilon(x, y)d(y) \, dy \text{ and } u_{\epsilon,n} = \int_{-L}^{L} G_\epsilon(x, y)n(y) \, dy \ . \qquad \text{(B.3)}$$

From (4.5) on page 55, the extremal energy is

$$E(u_\epsilon) = \int_{-L}^{L} (d + n)(d + n - u_{\epsilon,d} - u_{\epsilon,n}) \, dx + \alpha \qquad \text{(B.4)}$$

We are interested only in comparing energies; the energy difference is

$$\Delta E_\epsilon = E(u_\epsilon) - E(u_0) = \Delta E_{\epsilon,d} - (R_\epsilon - R_0) \qquad \text{(B.5)}$$

$$\text{where } R_\epsilon = \int_{-L}^{L} (du_{\epsilon,n} + nu_{\epsilon,d} + nu_{\epsilon,n}) \, dx, \qquad \text{(B.6)}$$

and $\Delta E_{\epsilon,d}$ is the energy difference for the noise free case. Assuming $|\epsilon| \ll \lambda \ll L$ then, from (4.23) on page 66 (with $g = 0$):

$$\Delta E_{\epsilon,d} \approx h^2 |\epsilon|.$$

Now the third term in the integral in (B.6) is negligible if the noise is not too great. The first two terms are equal; this is because in any Sturm-Liouville problem a real Green's function must also be symmetric: $G_\epsilon(x, y) = G_\epsilon(y, x)$, so that, from (B.3),

$$\int_{-L}^{L} du_{\epsilon,n} \, dx = \int_{-L}^{L} nu_{\epsilon,d} \, dx \ .$$

The noise dependent part of ΔE_ϵ, which is $R_\epsilon - R_0$, becomes

$$R_\epsilon - R_0 = 2 \int_{-L}^{L} n(u_{\epsilon,d} - d) \, dx$$

($u_{0,d} = d$ for the particular data chosen) which has zero mean.
A bound on $|R_\epsilon - R_0|$ can be obtained as follows:

$$R_\epsilon - R_0 = 2 \left(\int_{-L}^{0} + \int_{0}^{\epsilon} + \int_{\epsilon}^{L} \right) n(u_{\epsilon,d} - d) \, dx$$

but $u_{\epsilon,d} = d$ for $x > \epsilon$, so the last interval of integration can be omitted. Solving for $u_{\epsilon,d}$ in the first interval, assuming $\epsilon \ll L$, gives $u_{\epsilon,d}(x) = A_\epsilon \exp(x/\lambda)$ so that

$$R_\epsilon - R_0 = 2A_\epsilon T + 2 \int_{0}^{\epsilon} n(u_{\epsilon,d} - h) \, dx \qquad (B.7)$$

where A_ϵ is a constant and

$$T = \int_{-L}^{0} n(x) \exp\left(\frac{x}{\lambda}\right) dx$$

which has expected value (B.2)

$$\langle |T| \rangle \leq \langle |T|^2 \rangle^{\frac{1}{2}} = \sigma \left(\int_{-L}^{0} \exp\left(\frac{2x}{\lambda}\right) dx \right)^{\frac{1}{2}}$$

$$\approx \sqrt{\frac{\lambda}{2}} \sigma.$$

It can be shown that $|A_\epsilon| \leq \epsilon h/\lambda$, so that

$$\langle |2A_\epsilon T| \rangle \leq \epsilon h \sigma \sqrt{\frac{2}{\lambda}} = \epsilon h n_0 \sqrt{\frac{2\rho}{\lambda}}. \qquad (B.8)$$

Now, as for the other term in $|R_\epsilon - R_0|$,

$$\left| 2 \int_{0}^{\epsilon} n(u_{\epsilon,d} - h) \, dx \right| \leq 2 \left(\int_{0}^{\epsilon} n^2(x) \, dx \right)^{\frac{1}{2}} \left(\int_{0}^{\epsilon} (h - u_{\epsilon,d}(x))^2 \, dx \right)^{\frac{1}{2}}$$
$$(B.9)$$

by the Cauchy-Schwartz inequality. But $|h - u_{\epsilon,d}(x)| \leq h$ so that

$$\left| 2 \int_{0}^{\epsilon} n(u_{\epsilon,d} - h) \, dx \right| \leq 2h\sqrt{\epsilon} \left(\int_{0}^{\epsilon} n^2 \, dx \right)^{\frac{1}{2}}. \qquad (B.10)$$

This term dominates, if it is assumed that $\rho \ll \lambda$. The first term (B.8) can be neglected.

A necessary condition for some $\epsilon > 0$ to be optimal is that

$$\Delta E_\epsilon = h^2 \epsilon - (R_\epsilon - R_0) < 0. \tag{B.11}$$

We need to find the smallest value e such that

$$\forall \, \epsilon > e, \quad \Delta E_\epsilon > 0 \tag{B.12}$$

- which would mean that for all $\epsilon > e$ the energy for a discontinuity at $x = \epsilon$ must be higher than for one at $x = 0$. Thus there could not be a discontinuity at $x = \epsilon > e$, and e is the desired bound on localisation error. From (B.11), the required condition is that

$$\forall \, \epsilon > e, \quad \frac{|R_\epsilon - R_0|}{\epsilon} < h^2, \tag{B.13}$$

and from (B.7) and (B.10), neglecting (B.8),

$$\max_{\epsilon > e} \frac{|R_\epsilon - R_0|}{\epsilon} \leq \max_{\epsilon > e} \, 2h \left(\frac{1}{\epsilon} \right)^{\frac{1}{2}} \left(\int_0^\epsilon n^2 \, dx \right)^{\frac{1}{2}}$$

$$\approx \quad 2h n_0 \tag{B.14}$$

from (B.1). So now a sufficient condition for (B.13) is that

$$\frac{h}{n_0} \geq 2. \tag{B.15}$$

This means that provided signal-to-noise exceeds 2, there is negligible localisation error.

B.2   Spurious response

Consider data $d(x) = 0, x \in [-L, L]$ with additive noise as above. A comparison can be made between the energy $E(u_\epsilon)$ of the optimal solution with a single discontinuity at $\epsilon \in [-L, L]$ and the energy $E(u_c)$ of an entirely continuous solution.

Solutions with a discontinuity at ϵ are denoted $u_\epsilon = u_{\epsilon,d} + u_{\epsilon,n}$ as in (B.3) and continuous solutions are $u_c = u_{c,d} + u_{c,n}$, with associated Green's function $G_c(x, x')$. The energy difference is

$$E(u_\epsilon) - E(u_c) = \int_{-L}^{L} (d + n)(u_{c,d} + u_{c,n} - (u_{\epsilon,d} + u_{\epsilon,n})) \, dx + \alpha, \tag{B.16}$$

$$= \int_{-L}^{L} n(u_{c,n} - u_{\epsilon,n})\, dx + \alpha,$$

since $u_{\epsilon,d} = u_{c,d} = d = 0$. Now

$$u_{c,n} - u_{\epsilon,n} = \int_{-L}^{L} \Delta G_\epsilon(x, x') n(x')\, dx'$$

where $\Delta G_\epsilon = G_c - G_\epsilon$, so

$$E(u_\epsilon) - E(u_c) = \int_{-L}^{L} \int_{-L}^{L} n(x) \Delta G_\epsilon(x, x') n(x')\, dx\, dx' + \alpha. \qquad \text{(B.17)}$$

From the formula (A.5) for the weak string Green's function in a finite domain

$$G_c(x, x') = \frac{1}{\lambda \sinh\left(\frac{2L}{\lambda}\right)} \cosh\left(\frac{x_< + L}{\lambda}\right) \cosh\left(\frac{x_> - L}{\lambda}\right) \qquad \text{(B.18)}$$

and

$$G_\epsilon(x, x') = \begin{cases} \frac{1}{\lambda \sinh\left(\frac{L+\epsilon}{\lambda}\right)} \cosh\left(\frac{x_< + L}{\lambda}\right) \cosh\left(\frac{x_> - \epsilon}{\lambda}\right) & \text{if } x, x' < \epsilon \\ \frac{1}{\lambda \sinh\left(\frac{L-\epsilon}{\lambda}\right)} \cosh\left(\frac{x_< - \epsilon}{\lambda}\right) \cosh\left(\frac{x_> - L}{\lambda}\right) & \text{if } x, x' > \epsilon \quad \text{(B.19)} \\ 0 & \text{otherwise.} \end{cases}$$

Assuming $\lambda \ll L$, it can be shown that

$$\Delta G_\epsilon(x, x') \approx \begin{cases} -\frac{1}{2\lambda} \exp\left(-2\epsilon + (x + x')\right)/\lambda & \text{if } x, x' < \epsilon \\ -\frac{1}{2\lambda} \exp\left(2\epsilon - (x + x')\right)/\lambda & \text{if } x, x' > \epsilon \quad \text{(B.20)} \\ \frac{1}{2\lambda} \exp\left(-\frac{|x - x'|}{\lambda}\right) & \text{otherwise.} \end{cases}$$

From (B.17) and (B.20),

$$E(u_\epsilon) - E(u_c) = \alpha - R^2 \qquad \text{(B.21)}$$

where R is a Gaussian random variable

$$R = \frac{1}{\sqrt{2\lambda}} \left(\int_{-L}^{\epsilon} n(x) \exp\left(\frac{x - \epsilon}{\lambda}\right) dx - \int_{\epsilon}^{L} n(x) \exp\left(\frac{\epsilon - x}{\lambda}\right) dx \right)$$

$$\text{(B.22)}$$

with mean 0, and standard deviation S which can be computed from (B.2):

$$S^2 = \frac{1}{2\lambda} \sigma^2 \left(\int_{-L}^{\epsilon} \left(\exp\left(\frac{x - \epsilon}{\lambda}\right) \right)^2 dx \qquad \text{(B.23)} \right.$$

$$\left. + \int_{\epsilon}^{L} \left(\exp\left(\frac{\epsilon - x}{\lambda}\right) \right)^2 dx \right) = \frac{\sigma^2}{2},$$

so

$$S = \frac{\sigma}{\sqrt{2}}. \tag{B.24}$$

The conclusion is that, with at least 95% certainty (the 95% two-tail confidence limit is approximately 2 standard deviations), choosing

$$\alpha > 2\sigma^2 \tag{B.25}$$

guarantees (B.21) that

$$E(u_\epsilon) > E(u_c) \tag{B.26}$$

- no spurious discontinuity. This result is independent of ϵ.

B.3   Comparison with a linear operator

Results from the previous 2 sections can now be combined to make a comparison of the performance of the weak string in noise, with that of a linear (Gaussian) operator. Canny's measures of localisation and signal to noise performance (for an isolated step) are used (Canny 1983). For the same signal to noise performance in each case, localisation accuracy is compared. The following notation is used: $s_g, \delta x_g$ denote signal to noise ratio and localisation error for the output of a Gaussian fiter; $s_c, \delta x_c$ similarly for the weak string. From (Canny 1983) we have, approximately, that

$$\delta x_g = \sqrt{w} \left(\frac{h}{\sigma} \right)^{-1} \tag{B.27}$$

and

$$s_g = \sqrt{w} \frac{h}{\sigma}, \tag{B.28}$$

where w is the half-width of the Gaussian filter. For the weak string, we know from chapter 4 that a step is detected only if its height h satisfies

$$h > h_0 = \sqrt{\frac{2\alpha}{\lambda}}$$

and from the working leading up to (B.26) false positive discontinuities are avoided (at 1 standard deviation) if

$$\alpha > \sigma^2/2$$

and combining these 2 inequalities gives

$$\frac{h}{\sigma} > \sqrt{\frac{1}{\lambda}},$$

so that the effective signal to noise ratio is

$$s_c = \sqrt{\lambda}\frac{h}{\sigma}. \tag{B.29}$$

Thus, when $\lambda = w$, $s_c = s_w$, so that the weak string and the Gaussian filter can be regarded as "equivalent" in signal-to-noise performance.

We saw earlier that the weak string is free of localisation error for data in which $h/n_0 > 2$. But for the same data, localisation error in the equivalent directional Gaussian filter would be

$$\delta x_g = \frac{\sqrt{\rho w}}{2} = \frac{\sqrt{\rho \lambda}}{2}.$$

Appendix C

Energy Calculations for the Rod and Plate

The purpose of this appendix is to summarise the methods used for the energy calculations of the rod and plate in chapter 5. The derivations of many of the expressions are analogous to those given in the string and membrane appendices, and are not reproduced here. Methods for the mixed rod and string are similar to those given here for the rod, but details will not be given.

C.1   Energy calculations for the rod

The rod has the energy functional

$$E = \int_{-a}^{b} \{(u(x) - d(x))^2 + \mu^4(u'')^2\}\, dx. \tag{C.1}$$

The function $u(x)$ which minimises E is found using the Calculus of Variations. It satisfies the Euler Lagrange equation

$$u + \mu^4 \frac{d^4 u}{dx^4} = d \tag{C.2}$$

with the boundary conditions

$$u''|_{x=-a,b} = 0, \quad u'''|_{x=-a,b} = 0, \tag{C.3}$$

and over a bi-infinite region $u(x)$ can be found from the Green's function

$$G(x, x') = \frac{1}{2\mu} e^{\frac{-|x-x'|}{\sqrt{2}\mu}} \cos\left(\frac{|x - x'|}{\sqrt{2}\mu} - \frac{\pi}{4}\right) \tag{C.4}$$

For finite and infinite regions

$$E = \int d(x)(d(x) - u(x))\, dx, \qquad (\text{C.5})$$

just as for the string.

In a bi-infinite domain the energy can be obtained directly from the Fourier transform of $d(x)$

$$E = \mu^2 \int_{-\infty}^{\infty} \frac{\omega^4 |\hat{d}(\omega)|^2}{1 + \mu^4 \omega^4}\, d\omega. \qquad (\text{C.6})$$

C.2   Energy calculations for the plate

The two varieties of the energy functional for the plate, quadratic variation (5.4) and square Laplacian (5.5), have the same Euler Lagrange equation namely

$$u + \mu^4 \nabla^4 u = d \qquad (\text{C.7})$$

but the boundary conditions are different (Grimson 1981). However, for an infinite domain the Green's function in both cases is given by

$$G(\mathbf{x}, \mathbf{x}') \;\; = \;\; \frac{i}{4\pi\mu^2} \left\{ K_0\left(\frac{\sqrt{i}r}{\mu}\right) - K_0\left(\frac{r}{\sqrt{i}\mu}\right) \right\} \qquad (\text{C.8})$$

$$\;\; = \;\; \frac{-1}{2\pi\mu^2} \text{kei}\left(\frac{r}{\mu}\right) \qquad (\text{C.9})$$

where kei is a Kelvin function (McLachlan 1961), and $r = |\mathbf{x} - \mathbf{x}'|$. The energy is obtained from

$$E = \int d(\mathbf{x})(d(\mathbf{x}) - u(\mathbf{x}))\, dA \qquad (\text{C.10})$$

or from the Fourier transform

$$E = \mu^4 \int_{-\infty}^{\infty} \int_{-\infty}^{\infty} \frac{k^4 |\hat{d}(\mathbf{k})|^2}{1 + \mu^4 k^4}\, d^2 k \qquad (\text{C.11})$$

The derivation of these expressions is analogous to that given for the membrane.

Circular symmetry

The Green's function takes the form

$$
G(\rho, \rho') = \frac{1}{\mu^2} \left\{ K_0 \left(\frac{\sqrt{i}\rho_<}{\mu} \right) I_0 \left(\frac{\sqrt{i}\rho_>}{\mu} \right) \right.
$$

$$
\left. - K_0 \left(\frac{\rho_<}{\sqrt{i}\mu} \right) I_0 \left(\frac{\rho_>}{\sqrt{i}\mu} \right) \right\} \tag{C.12}
$$

$$
= \frac{1}{\mu^2} \left\{ \mathrm{ker} \left(\frac{\rho_>}{\mu} \right) \mathrm{bei} \left(\frac{\rho_<}{\mu} \right) \right.
$$

$$
\left. + \mathrm{kei} \left(\frac{\rho_>}{\mu} \right) \mathrm{ber} \left(\frac{\rho_<}{\mu} \right) \right\} \tag{C.13}
$$

where $\mathrm{ker}(x), \mathrm{ber}(x)$ and $\mathrm{bei}(x)$ are also Kelvin functions (McLachlan 1961). The energy expression involving the Fourier transform becomes

$$
E = 2\pi\mu^4 \int_0^\infty \frac{k^5 |\hat{d}(k)|^2}{1 + \mu^4 k^4} \, dk \tag{C.14}
$$

Top hat example

Using expression (C.14) the energy for the 2D top hat is given by

$$
E = \pi a^2 h^2 \left\{ K_1 \left(\frac{a}{\sqrt{i}\mu} \right) I_1 \left(\frac{a}{\sqrt{i}\mu} \right) \right.
$$

$$
\left. + K_1 \left(\frac{\sqrt{i}a}{\mu} \right) I_1 \left(\frac{\sqrt{i}a}{\mu} \right) \right\} \tag{C.15}
$$

$$
= 2\pi a^2 h^2 \left\{ \mathrm{ker}_1 \left(\frac{a}{\mu} \right) \mathrm{ber}_1 \left(\frac{a}{\mu} \right) \right.
$$

$$
\left. - \mathrm{kei}_1 \left(\frac{a}{\mu} \right) \mathrm{bei}_1 \left(\frac{a}{\mu} \right) \right\}. \tag{C.16}
$$

This has limits

$$
E = \frac{\pi h^2 a \mu}{\sqrt{2}}, \qquad a \gg \mu \tag{C.17}
$$

and

$$
E = \pi h^2 a^2, \qquad a \ll \mu. \tag{C.18}
$$

Appendix D

Establishing Convexity

D.1 Justification of "worst-case" analysis of the Hessian

In the worst-case analysis of H, we examined the Hessian of $F^*(\mathbf{u})$, for values of $\mathbf{u}$ at which every instance of the neighbour interaction function $g^*(t)$ is at its "least convex" - has its most negative 2nd derivative $(g^*)''(t) = -c$ (7.2). This analysis can be regarded as applying for all $\mathbf{u}$, to a hypothetical cost function $F^+(\mathbf{u})$, defined as F^* but with interaction function

$$g^+(t) = -\frac{1}{2}ct^2 \qquad (D.1)$$

in place of g^*. The worst-case analysis shows that F^+ is convex, for all $\mathbf{u}$. Hence F^* is convex if $F^*(\mathbf{u}) - F^+(\mathbf{u})$ is convex (a sum of convex functions is itself convex). It is sufficient that $\forall t \; g^*(t) - g^+(t)$ is convex, that is:

$$\forall t \; (g^*)''(t) - (g^+)''(t) \geq 0 \qquad (D.2)$$

From (7.2) and (D.1), (D.2) does indeed hold.

D.2 Positive definite Hessian is sufficient for convexity

A positive definite Hessian is only a general guarantee of convexity for a function with continuous 2nd derivatives (Roberts and Varberg 1976). The 2nd derivatives of F^* are not continuous, so a special proof is needed. It relies on the special form of $F^*(\mathbf{u})$ - that it can be decomposed as a sum of functions of one variable whose arguments are linear combinations of the u_i.

The definition of convexity is that, given two vectors $\mathbf{v}$ and $\mathbf{w}$, then

$$\forall r, \ 1 \geq r \geq 0, \ F^*(\mathbf{u}) \leq rF^*(\mathbf{v}) + (1-r)F^*(\mathbf{w}) \tag{D.3}$$

where

$$\mathbf{u} = r\mathbf{v} + (1-r)\mathbf{w}. \tag{D.4}$$

Now it is sufficient to prove that, for all such $\mathbf{v}, \mathbf{w}$ that $T(r) \equiv F^*(\mathbf{u}(r))$ is convex as a function of r, for $1 \geq r \geq 0$. This is done in 2 stages:

1. First we show that if the Hessian H of F^* is positive definite, then $T''(r) \geq 0$, for $1 \geq r \geq 0$.

2. Then we show that, given this condition on T'', T is convex.

Here are the proofs:

1. From (D.3),

$$T'' = \mathbf{s}^T H \mathbf{s} \text{ where } \mathbf{s} = \mathbf{v} - \mathbf{w}. \tag{D.5}$$

It is at this point that the decomposition of F^* is used implicitly: because each of the component functions in the decomposition has a piecewise continuous 2nd derivative, so $T''(r)$ must be piecewise continuous and hence integrable. Since H is positive definite then, using (D.5),

$$\forall r \ T''(r) \geq 0. \tag{D.6}$$

2. First, by integrating the inequality (D.6),

$$\forall h > 0, \ T'(r+h) > T'(r)$$

and, integrating again, it is easily shown that, for all $h > 0$,

$$T(r+h) \geq T(r) + hT'(r) \text{ and } T(r) \geq T(r+h) - hT'(r+h) \tag{D.7}$$

and hence,for all $h > 0$, $1 \geq t \geq 0$,

$$T(r+h) \geq T(r+th) + h(1-t)T'(r+th) \tag{D.8}$$

and

$$T(r) \geq T(r+th) - thT'(r+th). \tag{D.9}$$

Multiplying the first of these inequalities by t and the second by $1-t$, adding and rearranging, we obtain:

$$T(r+th) \leq tT(r+h) + (1-t)T(r). \tag{D.10}$$

so that $T(r)$ is convex, as required.

D.3   Computing circulant eigenvalues

To choose the parameter c^* in chapter 7, using (7.9) on page 134, it is necessary to calculate the appropriate largest eigenvalue v_{max}. Recall that v_{max} is defined to be the largest eigenvalue of the matrix $Q^T Q$, where Q is a matrix that describes a linear transformation, as in (7.11). This linear transformation is in fact a discrete representation of the differential operator that defines the energy of the fitted surface. Now when Q is a circulant matrix it can be represented by a convolution C:

$$Q_{k,l} = C_{l-k} \text{ for some array } C. \tag{D.11}$$

(The index $l - k$ must be evaluated *modulo* the size of the array C.) Note that for 2D data the index k becomes a double index $k = (i, j)$ and similarly for l. And a cautionary note is necessary: in fact Q is not quite a circulant because of behaviour on the boundary of the finite data array. In fact, if the data $\mathbf{d}$ and the discrete representation $\mathbf{u}$ of the fitted function were defined with "wrapped-around" boundaries (i.e. on a circle in 1D or a torus in 2D) then Q would be exactly a circulant. The following assumes that Q really is a circulant, and modifications for the finite boundaries case are given in appendix D.4. Similarly, the matrix $Q^T Q$ is represented by the convolution C^2, defined by

$$C_m^2 = \sum_p C_{m+p} C_p. \tag{D.12}$$

From (Davies 1979), the eigenvalues of a circulant that is represented by a convolution C^2 applied to 1D vectors of length N, are

$$v_m = \sum_r C_r^2 \exp(2\pi i m r / N), \ 0 \le m < N, \tag{D.13}$$

and the equivalent formula for 2D $N \times N$ vectors is

$$v_{m,n} = \sum_{r,s} C_{r,s}^2 \exp(2\pi i m r / N) \exp(2\pi i n s / N) \ 0 \le m, n < N. \tag{D.14}$$

The string

The circulant Q for the string is defined by its convolution (7.12)

$$C = \left(\ \dots \quad 0 \quad -1 \quad 1 \quad 0 \quad 0 \quad \dots \ \right)$$

and C^2 is easily shown, using (D.12), to be

$$C^2 = \left(\ \dots \quad 0 \quad -1 \quad 2 \quad -1 \quad 0 \quad \dots \ \right).$$

Now applying (D.13),

$$v_m = 2 - (\exp(2\pi im/N) + \exp(-2\pi im/N))$$

$$= 2(1 - \cos(2\pi m/N)),$$

so that

$$v_{max} = 4.$$

The membrane

The membrane energy is slightly different from the other three, in that its energy (6.10) leads to a sum of two terms in the Hessian, expressed in terms of two circulants Q, R with corresponding 2D convolutions C, D:

$$C = \begin{pmatrix} \cdots & \cdots & \cdots & \cdots & \cdots \\ \cdots & 0 & -1 & 0 & \cdots \\ \cdots & 0 & 1 & 0 & \cdots \\ \cdots & 0 & 0 & 0 & \cdots \\ \cdots & \cdots & \cdots & \cdots & \cdots \end{pmatrix}$$

$$D = \begin{pmatrix} \cdots & \cdots & \cdots & \cdots & \cdots \\ \cdots & 0 & 0 & 0 & \cdots \\ \cdots & 0 & 1 & -1 & \cdots \\ \cdots & 0 & 0 & 0 & \cdots \\ \cdots & \cdots & \cdots & \cdots & \cdots \end{pmatrix}.$$

These are essentially the same as C for the string above, but padded out with zeros to fill a 2D array. Now it is required to find the eigenvalues $v_{m,n}$ of $Q^T Q + R^T R$, which from (D.14), are:

$$v_{m,n} = 4 - 2\cos(2\pi m/N) - 2\cos(2\pi n/N),$$

so that

$$v_{max} = 8.$$

The rod

The energy of the plate is given in (6.13) and the equivalent in 1D, for the rod, is described by a single circulant Q with convolution

$$C = (\ \cdots\ \ 0\ \ -1\ \ 2\ \ -1\ \ 0\ \ \cdots\ ).$$

The symmetry of C means that Q is symmetric so that $Q^T Q = Q^2$. If v is an eigenvalue of Q then v^2 is an eigenvalue of $Q^T Q$. Now C here is the same as C^2 for the string, so clearly v_{max} here is v_{max}^2 for the string, i.e

$$v_{max} = 16$$

for the rod.

The plate

The square Laplacian energy for a plate is given in (6.13) yielding a convolution

$$C = \begin{pmatrix} \cdots & \cdots & \cdots & \cdots & \cdots \\ \cdots & 0 & -1 & 0 & \cdots \\ \cdots & -1 & 4 & -1 & \cdots \\ \cdots & 0 & -1 & 0 & \cdots \\ \cdots & \cdots & \cdots & \cdots & \cdots \end{pmatrix}.$$

As before, $Q^T Q = Q^2$ so, using (D.14) to obtain the eigenvalues of Q, they are squared to give eigenvalues of $Q^T Q$:

$$v_{m,n} = (4 - 2\cos(2\pi m/N) - 2\cos(2\pi n/N))^2,$$

so that

$$v_{max} = 8^2 = 64.$$

D.4 Treating boundary conditions

In the worst case analysis in chapter 7 and in (D.1), the neighbour interaction function for the convex function F^* has the form $g^*(t) = -\frac{1}{2}ct^2$. Thus $-g^*(t)$ is convex. Now given the worst-case F^* for the circulant case - when opposite edges of the array are connected toroidally - it is a simple matter to obtain the worst case F^* for the bounded array. Removing the toroidal connections involves simply subtracting from F^* the relevant neighbour interaction terms $g^*(t)$ - i.e. adding $-g^*(t)$. Now each such $-g^*(t)$ is convex, so any sum of them is convex. Hence if the toroidal worst case is convex, the corresponding bounded array worst-case must also be convex. So the proof using circulants, of convexity for the worst-case, holds also for a bounded array.

Appendix E

Analysis of the GNC Algorithm

In this appendix, we analyse the performance of the convex approximation F^* to the discrete cost function F, and the non-convex sequence $F^{(p)}, p \in [0, 1]$, for the weak elastic string. This is analogous to the analysis of the continuous problem in chapter 4, but instead of using variational methods to obtain Euler Lagrange equations, recurrence relations are obtained as an extremum condition for the discrete minimisation. Solutions of the recurrence relations are obtained with exponential decay similar to the extremal functions obtained by variational calculus.

With regard to sensitivity and scale behaviour, the solution of the discrete problem agrees with that of the continuous problem, with errors that are second order in element size, as expected with linear elements (Zinkiewicz and Morgan 1983).

As for the performance of the GNC algorithm, it is shown that it is correct - that is, it correctly finds the global minimum of the non-convex function F - for an important class of problems: those in which the potential discontinuities are non-interacting (separated by distances large compared with λ). Some generalisation to interacting discontinuities is possible.

E.1   Setting up the discrete analysis

The family of cost functions used in the GNC algorithm is

$$F^{(p)} = \sum_i (u_i - d_i)^2 + g^{(p)}(u_i - u_{i-1}), \tag{E.1}$$

where $g^{(p)}$ is shorthand for $g^{(p)}_{\alpha,\lambda}$, as defined in (7.23) on page 141. Local minima occur when

$$\partial F^{(p)}/\partial u_i = 0, \ \forall i$$

which, differentiating (E.1), gives:

$$\forall i \ u_i = d_i - \frac{1}{2}g^{(p)\prime}(u_i - u_{i+1}) + \frac{1}{2}g^{(p)\prime}(u_{i-1} - u_i). \qquad (E.2)$$

It assumed in the following analysis that, except at one possible discontinuity between $i = 0, 1$ (over the set $i \in \{-L_1, ..0, ..L_2\}$) the interaction functions $g^{(p)}(u_i - u_{i-1})$ are in their central quadratic regions (figure 7.1 on page 133). (It is possible to check, when the analysis is complete, that this assumption did indeed hold. This is done later.) The assumption means that

$$\forall i \neq 0, \ \Delta_i \leq q \text{ where } \Delta_i = |u_{i+1} - u_i|. \qquad (E.3)$$

so that

$$\forall i \neq 1 \ g^{(p)}(u_i - u_{i-1}) = \lambda^2 (u_i - u_{i-1})^2$$

and, differentiating,

$$\forall i \neq 1 \ g^{(p)\prime}(u_i - u_{i-1}) = 2\lambda^2 (u_i - u_{i-1}).$$

The recurrence relation (E.2) becomes, for $i < 0$ and $i > 1$,:

$$u_i = d_i - \lambda^2 (2u_i - u_{i+1} - u_{i-1}), \qquad (E.4)$$

which is analogous to the Euler-Lagrange equation (A.2) that describes an elastic string. For data $d_i = 0$ the solution has the form

$$u_i = An^i \qquad (E.5)$$

where n satisfies

$$n = \lambda^2 (1 - n)^2. \qquad (E.6)$$

Note that n can be expressed in terms of a length parameter Λ:

$$n = 1 - 1/\Lambda \qquad (E.7)$$

where

$$\Lambda^2 - \Lambda = \lambda^2 \qquad (E.8)$$

so that

$$\Lambda \approx \lambda \text{ for large } \lambda. \qquad (E.9)$$

This is the scale over which solutions decay exponentially, corresponding to λ in the variational analysis.

E.2 Constraining the discrete string

Variational analysis showed (appendix A) that when a continuous string over an interval $[0, L]$ is constrained at one end, moved from its natural value there of $\bar{z}$, to a new value z, then the increase in energy is $\Delta E = \mathcal{E}(z - \bar{z})^2$, where $\mathcal{E}$ depends only on λ and L. A similar result can be obtained from discrete analysis. The proof is similar.

The increase in discrete energy is

$$\Delta F = \mathcal{F}(z - \bar{z})^2 \qquad (E.10)$$

and again $\mathcal{F}$ is obtained by "calibration", once, on any convenient data. Taking $d_i = 0$ on $i \in \{0, .., L\}$ with $u_0 = 1$, the solution of the recurrence relation is $u_i = n^i$ and the energy is determined from (E.1) (with $g^{(p)}(t) = \lambda^2 t^2$) and simplified using (E.8) so that, assuming $L \gg \Lambda$,

$$\mathcal{F} \approx \Lambda. \qquad (E.11)$$

In any case, whatever the value of L,

$$1 \leq \mathcal{F} \leq \Lambda \qquad (E.12)$$

increasing from one bound to the other as L increases from 1. Of course $\mathcal{F}$ in (E.11) agrees closely with $\mathcal{E}$ since $\Lambda \approx \lambda$, differing only because of discretisation error.

Constraining both ends of an interval also acts as in the variational analysis (A.23) to give

$$F = F_0 + \mathcal{F}_- \left((z_1 - \bar{z}_1) - (z_2 - \bar{z}_2)\right)^2 + \mathcal{F}_+ \left((z_1 - \bar{z}_1) + (z_2 - \bar{z}_2)\right)^2 \quad (E.13)$$

acting as two independent constraints ($\mathcal{F}_- \approx \mathcal{F}_+ \approx \Lambda/2$) when $L \gg \lambda$.

E.3 Isolated discontinuity

As before, it is possible to compute the increase ΔF in energy, this time discrete energy, when a continuity constraint is imposed between two points. Assume the points are $i = 0, 1$ in an interval $i \in \{-L_1, ..0, ..L_2\}$ ($L_1, L_2 \gg \lambda$) and continuity is imposed by coupling the points with the usual elastic connection. The result is proportional to h^2 where the "effective" step height h is now defined to be the value taken by Δ_0 when u_0, u_1 are uncoupled. Calibration is done to obtain the constant of proportionality, for a bi-infinite interval, using an ideal step

$$d_i = \begin{cases} -h/2 & \text{for } i \leq 0, \\ h/2 & \text{for } i > 0, \end{cases} \qquad (E.14)$$

and exploiting its antisymmetry. Formula (E.10) is used once for each side of the step, and the interaction energy between u_0, u_1 must be added in to give

$$\Delta F = \min_{\Delta_0} \; 2\mathcal{F}\left(\frac{1}{2}(h - \Delta_0)\right)^2 + \lambda^2 \Delta_0^2 \tag{E.15}$$

which, after some algebra, turns out to be

$$\Delta F \;\; = \;\; h^2 \mathcal{F} \frac{\Lambda - 1}{2\Lambda - 1} \tag{E.16}$$

$$\approx \;\; \frac{1}{2}\mathcal{F}h^2 \tag{E.17}$$

in the limit that $L_1, L_2 \gg \lambda$. In fact ΔF agrees with the variational equivalent $\Delta E = \frac{1}{2}h^2\lambda$, within $O(1/\lambda^2)$. If the data is not bi-infinite then constants $\mathcal{F}_1, \mathcal{F}_2$ are associated with each side of the discontinuity, and the effective $\mathcal{F}$ for (E.16) is their harmonic mean.

E.4   Cost function sequence

What happens when string energy (E.15) is replaced by a cost function $F^{(p)}$ in the GNC sequence? Continuing to assume (E.3), behaviour of u_i for $i < 0, i > 0$ is entirely determined. The whole problem depends just on Δ_0, so that $F^{(p)}$ can be regarded as $F^{(p)}(\Delta_0)$.

$$F^{(p)}(\Delta_0) = F^{(p)}(h) + \frac{1}{2}\mathcal{F}(h - \Delta_0)^2 + g^{(p)}(\Delta_0) - g^{(p)}(h). \tag{E.18}$$

Differentiating twice, $d^2 F^{(p)}/d\Delta_0^2$ is positive except when $q < \Delta_0 < r$, in which case

$$\frac{d^2 F(p)}{d\Delta_0^2} = \mathcal{F} - c. \tag{E.19}$$

This means that $F^{(p)}(\Delta_0)$ is convex as c increases (p decreases) up to $c = \mathcal{F}$. At that point $F^{(p)}(\Delta_0)$ must be the convex envelope of $F(\Delta_0)$ because they are equal except over $q < \Delta_0 < r$, where $F^{(p)}(\Delta_0)$ is linear (figure 7.6, page 145).

At $c = \mathcal{F}$, Δ_0 *must* move to find the global minimum of $F(\Delta_0)$. At this point $F^{(p)}(\Delta_0) = F(\Delta_0)$ (7.17), so that Δ_0 does not change thereafter as $p \to 0$ in the GNC algorithm.

E.5   Discreteness of the function sequence

Ideally, the GNC algorithm would use the whole family of functions $F^{(p)}$, $p \in [0, 1]$. In practice it is restricted to a discrete sequence of p. Clearly there will be some error in c, compared with the ideal $c = \mathcal{F}$ that makes $F^{(p)}(\Delta_0)$ just convex, as above. If c is too small then $F^{(p)}$ is "over-convex" and its minimum may not be the global minimum of F. If c is too large then $F^{(p)}$ is non-convex and may have two local minima.

Referring to figure 7.6 again, it is apparent that, in either of the two cases, $F^{(p)}$ has a unique minimum that is the same as the global minimum of F provided

$$\text{sign}\left(F^{(p)'}(q)\right) = \text{sign}\left(F^{(p)'}(r)\right). \tag{E.20}$$

From (E.18) (and (7.24) on page 141)

$$F^{(p)'}(r) = \mathcal{F}(r - h)$$

and

$$F^{(p)'}(q) = \mathcal{F}(q - h) + 2\lambda^2 q.$$

Defining values h_r, h_q of h to be those at which $F^{(p)'}$ vanishes at r, q respectively:

$$h_r = r \text{ and } h_q = \frac{\mathcal{F} + 2\lambda^2}{\mathcal{F}}q. \tag{E.21}$$

When $c > \mathcal{F}$ error may occur if

$$h \in [h_r, h_q]$$

where, assuming $\mathcal{F}, c \ll \lambda^2$, and substituting $r^2 = 2\alpha/c$, $q = \alpha/(\lambda^2 r)$,

$$\frac{h_r}{h_q} = \frac{\mathcal{F}}{c}. \tag{E.22}$$

So when $c = \mathcal{F}$, the interval disappears, as expected since it is the ideal c above. And when $c < \mathcal{F}$ error occurs if

$$h \in [h_r, h_q], \tag{E.23}$$

with h_r, h_q again related by (E.22). This is also useful for analysing the performance of $F^* \equiv F^{(1)}$ on its own. For example, for a weak string $c = c^* = \frac{1}{2}$, and in the bi-infinite case $\mathcal{F} \approx \lambda$. From (E.21) and (7.8), assuming $\lambda \gg 1$,

$$h_q \approx \frac{h_0}{\sqrt{2\lambda}} \text{ and } h_r \approx h_0\sqrt{2\lambda}$$

These are the endpoints of the interval of ambiguity $[h_-, h_+]$ as in (7.20).

E.6   Checking for continuity of the discrete solution

Consider an ideal bi-infinite step (E.14): To check that condition (E.3) holds $\forall i \neq 0$, it is sufficient to check just for $i = 1$. This is justified by noting the antisymmetry of u_i and hence the symmetry of Δ_i, and by observing from (E.6) that

$$\Delta_i = An^i(1 - n) \tag{E.24}$$

so that $\forall i > 1 \ \Delta_i < \Delta_1$.

It is assumed that

$$\Delta_0 < r, \tag{E.25}$$

otherwise a discontinuous solution must already have been found. During GNC

$$\Lambda \geq c \geq 1 \tag{E.26}$$

(see chapter 7). So $\Delta_1 \leq q$ if

$$\frac{\Delta_0}{\Delta_1} \geq \frac{r}{q} \ \forall \Lambda \geq c \geq \frac{1}{2}. \tag{E.27}$$

From the definitions of r, q in (7.24),

$$\frac{r}{q} = 1 + \frac{2\lambda^2}{c}. \tag{E.28}$$

Minimising $F^{(p)}(\Delta_0)$ in (E.18), with $\mathcal{F} = \Lambda$ as the data is bi-infinite, it can be shown that

$$\frac{\Delta_0}{\Delta_1} = \frac{h\Lambda - rc}{(c/2)(h - r)(1 - n)} \tag{E.29}$$

which, from (E.28), (E.26) and (E.7)

$$\geq \frac{r}{q} + \frac{\Lambda}{c}. \tag{E.30}$$

So, using (E.26) again,

$$\frac{\Delta_0}{\Delta_1} > \frac{r}{q} \tag{E.31}$$

as required.

In fact, as there is a margin of Λ/c in inequality (E.31), it is clear that (throughout GNC)

$$|\Delta_1 - q| \geq M > 0,$$

for some bound M. That means that the above proof continues to hold, not just for an ideal step, but also for a step in a certain amount of noise. This is true provided that when the noise (or other variation) is filtered by a continuous string, no gradients of magnitude exceeding M are generated. It can be shown that the value of the gradient bound is

$$M \approx \frac{\sqrt{\alpha}}{4\lambda^3}. \tag{E.32}$$

Glossary of notation

SYMBOL	MEANING
α	penalty for step discontinuity
β	penalty for crease discontinuity
γ	decay time for convergence
ϕ	surface slant
κ	curvature
λ	scale parameter for string and membrane
μ	scale parameter for rod and plate
ρ	coherence length of noise
σ	standard deviation of mean noise
Δ_i	difference of adjacent u_i
Λ	discrete equivalent of λ
c	parameter used in definition of $g^{(p)}(t)$
$d(x),\ d(x,y)$	data signal
$d_i,\ d_{i,j}$	discrete forms of $d(x), d(x,y)$
$\mathbf{d}$	vector whose components are d_i or $d_{i,j}$
g	gradient of ramp
g_l	gradient limit
g_0	gradient difference threshold
$g(t)$	neighbour interaction function
$g^*(t)$	approximation to $g(t)$ (for F^*)
$g^{(p)}(t)$	neighbour interaction function for GNC
h	height of step
h_0	contrast threshold
$h(t,l)$	neighbour interaction function

SYMBOL	MEANING
l_i, $l_{i,j}$	line variable (flags discontinuities)
$\mathbf{l}$	vector of line-variables
$m_{i,j}$	line variable
n_0	standard deviation of noise
p	non-convexity parameter
$p(x,y)$, $q(x,y)$	components of ∇u
q, r	parameters in definition of $g^{(p)}$
$u(x)$, $u(x,y)$	function fitted to data
u_i, $u_{i,j}$	discrete forms of $u(x), u(x,y)$
$\mathbf{u}$	vector whose components are u_i or $u_{i,j}$
w	scale parameter of Gaussian
D	square error energy
$E(u), E(\mathbf{u},\mathbf{l})$	energy (continuous, discrete)
$\mathcal{E}$	elasticity of a piece of string (continuous)
$F(\mathbf{u})$	discrete energy with line variables eliminated
F^*	convex approximation to F
$F^{(p)}$	family of energy functions for GNC
$\mathcal{F}$	elasticity of a piece of string (discrete)
$G(x,x'), G(\mathbf{x},\mathbf{x}')$	Green's functions for string, membrane
S	smoothness term in energy
P	penalty term in energy

Index

activity flags, 163.
adaptive thresholding, 80.
Asada, H., 63.

Besag, J., 11.
Brady, J.M., 63, 93.
boundary condition, 56, 85, 183-184, 187, 189, 203, 211.

calculus of variations, 40, 51, 183, 189, 203.
Canny, J.F., 72, 200.
circulant matrix, 134, 209-211.
circular symmetry, 75, 191-193, 205.
Cole, W.S., 167.
complexity, 129.
continuity, 5-6.
contrast threshold:
    continuous data, 52, 58, 60, 64, 97, 100, 102.
    discrete data, 139, 216.
convergence:
    decay time, 159, 161.
    measure of, 158.
    optimum SOR, 159, 161.
    proof of, 152-155.
convexity, 11-12, 43-47, 110, 122, 132, 207-208.
cooperativity, 5-8, 110.
corner rounding, 77-78.
cost function, 40-43, 112.
crease discontinuity, 9, 20, 26, 32, 97, 99, 101-102, 107-108.

curve description, 33-35.

data compression, 4.
depth map, 3, 28-29.
Derin, H., 167.
descent algorithims, 49, 121-124, 152-157.
double edges, 61-62, 64, 80-81.
dynamic programming, 128-129.

edge detection, 18, 21-23, 78, 80-83.
effective step height, 57-58.
eigenvalue, 133-135, 158, 209-211.
energy minimization, 7, 40.
Euler Lagrange, 67, 85, 183, 189, 203, 204, 214.
extremal energy, 7, 11, 40, 55, 68.

Fahle, M., 85.
finite elements, 40, 111, 114-119.
first order plate, 98, 106, 120.
Fourier transform, 55, 184-185, 190, 204.
Frisby, J.P., 168.

Gaussian curvature, 109.
Gauss Seidel iteration, 122, 124, 159.
Geman, D., 13, 127, 169.
Geman, S., 13, 127.
global schemes, 21.
gradient difference threshold, 97, 101.

gradient limit: 52, 62-63, 97.
    remission, 95.
Graduated Non Convexity (GNC):
    46-50, 125, 131-151.
    correctness of, 142-151, 213-
    219.
granularity 163, 165, 216-217.
Green's function, 55-56, 60, 75,
    183, 185, 190, 203.
Grimson, W.E.L., 25, 99, 107, 121.

Hessian, 132, 207-208.
Hinton, G.E., 5.
Hopfield, J.J., 127.
hyperacuity, 84-86.
hysteresis, 52, 87-90, 105-106.

interacting steps:
    variational results, 52, 100.
    correctness of GNC, 146, 148-
    149.
iteration schemes:
    convex problems, 121.
    multigrid methods, 122.
    sparse data, 123.
    weak string, 156.
    weak membrane, 157.
Ising model, 7.

Julesz, B., 7.

lightness computation, 7, 167.
line process, 42, 112-114, 119.
linear filter, 21, 52.
local interaction, 7, 47, 49.
localisation:
    compared to linear operator,
    67, 71, 200-201.
    in noise, 52, 63-72, 195-198.

Markov Random Field (MRF), 11,
    13-15, 80, 167, 169.
Marr, D., 2, 4, 5, 27.

Marroquin, J., 28.
Mayhew, J.E.W., 168.
mechanical model, 15, 168-169.
MIMD, 168.
Montanari, U., 126.
Morgan, M.J., 171.
multigrid relaxation, 122-125.
Mumford, D., 52, 67-68.

neural networks, 127.
noise:
    effect on localisation, 52, 63-
    72, 195-198.
    effect on convergence, 151.
    rejection by GNC, 149-150.
    spurious response to, 52, 72,
    198-200.

parallelism, 7.
penalty functions:
    1D, 39, 51, 99.
    2D, 73, 99.
    numerical, 42-43, 112-116.
perceptron, 10.
Poggio, T., 10, 85.
Pollard, S.B., 168.
preservation of topology, 76-78.
probabilistic model, 13, 168-169.

quadratic variation, 99, 107, 109,
    119.

ramp data, 62, 101-104, 186.
range data, 3, 29.
regression, 8-9.
Reichardt, W., 10.
relaxation, 7.
run length encoding, 4.

scale:
    parameter, 40, 52, 53, 55, 75,
    99, 214.
    space filtering, 33-36, 63-72.

sensor frame noise, 93.

Shah, J., 52, 67-68.

simulated annealing, 46, 126.

sparse data, 81, 120, 121, 123, 136.

splines, 8-10, 98.

spurious response, 52, 72, 198-200.

square Laplacian, 99, 107, 109, 119.

stable description, 3.

step data, 40, 58.

step discontinuity, 9, 39.

stereopsis, 3, 5, 21.

Successive Over Relaxation (SOR), 122, 123, 152-161.

surface reconstruction, 21-33.

T junctions, 35, 37, 78-79.

template fitting, 21.

Terzopoulos, D., 25, 111, 121, 122.

tesselation, 117.

top hat data:
    1D, 58-60.
    2D, 75-76, 192, 205.

Ullman, S., 2.

uniformity, 63-72.

viewpoint invariance, 4, 90-94, 107-110.

Watt, R.J., 171.

weak continuity constraint, 5, 17, 39.

weak membrane, 18, 72-90, 114-117.

weak plate, 18, 97, 117-120.

weak rod, 17, 20, 97.

weak string, 17, 19, 39-72, 112.

wobble, 90.

Yuille, A.L., 93.

The MIT Press, with Peter Denning, general consulting editor, and Brian Randell, European consulting editor, publishes computer science books in the following series:

ACM Doctoral Dissertation Award and Distinguished Dissertation Series

Artificial Intelligence, Patrick Winston and Michael Brady, editors

Charles Babbage Institute Reprint Series for the History of Computing, Martin Campbell-Kelly, editor

Computer Systems, Herb Schwetman, editor

Exploring with Logo, E. Paul Goldenberg, editor

Foundations of Computing, Michael Garey, editor

History of Computing, I. Bernard Cohen and William Aspray, editors

Information Systems, Michael Lesk, editor

Logic Programming, Ehud Shapiro, editor; Fernando Pereira, Koichi Furukawa, and D. H. D. Warren, associate editors

The MIT Electrical Engineering and Computer Science Series

Scientific Computation, Dennis Gannon, editor